Transformation in *Theosis*

Transformation in *Theosis*
Embracing the Divine Nature

Yohanes Bambang Mulyono

WIPF & STOCK · Eugene, Oregon

TRANSFORMATION IN *THEOSIS*
Embracing the Divine Nature

Copyright © 2025 Yohanes Bambang Mulyono. All rights reserved. Except for brief quotations in critical publications or reviews, no part of this book may be reproduced in any manner without prior written permission from the publisher. Write: Permissions, Wipf and Stock Publishers, 199 W. 8th Ave., Suite 3, Eugene, OR 97401.

Wipf & Stock
An Imprint of Wipf and Stock Publishers
199 W. 8th Ave., Suite 3
Eugene, OR 97401

www.wipfandstock.com

PAPERBACK ISBN: 979-8-3852-3379-3
HARDCOVER ISBN: 979-8-3852-3380-9
EBOOK ISBN: 979-8-3852-3381-6

VERSION NUMBER 02/14/25

Where indicated, Scripture translations are taken from Holy Bible, New International Version®, NIV® Copyright ©1973, 1978, 1984, 2011 by Biblica, Inc.® Used by permission. All rights reserved worldwide.

Where indicated, Scripture translations are taken from The Holy Bible, English Standard Version. ESV® Text Edition: 2016. Copyright © 2001 by Crossway Bibles, a publishing ministry of Good News Publishers.

Where indicated, Scripture translations are taken from New American Standard Bible®, Copyright © 1960, 1971, 1977, 1995, 2020 by The Lockman Foundation. All rights reserved.

Contents

Preface | vii

Chapter 1   Theosis and the Restoration of the *Imago Dei*: A Path to Divine Likeness | 1
Chapter 2   The Divine Quality of Divinization | 16
Chapter 3   Theosis in Christian Theology | 29
Chapter 4   Historical Development of Theosis | 41
Chapter 5   The Biblical Foundations of Theosis | 57
Chapter 6   Transfiguration of Christ as a Theosis Event | 78
Chapter 7   Theosis in Catholic and Protestant Theology | 96
Chapter 8   Comparing Theosis in Many Denominations | 116
Chapter 9   Theosis in Contemporary Christian Spirituality and Ethics | 138
Chapter 10   Theosis in Teilhard de Chardin's Thought | 161
Chapter 11   Theosis in Social and Environmental Challenges | 181
Chapter 12   Theosis in the Digital Age | 199

Conclusion | 217

Glossary | 223
Bibliography | 239
Subject Index | 245
Author Index | 247
Scripture Index | 249

Preface

THEOSIS, ALSO KNOWN AS deification, stands as one of the most profound and mystical concepts in Christian theology. It explores humanity's potential to share in the divine nature and achieve union with God through a process of transformation. This book, *Transformation in Theosis: Embracing Divine Nature*, delves into this transformative journey, inviting readers to explore the depths of faith and the promise of spiritual growth.

In contrast to a world often focused on material wealth and superficial achievements, theosis presents a radical alternative. It calls individuals to uncover their true nature and life's purpose by aligning themselves with the divine essence believed to reside within each person. This journey encompasses self-discovery, inner change, and spiritual enlightenment. The concept of theosis challenges readers to look beyond conventional pursuits and consider a path of profound spiritual development. It suggests that humans have the capacity to participate in the divine life, offering a perspective that goes beyond traditional religious boundaries and speaks to the core of human spiritual aspirations.

Transformation in Theosis draws on insights from various religious and philosophical traditions to encourage readers to ponder life's fundamental questions and pursue a deeper sense of purpose and fulfillment. The book aims to inspire and guide readers on their personal journey toward theosis through contemplation of the nature of reality, the human condition, and life's mysteries.

The work explores the rich historical, theological, and spiritual contexts that have shaped our understanding of theosis. It traces the concept from the early church fathers to modern theologians, highlighting how theosis has consistently served as a source of hope and a reminder of humanity's ultimate calling. The book emphasizes that theosis is not just a theoretical concept but a practical, lived experience. It requires both intellectual understanding and active engagement, suggesting a holistic approach to spiritual growth that encompasses both mind and action.

The book offers a comprehensive view of theosis, encouraging readers to reconsider their spiritual journey from a fresh perspective. It proposes that the path of theosis provides a life-changing approach that transcends traditional religious practices, reaching into the core of human existence and potential. The exploration begins by examining the biblical foundations of theosis, showing how this concept is rooted in Scripture. The study then traces the development of theosis through the writings of the early church fathers, who articulated and championed the idea of deification with deep insight and fervor.

The journey continues into the Middle Ages, highlighting the contributions of rich mystical traditions to the understanding of theosis. It then moves on to the Reformation period, exploring how the renewed focus on grace and sanctification during this time further shaped and diversified the doctrine. By following this historical and theological progression, the book aims to provide a comprehensive understanding of theosis. It shows how the concept has evolved and been interpreted across different eras and traditions of Christian thought, while maintaining its central focus on the transformative potential of human beings in relation to the divine. This approach not only provides a historical context for theosis but also invites readers to consider how these various interpretations and developments might inform their own spiritual journeys and understanding of human potential for divine connection.

The book extends its exploration into the modern era, examining how contemporary theologians have engaged with and expanded the concept of theosis to address new challenges and opportunities in our evolving world. It investigates the connections between theosis and other theological areas such as Christology, soteriology, and ecclesiology, demonstrating how this doctrine is integrated into the broader framework of Christian belief. Emphasizing practicality, the book offers insights on living out theosis in everyday life. It suggests that the journey towards embracing the divine nature extends beyond theological texts and should be embodied in actions, relationships, and spiritual practices. The work considers how prayer, sacraments, community involvement, and personal discipline contribute to transformation and union with God.

PREFACE

Transformation in Theosis is intended for a wide audience, including theologians, religious studies students, and laypeople seeking spiritual growth. It aims to illuminate the path towards deification by providing both scholarly analysis and practical guidance. By bridging theoretical understanding with practical application, the book invites readers to consider how the concept of theosis can be relevant and transformative in their personal lives. It suggests that the journey towards the divine nature is not an abstract concept but a lived experience that can profoundly impact one's approach to faith, relationships, and daily existence.

This book is presented not as a definitive guide to a destination, but as a companion for an inward journey of self-discovery. It invites readers to explore life's mysteries, to question, and to awaken to the untapped potential within themselves. The text encourages approaching these profound teachings with openness and readiness to embrace the divine nature that seeks expression through each individual. It offers reassurance that this spiritual path is a shared journey, enriched by the diverse insights and experiences of fellow seekers.

As readers engage with the following pages, they are challenged to recognize and actualize their divine potential. Theosis is portrayed not as a distant aspiration, but as a present reality that invites individuals to transcend human limitations and fully participate in divine life. The passage concludes with an invitation to embark on this journey collectively, with hearts receptive to the transformative power of divine grace. It emphasizes the goal of not just understanding, but truly embracing and embodying the divine nature. This approach frames the exploration of theosis as a deeply personal yet universally relevant journey. It suggests that the concept is not merely an abstract theological idea but a practical path for spiritual growth and self-realization that can profoundly impact one's life and understanding of existence.

The book presents a spiritual journey through twelve chapters, exploring the concept of theosis from various theological, historical, and contemporary Christian perspectives. This work delves into theosis, understood as the process of human transformation towards divine likeness. It examines the concept from multiple angles, revealing its theological depth and practical implications for both spirituality and ethics.

The journey commences in chapter 1 with an exploration of theosis in relation to the restoration of the *imago Dei* (image of God). This initial chapter emphasizes the concept's significance in understanding humanity's purpose and ultimate destiny. It sets the foundation for comprehending how theosis permeates various aspects of Christian theology and spiritual practice. By structuring the exploration over twelve chapters, the book offers a comprehensive pilgrimage of faith, allowing readers to progressively deepen their understanding of theosis. This approach suggests that the concept of theosis is not just a single idea but a multifaceted principle that touches on numerous aspects of Christian thought and practice.

The book aims to provide readers with a thorough understanding of theosis, from its theological roots to its practical applications in contemporary Christian life. It invites readers to consider how this transformative concept might inform and enrich their own spiritual journeys and understanding of human potential in relation to the divine.

The book's exploration deepens in chapter 2, which examines the divine qualities inherent in theosis. This chapter illustrates how these qualities shape our understanding of God and influence our journey towards divine union. Chapters 3 and 4 offer a comprehensive overview of theosis and its historical development in Christian theology. These chapters highlight how the concept has evolved within various theological traditions and maintained its relevance throughout different historical periods.

Building on this historical context, chapter 5 investigates the biblical foundations of theosis. This chapter grounds the theological concept in scriptural narratives and teachings, demonstrating how theosis is deeply rooted in the biblical account of God's relationship with humanity. This biblical exploration provides a solid theological framework for the discussions that follow, showing how theosis is not a later theological invention but a concept embedded in the core of scriptural teaching. By structuring the exploration in this way, the book offers a progressive deepening of understanding. It moves from the foundational concept of the *imago Dei* through the divine qualities associated with theosis into its historical and theological development and then grounds all of this in biblical teachings. This approach allows readers to grasp the multifaceted nature of theosis and its central importance in Christian thought and spirituality.

Chapter 6 examines the transfiguration of Christ as a pivotal moment of theosis, illustrating the transformative potential inherent in divine encounters. This exploration highlights the practical and experiential aspects of theosis within the Christian narrative.

Chapters 7 and 8 offer a comparative analysis of theosis across Catholic, Protestant, and other denominational perspectives. This comparison reveals both shared understandings and unique interpretations of theosis within diverse Christian traditions. By doing so, these chapters demonstrate the dynamic interplay between theological unity and diversity in expressing the concept of theosis.

The focus shifts in chapters 9 and 10 to theosis in contemporary Christian spirituality and in the thought of Teilhard de Chardin, respectively. These chapters illustrate how the concept of theosis continues to inspire spiritual growth and theological discourse in modern contexts, emphasizing that theosis is not merely a historical or theoretical concept but one that actively shapes contemporary Christian thought and practice. This portion of the book demonstrates the ongoing relevance of theosis, showing how it informs ethical decision making and spiritual practices in today's world. By connecting historical understandings with contemporary applications, the book bridges past and present, theory and practice, offering readers a comprehensive view of theosis that is both deeply rooted and immediately relevant.

There is also a chapter on theosis and the public good that puts forward an argument for how it transforms believers in order to serve better and differently as they address contemporary challenges related to both society (injustice) and environmental care. The focus of this chapter emphasizes that theosis goes beyond individual spiritual formation and into broader social and environmental issues, in line with the holistic thinking of Christian discipleship.

Chapter 12 takes a forward-looking approach, attempting to reconcile ancient spiritual concepts with cutting-edge technological realities. It suggests a willingness to explore how traditional religious ideas might evolve or find new expression in a digital age. This pairing seeks to understand how the spiritual process of becoming more like God (theosis) can be understood or potentially enhanced through technological means. Such an exploration could lead to fascinating discussions about the nature of spirituality, the impact of technology on human consciousness, and the potential for digital tools to support (or potentially hinder) spiritual growth. This investigation shows that theosis is a living concept, which progresses to keep step with social transformation, inviting the faithful to contemplate where their faith meets and modifies current technology and culture. In these chapters, the theological idea is presented as a path of conversion, integrating spiritual growth with ethical commitment. The kingdom of God invites us to join the divine life and actively engage with our world, sharing in God's love and justice.

Each chapter will include a discussion on its relevance to daily life, with the exception of chapters 10–12, as these chapters already address the application of their ideas in real-life contexts.

Ultimately, *Transformation in Theosis: Embracing the Divine Nature* presents a wealth of riches about both what we mean by the term "theosis" as well as how life is lived inside this christological key. It demonstrates how theosis includes the process of restoration in God's divine image, acquiring his attributes over time and as a process of sanctification based on Scripture, tradition, and life in Christ. This book invites readers not only to abstract theosis but also into a transformed way of being in relationship with God and one another.

Now, as we reflect upon the fruits of each chapter, may we recall that theosis is not a destination or endpoint but an ongoing journey—a living invitation to manifest and express in our lives God's divine love-light and wisdom-luminescence.[1] Embracing theosis—this journey will continue to motivate us, and I hope it can embolden us more than ever to strive for self-transformation in ways that honor God, strengthen our communities, and care for all of creation, advancing together for a brighter future. This view of theosis could inspire individuals to see their spiritual path as having broad significance, prompting them to pursue personal growth not as a goal in itself but as a way to make a positive difference in the world.[2]

Most of all, may my twenty-third book be an agent for our personal and collective transformation, encouraging us to live with more compassion, wisdom, and a greater understanding of the divine spark within each one of us.

---

1. Leliovskyi, "Doctrine of Theosis."

2. Theosis is not a finite goal but a continuous process of growth and transformation. This aligns with the Orthodox understanding of salvation as a lifelong endeavor; the goal of theosis as expressing God's divine love-light and wisdom-luminescence in our lives. This poetic language evokes the idea of humans becoming vessels or conduits for divine qualities.

His divine power has given us everything we need for a godly life through our knowledge of him who called us by his own glory and goodness. Through these he has given us his very great and precious promises, so that through them you may participate in the divine nature, having escaped the corruption in the world caused by evil desires. (2 Pet 1:3–4 NIV)

Rev. Yohanes Bambang Mulyono

Chapter 1

Theosis and the Restoration of the *Imago Dei*

THEOSIS, ROOTED IN THE Greek term θέωσις ("theosis"), is a central concept in Christian spirituality that denotes the transformative process of union with God, wherein humans become increasingly conformed to the likeness of Christ and participate in the divine nature. Theosis is often referred to as deification or divinization, emphasizing the profound communion between humanity and God, which transcends mere moral or intellectual ascent with a mystical and transformative union.

Theosis holds profound significance in Christian spirituality, embodying the ultimate goal of human existence: the restoration of the divine image, manifest in the process of salvation and sanctification, participation in the divine nature, ethical living, communal worship, and eschatological hope. It beckons believers to embark on a transformative journey of union with God, becoming coheirs with Christ in the kingdom of God. Clendenin's statement underscores the importance of understanding theosis for anyone seeking to grasp Orthodox Christianity. It suggests that this concept is not just one doctrine among many but a lens through which the entire Orthodox faith and practice can be understood.[1] This centrality of theosis in Orthodoxy offers a distinctive perspective on the nature of human spiritual development and the ultimate goal of Christian life. It presents a vision of Christianity that is deeply transformative, seeing the end goal not just as moral

---

1. Clendenin, *Eastern Orthodox Christianity*, 120.

improvement or heavenly reward but as a profound participation in the divine nature itself.

Definition and Understanding of Theosis

Theosis provides a broader perspective that encompasses, yet surpasses, familiar Christian themes such as salvation and sanctification. It provides a rich vision of Christian spirituality as radically transformative, mystical, and directed towards union with God. And this is why theosis has been so captivating and lasting in Christian discourse, especially in the East. It is not a list of beliefs or moral codes but describes the journey of Christianity as one of becoming in which human nature itself evolves and is divinely transfigured. This definition presents theosis as both an inspiring vision of what humans can achieve and a reminder of the profound importance of spiritual life. In my humble opinion, it challenges us to view faith not merely as the means of salvation but as a transformative path. It is also an open invitation, welcoming everyone. This perspective on theosis could have significant implications for how one approaches spiritual practice, ethical living, and engagement with the world. It suggests a spirituality that is simultaneously deeply mystical and practically engaged, aimed at nothing less than becoming a living expression of divine love in the world.

Theosis is composed of transformation, unification, participation, and sharing in God's own being by nature. This includes being mingled, saturated, and breathed with divine qualities with the goal of becoming his expression—that is, so that God may live through us and express his love on earth. In the context of this rich, nuanced, and multilayered meaning lies our meta-spiritual perspective—that is, in his mercy God, by grace, is reaching out to bring a fallen human race into himself. This idea is beautifully articulated by Stavropoulos in *Partakers of the Divine Nature*: "The one true vocation that every human being has is that which must be achieved, understood soteriologically. Simply put, each of us is a ready-made God, a smaller copy of God destined to be consumed by Him."[2] As recipients of salvation in Christ, each individual uniquely experiences "theosis" and is destined by God to be "divinized"

---

2. Thomas, *Deification*, 208.

pursuit of spiritual goods and the cultivation of a deep, abiding love for God and one's fellow human beings.

Further, theosis speaks to salvation itself; that is to say, it speaks to what salvation means for us as individuals and how we are connected both with God and our neighbor in Christ. The great commandments of loving neighbor and identifying with the marginalized are central to Christian life, echoing satisfactorily in divine love seeking shalom for all creation. Theosis alludes to the fact that in the end, human beings are created for nothing else but a journey into God—or deification itself (*unio mystica*) through love and communion. It beckons us into our own spiritual journeys of our hearts through deep engagement with Christian teachings and practices, so that we can then live a life characterized by love, courage, and compassion toward others. Theosis is the work of calling human beings into who they are designed to be: beloved children, bearing God's image and likeness in creation.

Through theosis, humanity is restored to its original dignity and likeness to God. If previously humanity was marred by sin, theosis involves purification, illumination, and transformation of the entire person. It encompasses the idea that humanity, created in the image and likeness of God (*imago Dei*), has been distorted or marred by sin but can be restored to its original dignity and likeness to God through a process known as theosis. It involves the purification, illumination, and transformation of the entire person—body, soul, and spirit—bringing them into conformity with the image of Christ.

1. *Purification*: It is in this stage that the soul washes away impurity caused by sin and corrupting passions, which pervert God's image. This has to do with repentance, humility, and turning from sin. By means of those disciplines—confession (and the use of confessors), prayer, and fasting—they allow God to cleanse their hearts and minds, that they might be prepared for grace.

2. *Illumination*: The light of God's truth becomes clearer as individuals purify themselves. It is distinguished by the illumination of the mind and heart as one comes to gain more knowledge about God and thereby knowledge of his will. Through the enlightenment of Scripture, sacrament, and the providence of the Holy Spirit, they become better at seeing how to apply those unseen mysteries of life through a spiritual plane.

3. *Transformation*: The final stage in theosis is followed by the change of one's whole person into Christ. This is a process of growth in virtue, love, and holiness that lasts our whole life. Persons start by being molded into the image of God, loving as he loved and tendering mercy and righteousness in their thoughts, words, and deeds. But the end point of theosis is full participation in the life and glory of God himself.

Restoration of the Imago Dei

Restoration of the imago Dei through theosis is not merely about individual salvation but also about the renewal of all creation. As human beings are transformed into the likeness of Christ, they become agents of God's love and redemption in the world, working to bring about his kingdom of justice, peace, and reconciliation. Restoration of the imago Dei through theosis is a profound journey of spiritual growth and transformation in which human beings are restored to their original dignity and likeness to God, which has been marred by sin. Through purification, illumination, and transformation, individuals participate in the divine nature and become bearers of God's image in the world.

1. *Salvation and Sanctification*: Theosis can be thought of as a summation of both redemption and sanctification, with the former involving forgiveness for sins effected through Christ's redeeming work (also known as justification) and incorporation into the church while the latter involves progressing in union with Jesus to become more like him by means of divinization. Salvation and sanctification are basic terms in Christian theology that serve as key components of the ongoing process by which believers fulfill their purpose to be spiritually filled, healed, and reunited with God. At its most basic, salvation is the process by which people are saved from sin and reconciled with God through Jesus Christ's atoning work on the cross. It is the sinner's response to a holy God; yet this divine act of redemption or salvation, with the extension of mercy and grace, highlights that measure passed from an all loving eternal Creator: as lost sinners repent and place their faith in Christ, they are forgiven and reconciled. By his death on the cross, he paid for sin so that humanity may be justified before God and restored to right relationship with him.

2. *Life in Sanctification*: It is the continuing work by which God and man are brought together in righteousness; it is our sanctification. He is working in the new convert through the inner stream, purifying the character and attitudes of God as well. Sanctification is being made more like Christ and it isn't a one-time event but rather a lifetime of growth, maturity in the faith, as we learn to yield ourselves completely over to what the Holy Spirit wants us to do. Thereafter, his Spirit starts the work of renewal that molds a person's heart and character to look more like Jesus (2 Cor 3:18). While sanctification is a work of God through the Holy Spirit, it also involves an act of the believer's will. This cooperation consists of submitting to the leading of the Spirit, answering his nudges, and engaging in spiritual disciplines like talking (prayer), listening (word of God), worshiping, and fellowship with other believers. Such partnership is one of where the believer submit their will and desires to God, for him then be able to make something out his life as designed by being.

3. *Unity with God*: Theosis, a term closely related to Eastern Christian theology is the ultimate for salvation and sanctification; it signifies that the final purpose of the Christian life is unity with God. It points to the salvific and sanctifying power of God, in that he not only forgave our sins (saved) through Jesus but also calls us into a deep union with him where we are partakers of his divine nature. The key emphasis of theosis is that through Christ, humanity may truly share in the immaterial life of God; while man does not become one essence with he who dwells beyond creation, yet we indeed (in the words of the apostle Peter) "become partakers [κοινόω]of divine nature" (2 Pet 1:4).

   Both salvation and sanctification are dimensions of the Christian walk, functioning in complement with each other for the ultimate purpose of reconciling believers with God made possible through Christ. This is the essence of theosis, being incorporated now into a mystical union with God himself and moving onto the eternal and most ultimate fulfillment. Therefore, salvation and sanctification are not abstractions but an existential condition that fashions the identity and fate of every individual who follows Christ.

4. *Participation in the Divine Nature*: By grace, humans partake in the divine nature, entering into a profound communion of love and intimacy with God, characterized by unity of will and purpose.

Participation in the divine nature is a concept deeply rooted in Christian theology, particularly within the framework of the doctrine of grace. At its core, it signifies the remarkable relationship between humanity and the divine, facilitated by the grace of God. In Christian theology, God's nature is often described as infinite, transcendent, and characterized by perfect love, wisdom, and goodness. This divine nature is understood to be beyond the grasp of human comprehension or attainment through mere human effort. However, through the concept of grace, humans are invited to partake in this divine nature. Grace, in Christian understanding, is the unmerited favor and love of God extended towards humanity. It is through grace that humans are enabled to participate in the divine nature.[9]

This participation is not achieved through human striving or merit but is freely given by God as a gift. Entering into this participation involves a profound communion of love and intimacy with God. It is a relational union where humans are invited into a dynamic and reciprocal relationship with the divine. This communion is characterized by unity of will and purpose, where the desires and intentions of the individual align with the will of God. Through participation in the divine nature, humans experience a transformative union with God. This union brings about spiritual renewal and growth and a deepening of one's relationship with the divine. It involves the sharing of God's life and attributes, such as love, holiness, and righteousness.

This participation also implies a sharing in the mission and purposes of God in the world. As participants in the divine nature, humans are called to embody and express the love, compassion, and justice of God in their lives and relationships. This entails a commitment to living in accordance with the values and principles of the divine kingdom. Ultimately, participation in the divine nature is a profound expression of God's love and desire for communion with humanity. It reflects the beauty and mystery of the relationship between the Creator and the created, where humans are invited to experience the fullness of life in union with God.

---

9. The image of God in humanity, though marred by sin (Gen 3), is restored and renewed through Christ. Through faith in Christ and the process of sanctification (becoming more like Christ), humans are transformed into the likeness of Christ (2 Cor 3:18).

5. *Ethical and Moral Implications*: Theosis shapes ethical living, calling believers to embody virtues reflective of God's character, such as love, compassion, and holiness. At its core, theosis is the process through which individuals strive to become united with God, to attain a state of likeness or union with the divine. In this journey, ethical living becomes not just a set of rules to follow but a transformation of the entire being towards embodying virtues reflective of God's character. Central to theosis is the idea that humans are created in the image and likeness of God, and the ultimate goal is to grow into that likeness.

   This transformation involves not just adherence to a moral code but a profound internal change, a spiritual metamorphosis. Love, compassion, and holiness emerge as central virtues in this process. Love, as exemplified in the Christian tradition, transcends mere sentimentality or affection; it becomes an active force that seeks the well-being of others above oneself. Theosis calls believers to embody this selfless love, mirroring the divine love that embraces all humanity. Compassion, likewise, flows from the understanding of God's mercy and empathy towards his creation.

   Theosis calls us to realize a compassionate heart, connected with the pain of others and working toward its relief. This includes compassion for other humans, and even further for all creation as we are connected/interdependent in life. In theosis, however, this separation from sin is not a static holiness; it rather demands dynamism. Washing is not just about purity but a transformation from the inside out to become a god. The pursuit of holiness is the ongoing work and process in trying to be like Christ, constant refining or upgrading oneself morally, purging your heart from all impurities and assuring that every action you perform is obedient to God.

6. *Ethical Living*: The ethical implications of theosis are far reaching, touching every aspect of human existence. It challenges believers to engage in practices of prayer, fasting, almsgiving, and repentance, not as mere rituals but as means to deepen their union with God and cultivate virtuous living. It calls for a radical reorientation of priorities, placing spiritual growth and moral integrity above worldly pursuits.

   In addition, theosis underscores a social dimension of ethical life that is attentive to human relations and acknowledges our interconnected humanity. Believers are to create communities of love, justice, and reconciliation that reflect the unity and diversity characteristic in God himself. Theosis changes the theory and shapes ethical living by leading us through a transformative process aiming at union with God instead of just some virtues, like compassion or love. For me, it asks us to move beyond merely following the law and going through the motions of religious performance into a truer intimacy with God and our authentic selves.

7. *Communal and Ecclesial Dimension*: Theosis is not solely an individual pursuit but also communal, realized within the church through sacraments, liturgical worship, and spiritual fellowship. The communal and ecclesial dimension of theosis is a profound concept deeply rooted in the theology of Eastern Orthodox Christianity. At its core, theosis, or divinization, represents the transformative process through which individuals are called to become more like God, to participate in his divine nature, and to attain union with him. While theosis is often understood as an individual journey of spiritual growth and transformation, it is equally significant within the communal context of the church.

In Eastern Orthodox theology, the church is not merely a gathering of individuals but is understood as the body of Christ, a mystical and spiritual organism in which believers are united with Christ and with one another. Therefore, the process of theosis is not solely an isolated endeavor but is intricately linked to the communal life of the church. Sacraments play a central role in the communal dimension of theosis. These sacred rituals, such as baptism, chrismation, the Eucharist, and others, are seen as means of grace through which believers participate in the divine life of God. In the sacraments, individuals are not only united with Christ but are also integrated into the larger community of believers, strengthening the communal bonds that facilitate the journey toward theosis. Liturgical worship is another vital aspect of the communal dimension of theosis.

Believers gather in community to collectively worship God with praise, thanksgiving, and supplication. Far from being individualistic, liturgical worship is an equally corporate enterprise. It builds up the body of Christ and thus expresses that God makes people truly divine not as isolated individuals but in communion with each other. Additionally, church fellowship provides comradeship, encouraging and building up believers in their path to theosis while keeping one another accountable. Prayer, study, and service in community are ways for people of faith to engage in this, building one another up and deepening their transformation. Not only that, but this communal and eclesial dimension of theosis also reminds us of the fact that our personal spiritual life is intimately connected to others in a wider context within the church. In the sacraments, liturgy, and spiritual fellowship believers are bound together in Christ as one community on a journey toward union with God.

8. *Eschatological Hope*: Theosis points towards the fulfillment of God's plan for creation, offering hope of eternal life where humanity is fully transformed and united with God. At its core, eschatological hope embodies the belief that God's plan for creation will culminate in the complete transformation and union of humanity with the divine. This process of theosis involves a profound transformation of the human person, both spiritually and morally, towards likeness to God. Central to the concept of theosis is the belief that humanity was created in the image and likeness of God (Gen 1:26–27) and that through the incarnation of Christ human nature is united with the divine nature in the person of Jesus.

Through Christ's life, death, and resurrection, humanity is offered the possibility of participation in the divine life, reconciled to God, and restored to communion with him. Eschatological hope, therefore, is the anticipation of the fulfillment of this divine plan for humanity. It is the expectation that, at the end of time, all creation will be restored and transformed, and humanity will be fully united with God in a state of perfect communion.[10] This hope is grounded in the promises of God revealed in Scripture and affirmed through the life, death, and resurrection of Jesus Christ. The eschatological vision portrayed in Christian Scripture, particularly in the New Testament, depicts a future reality where God's kingdom is fully realized, where there is no more suffering, pain, or death, and where humanity experiences the fullness of life in God's presence. This vision is encapsulated in passages such as Rev 21:3–4, which speaks of

---

10. The belief is that Christ, being the perfect representation of God, shows us what God is like in human form. Humans, being created in the image of God, reflect certain aspects of God's nature in their own being. This includes capacities like reason, morality, creativity, and the ability to have relationships, which are seen as reflections of God's own attributes.

a new heaven and a new earth where God dwells among his people, wiping away every tear and making all things new.

Eschatological hope, therefore, offers believers a profound sense of purpose and assurance in the midst of life's struggles and challenges. It provides a perspective that transcends the limitations of earthly existence, reminding believers that their ultimate destiny lies in union with God. This hope sustains them in times of trial and suffering, knowing that their present experiences are but temporary and that a glorious future awaits them in the presence of God.

Eschatological hope, grounded in the concept of theosis, points towards the fulfillment of God's plan for creation, offering believers the assurance of eternal life where humanity is fully transformed and united with God. It is a hope that transcends earthly realities, providing meaning and purpose to the journey of faith and ultimately culminating in the realization of God's kingdom where all things are made new.

Theosis embodies the transformative power of God's grace, leading believers into ever-deepening communion with him. As the ultimate goal of Christian life and spirituality, theosis invites believers to embark on a journey of spiritual growth, striving towards union with the divine and the attainment of true human flourishing. The path to theosis is a lifelong journey that involves spiritual growth, discipline, and surrender to God's will. It requires a commitment to prayer, fasting, and service to others.

As believers deepen their relationship with God, they are gradually transformed into the image of Christ. Moreover, theosis holds profound eschatological implications. It anticipates the fulfillment of God's kingdom where believers, having attained union with God, reign as coheirs with Christ. This eschatological hope provides believers with a sense of purpose and anticipation, which guides their actions and attitudes in the present.

Relevance in Daily Life

1. *Personal Growth and Transformation*: As theosis involves becoming more like Christ, in daily life it encourages personal development. This means striving to embody qualities like compassion, humility, and patience. For example, if you're dealing with a challenging coworker, approaching the situation with patience and understanding can be seen as a step towards spiritual growth and transformation.

2. *Commitment to Spiritual Practices*: Theosis emphasizes practices like prayer, fasting, and service. In a practical sense, this translates to setting aside time for reflection and connection with God. Even small acts, such as setting aside a few minutes for meditation or engaging in acts of kindness, can be ways to integrate these practices into your routine.

3. *Living with Purpose*: The eschatological hope of theosis—that believers will eventually reign with Christ—can inspire a sense of purpose in daily actions. Understanding that your actions have eternal significance can motivate you to act with integrity and kindness, knowing that these choices contribute to your spiritual journey and have a broader impact.

4. *Developing Relationships*: The journey towards theosis involves deepening relationships, both with God and with others. This means investing in meaningful relationships, showing love and support to friends and family, and working towards reconciliation and forgiveness. For instance, making an effort to resolve conflicts and build stronger, more loving relationships reflects the transformative power of God's grace.

5. *Facing Challenges*: The process of theosis is about surrendering to God's will, which can be particularly relevant when facing life's difficulties. By accepting challenges as part of your spiritual journey and trusting in God's plan, you can find peace and purpose in struggles. This might look like practicing patience during hard times or seeking God's guidance in making tough decisions.

6. *Service to Others*: Theosis involves a commitment to serving others, which reflects the selfless love of Christ. In everyday life, this could be as simple as helping a neighbor, volunteering in your community, or offering support to someone in need. These acts of service are expressions of your spiritual growth and commitment to living out your faith.

7. *Hope and Anticipation*: The eschatological aspect of theosis gives believers a sense of hope and anticipation for the future. This hope can influence how you approach daily life, helping you to remain optimistic and resilient. For example, maintaining a hopeful attitude during challenging times or working towards long-term goals with faith in a greater purpose can be seen as living out this hope.

Chapter 2

Divinization in the Divine Quality

THE MEANING OF THEOSIS transcends a simple literal interpretation such as "divinization," which might imply that humans can become divine in the same nature as God. This interpretation would be erroneous because humans are mortal creations, while God is the eternal and divine Creator. Thomas Anastos clarifies that the Orthodox Church views God as uncreated, existing beyond all being, and thus incomprehensible and inexpressible.[1] God is eternal, uncreated, beyond all being, and therefore beyond human comprehension and expression. At the heart of this understanding lies the concept of divine transcendence, which asserts that God exists beyond the limitations of creation and human comprehension.

The Orthodox conception of God as existing beyond all being underscores the idea that God's essence transcends the categories of existence as we understand them. In philosophical terms, existence is often associated with contingent realities—things that have the potential not to exist. However, God, as the uncreated source of existence itself, transcends this notion of contingent being. Instead, God is understood to be the ground of being, the very essence from which all existence emanates. This acknowledges the limitations of human intellect and language in grasping the divine. While humans can apprehend aspects of

---

1. Anastos, "Palamas' Radicalization," 335–36. Thomas Anastos's clarification illuminates the Orthodox Church's profound understanding of God as uncreated, transcendent, incomprehensible, and inexpressible. This theological framework invites believers into a deeper encounter with the mystery of the divine and fosters a spirituality grounded in humility, awe, and wonder.

God through revelation, experience, and reason, the Orthodox tradition maintains that the totality of God's essence remains beyond human comprehension.[2] Consequently, any attempt to fully articulate or encapsulate God in human language ultimately falls short.

Unbridgeable Chasm Between God and Humanity

Humans cannot be divine nor can our existence approach that of the being of God. As a result, theosis has zero to do with human nature changing to become part of God's essence. Humanity is still human and cannot avoid it. Various religious traditions locate the insurmountable gap between humans and gods at their centers. This chasm is the rift that separates God as infinite, eternal, and transcendent from humanity: their finitude, temporality, and immanence. This discrepancy makes apparent the primary ontological difference between Creator and created. It shows the beyond-nature division between divine and human that can never be closed or bridged by any feat whatsoever of man. This concept brings with it substantial questions concerning the being of God, human beings, and our intermediate relation.

At the heart of this idea is the recognition of the transcendent nature of God. In many religious traditions, God is understood to be infinite, eternal, and omnipotent, possessing qualities that are fundamentally different from those of human beings. God is often seen as the Creator and Sustainer of the universe, existing outside of time and space, and possessing knowledge and power beyond human comprehension. This understanding of God as transcendent highlights the vast difference between the divine and the human. On the other hand, humanity is seen as finite, limited, and imperfect. While human beings may possess certain qualities or attributes that reflect the divine image, they are ultimately constrained by their mortality, their fallibility, and their inherent limitations. Despite our aspirations, achievements, and advancements, humans remain fundamentally distinct from God in terms of our nature and capabilities.

2. The Orthodox Church asserts the notion of God's uncreated nature. This concept distinguishes God from everything else in existence. While all created things, including humanity, owe their existence to a source outside themselves, God stands apart as the uncreated source of all that is. This understanding highlights the fundamental distinction between the Creator and the created, emphasizing God's eternal and self-sufficient nature. See Packer, "What Did the Cross Achieve?"; Stott, *Cross of Christ*.

This unbridgeable chasm between God and humanity has profound effects upon our religious thinking and doing. It highlights why we must be humble in our dealing with the divine, because only a fool would not consider limits of human intelligence and capabilities whilst engaging or seeking to appreciate divinity. It also teaches us the value of faith and trust in God, recognizing that we cannot earn our own salvation but must rather depend on grace from above. An awareness of this gap can be profoundly moving, leading us to worship after a mystical encounter with the divine. It encourages us to consider the expansiveness of God as well as holding our own value and dignity.

In light of this understanding, attempts to bridge the chasm between God and humanity through human means or methods are ultimately futile and misguided. While humans may strive for spiritual enlightenment or union with the divine, such efforts are inherently limited by our finite nature and can never fully overcome the inherent difference between God and humanity. Ultimately, the recognition of the unbridgeable chasm between God and humanity invites us to embrace a posture of humility, reverence, and awe in our relationship with the divine, recognizing our own limitations while also acknowledging the boundless love and mercy of God towards humanity. In the Christian tradition, for instance, the doctrine of theosis emphasizes the transformative journey of individuals toward divine likeness. However, this journey does not entail a metamorphosis of human nature into the essence of God. Rather, it involves the participation of humans in the divine nature through grace, leading to the cultivation of virtues and the alignment of one's will with the will of God.

A chasm between man and God that cannot be bridged highlights the humble nature of all references to God. For human beings, although they can aspire to copy divine qualities and draw near to God, humans cannot comprise the infinite existent nature of his divinity. Such a conception of the incomprehensibility of God cultivates an attitude in which it is recognized humility and reverence are required to address the divine. It requires a posture of humility and curiosity, which affirms the limits of our human capacity juxtaposed against the cavernous enigma that God is. Instead of trying to domesticate or encase God in human categories, the Orthodox tradition adopts a responsive posture that remains open and present before him; it chooses reverence over capture, exploration over mastery.

Misconstruing Theosis

Misconstruing theosis as the transformation of human nature into a part of God's essence would be a theological error, as it blurs the distinction between the Creator and the created. It would imply a pantheistic understanding where humans essentially become God, which contradicts the foundational beliefs of many religious traditions. Instead, theosis should be understood within the framework of divine-human communion, where humans, while remaining distinct beings, can partake in the life of God through a process of spiritual growth and transformation.[3] This understanding preserves the dignity of human nature as created by God while affirming the possibility of a deep and intimate relationship with the divine. In this light, Philip Schaff cites John Damascene, who explains that humans are "deified" not by becoming divine beings themselves, but by participating in the divine glory. The deification of humans occurs through sharing in the divine glory, not through a metamorphosis into the divine nature.[4]

So, what then does theosis entail? It signifies a profound union with God, where humans participate fully in his divine life and attributes. However, this union doesn't entail a transformation of human nature into divine nature. Instead, it involves the elevation of humans to a state of communion and likeness with God, wherein they reflect his glory and participate in his divine energies. In essence, theosis represents the pinnacle of human spiritual development, where individuals experience a deep, transformative union with the divine while retaining their distinct human identity.[5]

---

3. In theosis, human nature does not merge with or become a part of God's essence. The essence and nature of humanity remain distinct and created, while theosis entails a deepening of union with the divine. This transformation is not absolute but relative, as articulated by Maximus the Confessor, who remarked that through grace, individuals partake in all that God is, except for identity in essence. Cf. Palmer et al., *Philokalia*, 2:193.

4. Cf. Palmer et al., *Philokalia*, 2:189-90, 243, 246, 263, 267; 3:79. Human nature remains distinct from the divine nature; it does not undergo a metamorphosis into God's essence. The concept of theosis underscores that human nature, as a created entity, maintains its inherent identity. Therefore, theosis does not entail the transmutation of human nature into divine essence; rather, it signifies a relational and relative transformation.

5. Here Saint Irenaeus explains to us that through the incarnation, by which the Son of God became the Son of Man, we receive the adoption and become sons of God and thus attain incorruptibility and immortality. He makes it clear that the goal (or as he calls it the end) of the incarnation is that, because the word of God has taken our humanity into himself and united our corruptibility and mortality with his own

The meaning of deification in theosis is rooted in the event of the Word, who is God, taking on human form. Through the incarnation of Christ, the transcendent God became immanent, bridging the gap between divinity and humanity.[6] Consequently, through faith in Christ, humanity is drawn into communion with his divine essence. However, the process of theosis does not alter the fundamental essence or nature of humanity. Rather, it is understood as the gradual transformation of human beings to reflect the character and attributes of God. In Christ, the transcendent God became immanent, dwelling among humanity and intimately sharing in its experiences, struggles, and joys.

Through Christ's incarnation, humanity is offered a pathway to communion with God. By participating in the life, death, and resurrection of Christ, individuals are invited into a transformative process whereby they are gradually conformed to the likeness of Christ.[7] This transformation involves the purification of the soul, the cultivation of virtues, and the acquisition of divine grace through the sacraments and prayer.

Being merged in God as a new creation does not suggest an abolition of personal identity, nor is there any loss of self. Instead, it represents the realization of human potential, reflecting how humanity was created in the image and likeness of God. In theosis, human beings do not become God in his essence as if a part of them were absorbed into the divine essence; rather through participation in him, by participation in God's energies, they attain self-definition and thus more fully retain what people have recognized must be distinct for our humanity. Theosis effects not only a radical transformation of character in being set on the divine path but also the preservation of human nature in accordance with creaturely potential. And this path into theosis is truly an unending one, something lived out from day to day and year to year, wherein we always seek spiritual growth in union with God. This is a partnership

---

incorruptibility and immortality, we might receive the adoption of sons. See books 3 and 4 of Irenaeus, *Against Heresies*, where he discusses Christ's nature extensively.

6. Similarly, Lossky in *Orthodox Theology* emphasizes that the transformation brought about by Christ does not alter the essential nature of humanity but rather enhances its quality. When Christ, the Word, assumed human form and deified humanity, he elevated the quality of human nature without changing its essence.

7. Theosis represents the ultimate destiny of humanity—to become like God through participation in the life of Christ. It is a journey of profound significance, offering believers the hope of transcending their earthly limitations and attaining union with the divine.

between man and God, With the Holy Spirit being that which fulfills this fully divine life in each person.

The significance of embracing newness in shaping the quality of human character is beautifully exemplified in 2 Cor 5:17: "Therefore, if anyone is in Christ, the new creation has come: The old has gone, the new is here!" (NIV). The apostle Paul vividly portrays those united with Christ as "new creations" (*kainē ktisis*). When someone becomes "in Christ," they enter into a deep union with him. This union is not merely external or superficial but involves a profound inward change. The phrase "the new creation has come" suggests a radical transformation at the very core of one's being. It speaks to a spiritual rebirth, where old patterns of thought, behavior, and identity are replaced with new ones.

A Journey of Purification and Sanctification

Theosis involves a journey of purification and sanctification, where the old self, characterized by sin and separation from God, is gradually shed away. As this old self diminishes, the new self, conformed to the image of Christ, emerges. This new self is characterized by qualities such as love, holiness, humility, and compassion. The process of theosis is ongoing and dynamic. It is not a one-time event but a lifelong journey of growth and transformation.[8]

The verse 2 Cor 5:17 can be interpreted in relation to theosis as describing the transformative journey of believers who, through their union with Christ, are continually being renewed and conformed to his image. The phrase "the old has gone, the new is here" emphasizes the continual nature of this process. It speaks to the ongoing work of God's grace in the life of the believer, continually shaping them into the likeness of Christ. It speaks to the profound change that occurs within a person who participates in the process of theosis, where old ways of being are replaced by new ones, which reflect the character and likeness of Christ. This transformative process, termed deification, doesn't alter human essence; rather, individuals remain creations (*ktisis*), yet imbued with fresh spiritual dimensions and virtues (*kainē*). Through

---

8. Theosis encapsulates the transformative journey of humanity towards divine likeness and union with God. Rooted in the teachings of the early church fathers and deeply embedded in Eastern Orthodox tradition, theosis offers a unique perspective on the purpose and destiny of human existence.

this renewal, believers transcend the dictates of the flesh and instead align their lives with the Spirit's guidance.

In Gal 5:16, Paul exhorts believers to "walk by the Spirit" to overcome the allure of fleshly desires. The verse suggests a contrast between the desires of the flesh and the guidance of the Spirit. Theosis involves the gradual overcoming of worldly desires and the cultivation of virtues that reflect the divine nature. Walking by the Spirit implies a continual surrendering of one's own will to the will of God, which leads to spiritual growth and transformation. In the context of theosis, this verse encourages believers to actively participate in their own spiritual development by choosing to follow the leading of the Holy Spirit over the impulses of their flesh. Through this ongoing process, believers are transformed more and more into the likeness of God, ultimately fulfilling the divine purpose of human existence.

Those who undergo deification are inclined towards the Spirit's promptings (*epithimia pneuma*) and consequently forsake the impulses of the flesh (*epithimia sarkos*, Gal 5:16–17). Consequently, the deified exhibit the fruits of the Spirit (*karpos tou pneumatos*), exemplifying qualities such as "love, joy, peace, patience, kindness, goodness, faithfulness, gentleness, self-control" (Gal 5:21–23 NIV). The process of deification, as understood in the theological framework of the Orthodox Church, unfolds as believers respond to God's gracious gift of salvation, exercising their free will to align themselves with the divine will and thus become more like God.

St. Gregory of Nyssa articulates this concept, noting that humans possess the image of God inherently through their rationality, but they receive the fullness of this image by actively cultivating virtue through their free will. Humans have always been set apart as bearers of God's image due to their ability to reason. However, this is only the foundation. We can fully express this divine image by developing moral virtues. The reflection of God's characteristics becomes more direct as humans make conscious moral choices and cultivate their character, living according to the image of God in which they were created.[9] However, the question arises, How does God's salvific gift lead to deification or theosis? It's crucial to clarify that theosis does not entail humans becoming God or acquiring the divine essence. Rather, theosis involves the transformation and elevation of human nature towards godliness.

---

9. Cf. Gregory of Nyssa, *Making of Man*.

In essence, theosis unfolds as believers, responding to God's salvific grace, undergo a process of spiritual growth and refinement. Through the exercise of their free will, they actively engage in the pursuit of virtue and conformity to the divine will, thereby becoming increasingly united with God. This transformative journey, rooted in the relational dynamics between humanity and divinity, signifies not a dissolution of human nature into God, but rather a profound elevation towards the divine likeness.

The Richness and Depth of Theosis

We endeavor to unveil the richness and depth of theosis as a guiding principle for the spiritual life. Through the grace of God, humans participate in the divine nature and become increasingly conformed to the likeness of Christ. It is not merely a moral or intellectual ascent, but a mystical and transformative union with the triune God. Theosis involves the purification of the soul, the illumination of the mind, and the union of the will with God's will, resulting in a communion of love that transcends human understanding.[10] The ultimate goal of theosis is the union of the human will with God's will. Through prayer, obedience, and a life of virtue, believers seek to align their desires and choices with God's purposes and commands. This union of wills signifies a deep communion of love between the individual and God, where the believer's actions and motivations reflect God's love and righteousness.[11] This journey toward theosis encompasses the entire being, integrating body, mind, and spirit in a harmonious alignment with the divine, ultimately leading to the fulfillment of humanity's highest potential and the realization of unity with God.

The concept of theosis holds profound significance in Christian theology for several reasons:

1. *Biblical Foundation*: Theosis finds its roots in the Scriptures, where 2 Pet 1:4 speaks of believers becoming "partakers of the divine nature" through Christ. Interpreting this passage within the framework of theosis entails delving into the nature of God, humanity, and the

---

10. Theosis includes the illumination of the mind or enlightenment by divine grace. This stage involves the deepening of spiritual understanding, the reception of divine wisdom, and growth in the knowledge of God's truth. It enables believers to perceive spiritual realities more clearly and to discern God's will for their lives.

11. Stavropoulos, *Partakers of Divine Nature*, 17–18.

relationship between them as revealed in Christian theology. Analyzing 2 Pet 1:4 within this framework, it becomes evident that the passage speaks to the transformative nature of the Christian life.[12] Believers, by virtue of their relationship with Christ, are granted a share in the divine nature. This participation entails not only forgiveness of sins and reconciliation with God but also the ongoing process of spiritual growth and conformity to Christ.

2. *Nature of God and Incarnation.*
   a. *Nature of God*: Central to theosis is the understanding of God's nature as inherently relational and dynamic. Rather than a distant and aloof deity, the Christian God is depicted as immanent, desiring communion with humanity. This aligns with the biblical narrative of God's ongoing involvement with creation, culminating in the incarnation of Christ.
   b. *Incarnation*: Theosis emphasizes the significance of the incarnation—the belief that God became human in the person of Jesus Christ. Through the incarnation, God bridges the gap between the divine and the human, offering a pathway for humanity to participate in the divine life.
   c. *Union with Christ*: Theosis underscores the idea of union with Christ as the means by which believers partake in the divine nature. This union is not merely intellectual or moral but transformative, involving the whole person—body, soul, and spirit. Through faith in Christ and participation in the sacraments, believers are united with Christ and progressively conformed to his likeness.
   d. *Transformation*: Theosis involves a process of spiritual transformation whereby believers are gradually conformed to the image of Christ. This transformation encompasses moral purification, spiritual illumination, and union with God in love. It is a synergistic cooperation between divine grace and human response,

---

12. Interpreting 2 Pet 1:4 within the framework of theosis underscores the profound relationship between God and humanity in Christian theology. Believers, through their union with Christ and the work of the Holy Spirit, are invited into a transformative process where they become increasingly conformed to God's likeness and participate in his divine nature. This concept not only speaks to the theological depth of Christian faith but also to the practical implications for the Christian life of holiness, love, and eternal hope in God's promises.

wherein believers are empowered by the Holy Spirit to grow in holiness and likeness to Christ.

e. *Eternal Destiny*: Theosis points towards the ultimate destiny of humanity, which is communion with God in eternity. Believers, through their participation in the divine nature, are destined for union with God—a union characterized by love, joy, and eternal fellowship.[13]

f. *Christ-Likeness*: The concept of theosis offers a profound vision of human potential and divine-human communion within Christian theology. Grounded in Scripture and affirmed by the tradition of the church, theosis invites believers into a dynamic relationship with God wherein they are transformed into Christ's likeness and destined for eternal communion with the divine. Similarly, Jesus' invitation to "be perfect, therefore, as your heavenly Father is perfect" (Matt 5:48 NIV) reflects the ultimate goal of theosis—to attain the fullness of God's love and holiness and embody his divine attributes in our lives. To understand the connection between Jesus' invitation and theosis, it's important to delve into the context of the Sermon on the Mount, where this statement is found. In this sermon, Jesus presents a radical reinterpretation of the Mosaic law, emphasizing the inward transformation of the heart over mere adherence to external rules. He challenges his listeners to embody the values of the kingdom of God—love, mercy, humility, and righteousness—in their thoughts, attitudes, and actions.

g. *Gradual Transformation*: When Jesus speaks of being perfect as the heavenly Father is perfect, he isn't setting an impossible standard of flawlessness. Rather, he's calling believers to emulate the divine character of God—a character marked by boundless love, infinite mercy, unwavering justice, and complete holiness. In other words, Jesus is inviting his followers to participate in the divine life and to reflect God's nature in their own lives.[14] Theosis,

---

13. Theosis underscores the transformative journey of becoming more like Christ in this life and the glorious fulfillment of being united with God in eternity. This concept not only enriches Christian theology but also inspires believers to live in anticipation of the divine communion they will enjoy with their Creator and Redeemer.

14. In theosis, human nature is not obliterated or absorbed into the divine but rather elevated and perfected. St. Athanasius of Alexandria, who wrote "God became man so that man might become God" (*Incarnation*, 54.3).

then, can be seen as the process through which Christians strive to attain this perfection. It involves a gradual transformation of the entire person—body, soul, and spirit—in communion with God. Through prayer, repentance, ascetic practices, and participation in the sacraments, believers cooperate with the grace of God to purify their hearts, align their will with his, and grow in likeness to Christ. Therefore, Jesus' call to be perfect as the heavenly Father is perfect reflects the ultimate goal of theosis—the restoration of the divine image within humanity, the union of the created with the uncreated, and the fulfillment of God's plan for our transformation into beings of perfect love and holiness. It's a call to embrace our true identity as children of God and to live in communion with him for all eternity.

3. *Incarnational Theology*: Theosis is intricately intertwined with the incarnation of Christ, wherein he assumed human flesh to forge a union between humanity and divinity. Through Christ's earthly journey, sacrificial death, and triumphant resurrection, humanity is extended the opportunity for a restored relationship with God and engagement in the divine existence. As Athanasius boldly declared, "God became man so that man might become god." In the work where this statement can be found, *On the Incarnation of the Word*, Athanasius discusses the significance of the divine incarnation in Jesus Christ. The significance is rooted in the belief that through union with Christ humans can share in his divine nature and participate in the life of God.[15]

4. *Salvation and Sanctification*: Theosis illuminates the profound journey of salvation and sanctification in Christian theology. It articulates not only the redemption from sins but also the intricate restoration and exaltation of human nature to its pristine dignity and intended purpose. Through theosis, humanity transcends the shackles of sin and mortality, embracing a liberated existence marked by holiness and intimate communion with the divine.

Vladimir Lossky discusses this concept extensively in his works. Here are his key writings that address this theme: *The Mystical Theology of the Eastern Church* (1944), *Orthodox Theology: An Introduction*, which compiles Lossky's lectures at St. Denys Institute in Paris (published posthumously in 1978) and contains important sections on the doctrine of theosis. This teaching does not imply an ontological change in essence but rather a participation in the divine energies or attributes of God.

15. Athanasius, *Incarnation*, 54.3.

5. *Ecclesial and Sacramental Life*: Theosis infuses every aspect of the church's existence and its sacramental mysteries. Through the transformative rituals of baptism, chrismation, the Eucharist, and other sacraments, believers are not only initiated into but also continually nurtured by the divine life, advancing on the path towards theosis. The church, as the mystical body of Christ, stands as the sacred vessel of divine grace and communion; it is where the process of theosis finds its fullest expression, within the embracing folds of community.

6. *Eschatological Hope*: Theosis, as the culmination of God's plan for creation, beckons towards the ultimate fulfillment. It foresees the complete consummation of all existence in Christ, wherein humanity achieves total metamorphosis and eternal union with the divine. Theosis unveils a vista of hope and realization, where the sovereign love of God reigns supreme, every sorrow is tenderly erased, and eternal solace and joy are granted.

Theosis is a doctrine of Christian theology that depicts the nature and purpose of humanity. This book highlights the journey of transformation into divine union, through Christ's incarnation and embodied within the life of God's people. This process of theosis requires that, as we draw closer to God through our love, holiness, and compassion, we also become more like him by embodying these attributes in the world. In doing so, others will be able to see the purpose of their lives: to live according to his image. Theosis, therefore, continues to be an abiding and indispensable element of Christian spirituality, which calls Christians into full participation in the life divine through co-inhering with Christ both now and forevermore. In this union, humanity finds its highest realization, and the joy of divine communion sparkles in all creation as God's eternal plan is made known worldwide.

Relevance in Daily Life

1. *Embracing Humility and Reverence*: Recognize your limits and the distinction between human nature and divine nature. In practical terms, this means approaching spiritual practices, personal growth, and even relationships with a sense of humility and respect. Understanding that there is a vast difference between our capabilities and the divine can foster a more grounded, respectful attitude toward

others and ourselves. Approach spiritual practices, whether prayer, meditation, or acts of service, with a sense of awe and respect for the divine. This awareness can lead to a more mindful and sincere engagement with faith and spirituality.

2. *Pursuing Spiritual Growth*: View personal growth as a continuous journey rather than a destination. Engage in practices that help you grow in virtues such as love, patience, and kindness. This might include regular self-reflection, seeking mentorship, or actively working on personal weaknesses. Strive to live in a way that reflects the divine attributes you admire. This could manifest as increased compassion towards others, striving for honesty, or dedicating time to serve those in need.

3. *Balancing Aspiration and Acceptance*: Set spiritual and personal goals that are challenging yet attainable, understanding that complete perfection is not achievable in this life. Celebrate progress rather than expecting perfection. Embrace your human nature with its limitations and imperfections. This acceptance can lead to greater self-compassion and patience with others.

4. *Living Out Divine Qualities*: Regularly reflect on how you can embody virtues such as compassion, humility, and forgiveness. Take actionable steps to integrate these virtues into your daily interactions, whether in your family, workplace, or community. Engage in spiritual practices such as prayer, meditation, or reading inspirational texts that help you stay aligned with these virtues and keep you focused on your spiritual journey.

5. *Recognizing the Process of Transformation*: Embrace the idea of life as a journey of continuous improvement. Regularly reassess and adjust your actions and attitudes to align more closely with your spiritual values. Understand that spiritual growth often involves overcoming challenges and setbacks. Approach difficulties as opportunities for learning and growth, maintaining faith in the transformative process.

6. *Engaging with the Divine Grace*: Recognize and be grateful for the grace and support you receive in your spiritual journey. This can foster a sense of gratitude and reliance on divine assistance rather than purely relying on your own efforts. Approach spiritual practices and interactions with others with an open heart, welcoming the divine presence and grace into your life and recognizing the connection of your spiritual journey with a larger divine plan.

Chapter 3

Theosis in Christian Theology

THEOSIS FINDS ITS ROOTS in the Scriptures, where 2 Pet 1:4 speaks of believers becoming "partakers of the divine nature" through Christ. Similarly, Jesus' invitation to "be perfect, therefore, as your heavenly Father is perfect" (Matt 5:48) reflects the ultimate goal of theosis, which is not merely a standard of moral or ethical behavior, but is to attain the perfection of God's love and holiness.

Jesus is inviting his followers to strive towards the complete and unblemished nature of God's love, suggesting that through divine grace and transformation, believers can grow closer to the perfect nature of God. Theosis is about an intimate and transformative participation in God's divine attributes. These Scripture passages highlight the journey towards this divine union and transformation, where believers are called to embrace God's nature and attain a level of holiness and love that reflects God's perfection.

The Message of 2 Peter 1:4

The epistle of 2 Pet 1:4 in the Bible states, "Through these he has given us his very great and precious promises, so that through them you may participate in the divine nature, having escaped the corruption in the world caused by evil desires" (NIV).

Matthew Henry emphasizes the transformative power of the promises of God. He emphasizes that through the promises of God, believers are enabled to partake in the divine nature. This could be understood in a spiritual sense, indicating that believers are made like God in character and holiness through their relationship with him.[1] Matthew Henry's commentary on 2 Pet 1:4 may resonate with the broader theological concept of believers being transformed to reflect the divine nature through their union with Christ.[2]

Plummer emphasizes the transformative power of God's promises. He highlights that through these promises, believers are enabled to share in the divine nature, suggesting a deep union with God. Ellicott declares that this participation in the divine nature involves a transformation of character and a sharing in the holiness and attributes of God.[3] Therefore, although Plummer may not directly address the concept of theosis, his commentary on 2 Pet 1:4 could resonate with the idea that believers, through their union with Christ and participation in his promises, are transformed to become more like God in their character and conduct. This interpretation would be in line with the broader theological concept of theosis.

MacLaren emphasizes the transformative power of God's promises. He highlights that through these promises, believers are enabled to share in the divine nature, suggesting a deep union with God. He emphasizes that this participation in the divine nature involves a transformation of character and a sharing in the holiness and attributes of God.[4] He stresses the idea that believers are called to reflect God's char-

---

1. While Henry may not explicitly use the term theosis, his commentary could align with the idea that believers, through their union with Christ and participation in his promises, are transformed to become more like God in their character and conduct. This transformation reflects the process of theosis, where believers progressively become more united with God and share in his divine attributes.

2. Henry, *Commentary*.

3. Plummer, "Second Peter." Plummer's interpretation of believers sharing in the divine nature through God's promises underscores the depth of God's love and his desire for intimate communion with his people. It challenges believers to embrace the transformative work of God in their lives and to live in a manner that reflects the holiness and attributes of the divine nature they are called to share in. This perspective not only enriches understanding of Christian theology but also inspires a life of faith, hope, and active participation in God's redemptive plan.

4. MacLaren, "Partakers of the Divine." MacLaren's interpretation highlights the dynamic and transformative nature of Christian faith, where believers are not only recipients of God's promises but active participants in his divine nature. This perspective deepens our understanding of sanctification as a process of becoming more like Christ and underscores the profound intimacy and communion believers can experience with God through faith. It inspires a life of devotion, holiness, and spiritual vitality, rooted

acter in their lives, becoming more like him in love, righteousness, and purity. This interpretation would be consistent with the idea of theosis, where believers are progressively conformed to the image of Christ and grow in their likeness to him.

Barnes interprets this verse in a way that emphasizes the transformative power of God's promises. He highlights that through these promises, believers are enabled to share in the divine nature, suggesting a deep union with God. Barnes emphasize that this participation in the divine nature involves a transformation of character and a sharing in the holiness and attributes of God. He stresses the idea that believers are called to reflect God's character in their lives, becoming more like him in love, righteousness, and purity.[5] This interpretation would be consistent with the idea of theosis, where believers are progressively conformed to the image of Christ and grow in their likeness to him. The commentary explains that through God's promises believers become partakers of the divine nature. This participation implies a transformative process where believers are infused with the characteristics and attributes of God, such as holiness, righteousness, and love. This aligns with the broader theological concept of theosis, where believers are progressively transformed into the image of Christ through their union with him. The key words and most important meanings of the message in 2 Pet 1:4 include:

1. *Theias (divine)*: This term refers to something that is of or related to God, the divine. It conveys the essence of the divine, that which is transcendent, holy, and beyond the realm of mere human understanding. In the context of 2 Pet 1:4, the "divine nature" suggests that believers are invited to partake in the essence of God himself, to be in communion with the divine.

2. *Koinōnoi (participate)*: This term speaks to the idea of sharing, communion, or fellowship. It's not just a passive reception but an active engagement. In this verse, believers are not merely recipients

---

in the transformative power of God's promises and his gracious invitation to share in his divine nature.

5. Barnes, *Notes on the New Testament*. Barnes's interpretation offers a profound reflection on how 2 Pet 1:4 teaches believers about the transformative power of God's promises and their participation in the divine nature. It underscores the deep union with God made possible through Christ, the ongoing transformation of character into Christlikeness, and the call to reflect God's holiness and attributes in all aspects of life. This interpretation inspires believers to embrace God's promises with faith, pursue intimacy with him fervently, and strive for continual growth in likeness to Christ.

of God's promises but active participants in his divine nature. It implies a deep, intimate relationship with God, where believers are invited to share in his attributes, purposes, and character.

3. *Physeōs (nature)*: This term refers to the inherent characteristics or qualities that define a thing or being. In the context of this verse, it points to the essential nature of God himself. The invitation to partake in the divine nature suggests a transformational process where believers are conformed to the likeness of God, adopting his qualities such as love, holiness, righteousness, and eternity.

Putting it all together, 2 Pet 1:4 offers a profound insight into the nature of the Christian faith. It speaks of a divine invitation extended to believers to not only receive God's promises but to actively participate in his divine nature. This participation involves a deep communion with God, where believers are transformed to reflect his attributes and character. It speaks to the transformative power of the gospel, which not only offers forgiveness of sins but also invites believers into a profound and intimate relationship with the Creator of the universe.

This verse underscores the profound privilege and weighty responsibility inherent in being a Christian. Followers of Christ are not only beneficiaries of God's boundless grace, they are also beckoned to incarnate his virtues and conduct their lives in a manner that mirrors their transformed identity in Christ.

The Transformative Power of Faith in Jesus Christ

The verse states that through God's promises, believers can become "partakers of the divine nature." This highlights a profound aspect of Christian faith: it is not just about receiving God's promises but also about being invited into a transformative relationship with him. God's promises are not merely guarantees of future blessings but are also the means by which believers can experience a real, ongoing participation in the divine life.

The apostle who wrote 2 Pet 1:4 reveals that the Christian faith is about more than just following rules or traditions. It's about a profound, transformative relationship with God, where believers actively participate in his divine nature and are changed to reflect his character. This transformative process is both a gift and a call to live in a way that mirrors the divine attributes and love of God.

1. *"Through These"*: Refers to the promises of God, which include salvation, forgiveness, eternal life, and the indwelling of the Holy Spirit. These promises are central to the Christian faith.

2. *"Participate in the Divine Nature"*: This phrase is quite profound. It suggests that believers, through their relationship with Christ, can share in God's nature in some way. This doesn't mean that humans become gods, but rather that they are united with God in a spiritual sense, being transformed to reflect his character more closely. This transformation involves aspects like love, holiness, righteousness, and eternal life.

3. *"Having Escaped the Corruption in the World"*: Through Christ, believers are liberated from the sinful nature of the world. They are no longer slaves to their sinful desires but are empowered to live according to God's will.

4. *The Journey of Spiritual Growth*: Theosis, then, is not merely a concept but a profound reality for Christians. It encapsulates the journey of spiritual growth and transformation, where believers are continually conformed to the image of Christ, reflecting more and more of his divine nature as they walk in faith and obedience.

5. *Incarnational Theology*: Theosis is intimately connected to the incarnation of Christ, who took on human flesh to unite humanity with divinity. Through Christ's life, death, and resurrection, humanity is offered the possibility of reconciliation with God and participation in the divine life. As Athanasius famously proclaimed, "God became man so that man might become god." Theosis, also known as divinization or deification, is indeed closely linked to the incarnation of Christ in Christian theology. The concept is rooted in the belief that through the incarnation—where Jesus, the divine Son of God, became fully human while retaining his divine nature—humanity is given the opportunity to be united with the divine. By participating in Christ and partaking in the very life and nature of God, believers can ultimately attain a likeness to him.

    a. In Christian thought, the purpose of the incarnation transcends mere salvation from sin, though this remains central. It embodies God's profound longing for an intimate relationship with humanity. By assuming human nature, Jesus not only unveils God's boundless love and character to humanity but also serves as the bridge between humanity and divinity, enabling humans to partake in the very essence of the divine.

b. Theosis, then, is the profound journey wherein humanity is gradually transfigured into the very likeness of God, evolving ever closer to his divine character and essence. This sacred metamorphosis finds its roots in active engagement with the life of Christ, encompassing faith, the sacraments, prayer, and a devoted existence marked by obedience and holiness. The sublime pinnacle of theosis is the consummate union with God wherein humanity merges seamlessly with divinity, partaking fully in God's eternal life and radiance.

c. The concept of theosis, originating from Eastern Orthodox theology, stands as a pinnacle of human destiny and the culmination of God's design for humanity. Its essence transcends denominational boundaries, resonating also within Catholic and Protestant theological frameworks, albeit with nuanced distinctions in emphasis and interpretation. At its core, theosis magnifies the centrality of the incarnation in Christian doctrine, illuminating the transformative potency of divine love and grace within the hearts and souls of believers.

6. *Salvation and Sanctification*: Theosis completes and perfects the process of salvation and sanctification in Christian theology. It not only entails the forgiveness of sins but the full restoration and elevation of human nature to its original dignity and purpose. Through theosis, humanity is not only freed from the shackles of sin and death but empowered to lead lives of holiness and intimate communion with God. The concept of theosis, often referred to as "divinization" or "deification," is a cornerstone within Eastern Orthodox Christian theology, shedding unique light on the journey of believers as they increasingly reflect the likeness of God, participate in his divine nature, and ultimately achieve perfect union with him.

Illuminates the Intricate Process of Salvation and Sanctification

Theosis encapsulates the profound journey of believers as they are transformed into the likeness of God, culminating in a sacred union with him. This concept, central to Eastern Orthodox theology, illuminates the intricate process of salvation and sanctification, emphasizing the dynamic and intimate relationship between God and his people. Here's a breakdown of how theosis relates to salvation and sanctification:

1. Theosis begins with the foundational concept of salvation, representing the divine deliverance of humanity from the shackles of sin and its dire consequences. Rooted deeply in Christian theology, salvation finds its consummate expression in the sacrificial death and triumphant resurrection of Jesus Christ. By embracing Christ as their Savior and forging an intimate relationship with him, believers experience liberation from both the dominion and the punitive grip of sin, thereby embarking on the transformative journey of theosis.

2. Sanctification is the beautiful journey wherein believers are gradually and fully conformed to the likeness of Christ. It embodies the continuous operation of the Holy Spirit within the believer, refining their character and empowering them to lead lives of holiness and righteousness. This sanctifying work isn't a sudden occurrence but rather unfolds over time as believers actively engage with and yield to the grace of God.

3. Theosis, the pinnacle of sanctification, proposes that believers can transcend mere sanctification and actively partake in the divine nature of God. This profound concept finds its roots in biblical passages like 2 Pet 1:4, which elucidates believers' transformation into "partakers of the divine nature." Theosis expounds that through the indwelling presence of the Holy Spirit and the unmerited favor of God, believers can forge an intimate union with the divine, wherein God's life and attributes are increasingly mirrored and manifested in their own lives.

4. Theosis is the profound journey of metamorphosis, wherein the entirety of one's being—body, soul, and spirit—is transfigured into the radiant likeness of Christ. This transcendent process moves beyond mere moral and ethical evolution, delving into the depths of spiritual enlightenment and even corporeal refinement. The ultimate aspiration of theosis is for individuals to achieve seamless unity with the divine, basking in the boundless splendor of God's eternal presence and partaking in the ineffable essence of his divine existence. This emphasizes theosis as a dynamic, transformative process rather than a static state. The use of "metamorphosis" evokes a complete

and fundamental change, akin to a caterpillar becoming a butterfly. By specifying "body, soul, and spirit," the holy Scripture highlights the holistic nature of theosis. It's not just a spiritual or mental change but one that affects every aspect of human existence.

5. Theosis is not merely a theoretical concept but a lived reality for believers. It is actively pursued through the avenues of prayer, worship, engagement with sacraments, ascetic disciplines, and a dedicated life of obedience to Christ. By persistently seeking God's presence and endeavoring to align their will with his, believers actively participate in the transformative process of theosis, gradually growing in their likeness to Christ. This journey is marked by a deepening intimacy with the divine and a continual striving towards spiritual maturity and union with God.

6. Theosis permeates the life of the church and its sacramental mysteries. Through baptism, chrismation, the Eucharist, and other sacraments, believers are initiated into the divine life and nourished on the journey of theosis.

Theosis and Sacraments

The church, as the mystical body of Christ, serves as the locus of divine grace and communion where theosis is realized in community. In the life of the church, theosis permeates through various means, particularly through the sacraments. Here's how the sacraments contribute to this process:

a. *Baptism*: This is a sacred sacrament in which an individual is initiated into the church, thereby becoming a cherished member of the body of Christ. This profound ritual serves as a transformative gateway, purifying the soul from sin and forging an inseparable bond with Christ. Through baptism, one embarks upon the divine journey of theosis, a spiritual ascent towards unity with the divine, guided by the grace and love of God.

b. *Chrismation/Confirmation*: In this sacrament, the individual receives the gift of the Holy Spirit, infusing them with divine grace, fortifying their bond with Christ, and equipping them for a journey of sanctity and service. The Holy Spirit occupies a pivotal role in theosis, for it is through the Spirit's transformative power that we are molded ever closer to the image of Christ, reflecting his love, compassion, and righteousness in our lives.

c. *Eucharist*: The Eucharist, or Holy Communion, stands as the quintessential sacrament of the church, embodying the very essence of communion with the divine. Through the partaking of the sacred elements symbolizing the body and blood of Christ, believers engage in a transcendent union with the divine presence. This sacred communion not only nourishes the soul but also serves as a spiritual sustenance, enriching the believer's journey toward a deeper integration into the divine life.

d. *Confession/Repentance*: The sacrament of confession is a sacred rite that grants believers the opportunity to humbly acknowledge their sins, seeking forgiveness and reconciliation with both God and their community. Through this act of contrition, believers are restored to a state of grace, cleansed of their transgressions, and empowered to pursue the transformative journey of theosis, ultimately drawing closer to the divine likeness and fulfilling their spiritual potential.

e. *Marriage and Holy Orders*: These sacraments embody a profound commitment to selfless love and service, reflecting the unconditional love of Christ for his church. Through these sacred rites, individuals are summoned to mirror Christ's sacrificial love and actively engage in his redemptive mission.

The sacraments of the church serve as divine conduits of grace, facilitating the profound union of believers with Christ and endowing them with the strength for a sanctified existence. Through active engagement in the sacramental life and a commitment to prayer, asceticism, and virtuous conduct, believers undergo a gradual metamorphosis, becoming increasingly conformed to the image of Christ. This journey culminates in the participation of believers in the divine nature itself, attaining the lofty state of theosis, wherein human and divine realities harmoniously converge.

Eschatological Fulfillment

The term eschatological pertains to the ultimate fulfillment of God's plan for the world and is often associated with the end times or the final consummation of all things. In Christian theology, eschatological fulfillment is intimately tied to the notion of salvation and the restoration of all creation in harmony with God. Theosis, then, represents the pinnacle of this eschatological fulfillment, wherein human beings are fully united with God in a state of divine perfection.[6] Theosis, the divine process of human transformation, vividly illustrates the culmination of God's grand design for creation. It serves as a beacon, guiding us towards the ultimate realization of all existence in Christ, where humanity achieves complete metamorphosis and harmonious unity with the divine for eternity.

Theosis sweeps over a dazzling canvas of possibilities and satisfactions in which the limitless, endless love of God presides unopposed, sweeping up every teardrop that falls. Basically, what it does is posit the powerful idea that you and I, when connecting with God in an intimate way, can literally share in his divinity. Theosis is the highest goal of human destiny, whereby men and women become fully united with God at his parousia, the ultimate end (telos) of his divine will for creation. At this juncture, humanity will bask in profound communion with the divine, partaking fully in his glory and essence.

Eschatological fulfillment, as embodied in theosis, transcends temporal and spatial limitations, pointing towards the ultimate destiny of humanity in the eternal kingdom of God. It is a process that begins in this life but extends into eternity, culminating in the full realization of God's kingdom where all things are made new.

At the heart of theosis is an understanding of synergy between God's grace and human free will. Theosis, eschatological realization, leads to finality as the purpose of creation in all of its complexity is understood: the deification or transformation of humans into God and finally participating completely with his divine nature. This passage of transformation includes spiritual growth, the harmony between God's grace and human wills, relational communion in church bodies, and perhaps even the full consummation of God's kingdom in eternity.

---

6. Eschatological fulfillment encompasses the culmination of God's purposes for creation, where his sovereignty and justice are fully realized. It involves the restoration of all things to their intended state of harmony and perfection as originally intended by God. Eschatology is also intimately linked with the Christian doctrine of salvation. It encompasses the belief that through Christ's redemptive work, humanity and creation will be restored to their original intended state before the fall. This restoration includes not only the reconciliation of humans with God through forgiveness of sins but also the renewal of creation itself (Rom 8:18–25).

Relevance in Daily Life

1. *Understanding Divine Promises and Transformation*: God's promises are not just assurances of future blessings but are transformative tools meant to align believers with his divine nature. By embracing these promises, believers can find motivation and strength to transform their character and actions. For example, the promise of forgiveness can lead to genuine personal change, helping someone to forgive others and cultivate a spirit of reconciliation. When facing challenges or temptations, reflecting on God's promises can provide the strength to overcome difficulties. For instance, the promise of God's guidance can offer clarity and peace when making difficult decisions.

2. *Participation in the Divine Nature*: To participate in the divine nature means to be transformed to reflect God's character—his love, holiness, and righteousness. This involves living out virtues such as compassion, integrity, and patience in everyday interactions. For instance, a believer might strive to show kindness and understanding in a contentious workplace or demonstrate honesty in personal and professional dealings. In practical terms, this could mean engaging in acts of service, practicing patience in relationships, or striving for ethical behavior at work. By doing so, believers mirror the divine nature and contribute positively to their communities.

3. *Escaping Corruption and Evil Desires*: Through participation in divine promises, believers escape the moral and spiritual corruption prevalent in the world. This aspect emphasizes living a life distinct from societal norms that may promote unethical behavior. It challenges believers to resist temptations and harmful practices that lead to moral decay. For example, a believer might avoid gossip, resist consumerism, or uphold justice and fairness, even when these actions go against prevailing societal trends. This choice not only aligns with divine nature but also sets an example for others.

4. *Incorporating Theosis into Life*: Theosis, or deification, involves growing into the likeness of God and reflecting his divine attributes more fully. This long-term goal affects daily behavior and spiritual practices. It's not merely about achieving moral perfection but about cultivating a deep, intimate relationship with God. Engaging in regular prayer, participating in worship, and seeking spiritual

growth through study and fellowship are ways to pursue theosis. This continuous growth impacts how one lives out their faith and interacts with others.

5. *Eschatological Fulfillment and Hope*: Theosis also looks towards the final, eschatological fulfillment where believers fully realize their unity with God. This future hope provides encouragement and perspective in daily struggles. Knowing that life's trials are temporary and that there's a promised future can offer solace and strength. This hope can shape one's response to adversity, making it easier to endure difficulties with patience and faith. It also encourages a forward-looking attitude that helps believers live in light of their ultimate destiny with God.

Chapter 4

Historical Development of Theosis

THE ROOTS OF THEOSIS can be traced back to the New Testament, particularly the epistles of Peter and of John. They speak of believers becoming "partakers of the divine nature" (2 Pet 1:4) and "children of God" (1 John 3:1). These passages suggest an intimate union between believers and God, a concept that would later be elaborated upon in the early church.

The Byzantine period witnessed a significant development of the teaching on Christian theosis. The Cappadocian Fathers—Basil the Great, Gregory of Nazianzus, and Gregory of Nyssa—played a crucial role in formulating the concept. The Cappadocians laid the groundwork for the concept of human participation in the divine life. Later, Gregory Palamas would emphasize the distinction between the divine essence and the divine energies, arguing that while humans cannot directly partake of the divine essence, they can participate in the divine energies.

Theosis remains a central theme in Eastern Orthodox theology today. It continues to be explored and discussed in various contexts, including interfaith dialogues and theological education. Modern Orthodox theologians have sought to articulate the concept in ways that are relevant to contemporary culture and address the challenges of the modern world. Theosis is a rich and multifaceted concept, which has played a central role in Christian thought for centuries. It continues to be a vital aspect of Eastern Orthodox theology and offers a profound understanding of the believer's relationship with God.

Review of the Historical Evolution of Theosis

1. *The Early Church Fathers*:

    a. The roots of theosis can be traced back to the writings of the early church fathers, particularly in the Eastern Christian tradition. Figures such as Athanasius of Alexandria, Gregory of Nyssa, and Maximus the Confessor articulated the idea of humanity's participation in the divine nature and the transformative union with God. Their profound insights into theosis emphasized not merely a superficial understanding of salvation, but rather a deep spiritual journey towards the likeness of God, whereby human beings are invited into a communion of love and grace that transcends earthly limitations. Through their writings and teachings, these venerable figures illuminated the path of spiritual growth and union with the divine, inspiring generations of believers to pursue holiness and spiritual perfection.

2. *Byzantine Era*:

    a. During the Byzantine era, the concept of theosis flourished, especially amidst theological debates concerning the essence of Christ and the pathway to salvation. The insights of theologians such as Gregory Palamas took precedence, stressing the potential for individuals to directly encounter God's energies and attain theosis through mystical devotion and rigorous asceticism. This emphasis reshaped Eastern Orthodox spirituality, highlighting the transformative journey towards union with the divine.

    b. The teachings of theologians like Gregory Palamas, who emphasized the possibility of direct experience of God's energies and theosis through mystical prayer and ascetic practice, became central to Eastern Orthodox spirituality.[1]

3. *Western Reception*:

    a. While theosis has deep roots in Eastern Christian thought, its reception in the Western Christian tradition has been more limited, often overshadowed by alternative theological emphases such as justification by faith.[2]

---

1. Lossky, *Mystical Theology*.

2. The doctrine of justification by faith holds that humans are made righteous before God through faith in Jesus Christ, apart from any merit or works of their own. This

b. The concept of sanctification through grace has also played a prominent role in Western Christian thought, particularly in the Wesleyan tradition and within certain strands of Catholic theology. Sanctification emphasizes the ongoing work of the Holy Spirit in the lives of believers, progressively conforming them to the image of Christ and empowering them to live holy and righteous lives.[3]

c. Western theologians such as Augustine of Hippo and Thomas Aquinas addressed themes related to divinization, albeit within the framework of sanctification and participation in God's grace rather than explicit deification.[4] Aquinas focused more on the forensic aspect of salvation and the juridical language of justification. His theology of sanctification and participation in the divine life, however, bears some similarities to the Eastern Orthodox concept of theosis.

d. Augustine's emphasis on the fallen nature of humanity due to original sin highlights the profound impact of sin on the divine image within humans and their alienation from God. However, he also affirmed that through divine grace, made available through Christ, believers can experience a form of restoration and transformation that aligns with the broader concept of theosis, acknowledging the ongoing struggle and dependence on God's grace for this process.

---

doctrine, championed by figures like Martin Luther during the Protestant Reformation, has been central to much of Western Protestant theology and has tended to frame discussions on salvation and the Christian life.

3. These theological emphases do not necessarily conflict with the idea of theosis, though they have often taken precedence in Western Christian discourse, leaving comparatively less room for the explicit exploration and development of the concept of deification.

4. Augustine, "Tractate 17." Here he connects baptismal rebirth with divine participation: "For God wishes to make you gods, not in relation to God by nature, like Him whom He begot, but by His gift and adoption. For just as He through humanity was made partaker of your mortality, so through lifting you up He makes you partakers of His immortality." Other Western theologians, such as Thomas Aquinas and John Wesley, have also affirmed elements of theosis within their theological frameworks. Aquinas, for instance, spoke of the beatific vision, wherein the saints behold the essence of God and are transformed into his likeness. See Aquinas, *Summa Theologiae*, I-II.110.1–4; I-II.112; and I.4.3. Wesley, similarly, emphasized the idea of Christian perfection, wherein believers are enabled by grace to love God with all their heart, soul, and mind. See Collins, *Theology of Wesley*.

e. For Augustine, divinization involves the process of restoration and transformation, wherein human beings are restored to their original likeness to God through the redemptive work of Christ. This process begins with grace, which Augustine understands as God's unmerited favor and assistance given to humanity for salvation. Grace, in Augustine's theology, is essential for initiating and sustaining the process of divinization.[5] Augustine also cautioned against a simplistic understanding of divinization. He recognized the tension between the already and the not yet—the reality that divinization begins in this life but is not fully realized until the eschaton, in the final fulfillment of God's kingdom. Augustine acknowledges the ongoing struggle with sin and the limitations of human nature, even for those who are being divinized.

f. Crucial to Augustine's understanding of divinization is the concept of love. Augustine famously wrote, "Love, and do what you will."[6] He believed that love, particularly love of God, is the primary catalyst for divinization. Through love, humans are drawn closer to God and participate in his divine nature. This participation involves not only intellectual ascent but also a transformation of the will and affections, aligning them with the divine will.

4. *Reformation and Post-Reformation Era*:

a. The Protestant Reformation catalyzed profound theological shifts within Western Christianity, heralding a resurgence in doctrines such as *sola fide* (faith alone) and justification by faith. Despite the marginalization of the concept of theosis within Protestant theology, certain branches, notably the Wesleyan tradition, accentuated themes of Christian perfection and sanctification.[7] These emphases, akin to theosis in some

---

5. Augustine's theology of divinization is deeply sacramental. He saw the sacraments, especially baptism and the Eucharist, as means of grace through which God communicates his divine life to believers. In the sacraments, Augustine saw the transformative power of God's grace at work, gradually conforming believers more closely to the image of Christ.

6. Augustine, "Homily 7," para. 8. The full Latin phrase is "Dilige et quod vis fac."

7. Collins, *Theology of Wesley*. John Wesley, the founder of Methodism, and the Wesleyan tradition have engaged with themes related to theosis, albeit using different terminology. Wesley taught the doctrine of Christian perfection or entire sanctification,

respects, underscored the pursuit of spiritual maturity and the transformative journey towards alignment with the divine. In this context, Clendenin is correct to conclude his analysis with this statement: "Western theologians in general and Protestants in particular have given only scant attention to the central importance of theosis in Orthodox thought.[8]

b. These concepts were deeply intertwined with the broader theological critique of the Catholic Church's teachings and practices.

  i. *Sola fide*, or "faith alone," emphasizes the belief that salvation comes solely through faith in Jesus Christ, rather than through good works or adherence to sacraments administered by the church. This doctrine challenged the prevailing Catholic teaching that salvation was attained through a combination of faith and good works. For Reformers like Martin Luther, *sola fide* was not merely a theological assertion but a fundamental reorientation of the Christian understanding of salvation. It underscored the belief that individuals could have a direct and personal relationship with God through faith, without the need for intermediary figures or institutions.

  ii. Justification by faith, closely related to *sola fide*, emphasizes the idea that individuals are justified or made righteous in the eyes of God by their faith in Christ, rather than by their own merit or efforts. This concept is deeply rooted in the writings of the apostle Paul, particularly in his letters to the Romans and Galatians, but had become obscured or downplayed within medieval Catholic theology. Reformers sought to recover and emphasize this biblical teaching as a corrective to what they saw as the legalism and works-based righteousness of the Catholic Church.

  iii. The emphasis on *sola fide* and justification by faith had profound implications for the understanding of salvation, the role of the church, and the relationship between individuals and God. It placed a greater emphasis on the authority

---

which he understood as the process of being made perfect in love and attaining a state of holiness in this life.

8. Clendenin, "Partakers of Divinity," 367.

of Scripture as the ultimate source of religious truth and encouraged a more personal and direct engagement with biblical texts among lay Christians. Additionally, it challenged the hierarchical structure of the Catholic Church and paved the way for the proliferation of diverse Protestant denominations, each with its own interpretation of these key doctrines.

c. Beyond their theological significance, *sola fide* and justification by faith also had profound social and political implications. They contributed to the erosion of the Catholic Church's monopoly on religious authority and sparked conflicts that would shape the course of European history for centuries to come, including wars of religion and the rise of nation-states.[9]

5. *Contemporary Theological Dialogue*:

a. The growing interest in theosis across Eastern Orthodox and Western Christian circles reflects a broader engagement with and exploration of this profound concept. This renewed attention is driven by efforts to integrate traditional teachings with contemporary issues, enrich theological dialogue, and deepen personal spiritual practices.

b. Ecumenical dialogue between Eastern Orthodox, Catholic, and Protestant theologians is increasingly exploring the theological implications of theosis. This exploration helps identify common spiritual goals, promote an understanding the role of divine grace, and fosters unity and mutual enrichment among Christian traditions. The ongoing discussions aim to build bridges across denominations, enhancing collaborative efforts and deepening shared spiritual and theological insights.

The historical development of theosis reflects the rich diversity and theological dialogue within the Christian tradition. While the concept has deep roots in Eastern Christian thought, its reception and interpretation have varied across different theological traditions. Nonetheless, theosis remains a central and enduring theme within Christian spirituality, inviting believers into a transformative journey of union with God.

---

9. Calvin, *Institutes*, vol. 1.

Key Figures in the Historical Development of Theosis

The concept of theosis, although not always articulated using that precise term, can be traced through the writings of key figures in early Christian thought, particularly the Cappadocian Fathers, Athanasius of Alexandria, and Maximus the Confessor. Here's a brief overview of their contributions to the development of theosis:

1. *Cappadocian Fathers (fourth century)*:

    a. Basil the Great, Gregory of Nyssa, and Gregory of Nazianzus, collectively known as the Cappadocian Fathers, played a crucial role in shaping early Christian theology, particularly in the Eastern Orthodox tradition.[10] They emphasized the transformative nature of the Christian life, teaching that through participation in the sacraments and the pursuit of virtue, believers could become increasingly conformed to the image of Christ.

    b. Gregory of Nyssa developed a robust theology of theosis, emphasizing humanity's potential to participate in the divine nature through communion with God. He articulated the idea of an ascent towards God, wherein humans progressively become more like God through the work of the Holy Spirit.[11]

    c. Gregory of Nazianzus, in his theological writings and sermons, emphasized the importance of Christ's incarnation for theosis, teaching that through the union of divine and human natures in Christ, humanity is elevated and deified.[12]

---

10. The Cappadocian Fathers made significant contributions to the understanding of theosis through their theological writings and debates, particularly in the fourth century. Basil the Great emphasized the transformative power of the Holy Spirit in the Christian life, leading believers to become more like God through a process of spiritual growth and purification. See Russell, *Greek Patristic Tradition*.

11. Gregory of Nyssa, influenced by Origen's teachings, elaborated on the concept of theosis by highlighting the inherent desire within human beings for union with God. He described theosis as the ultimate goal of human existence, where individuals participate in the divine nature through the grace of God. See Catherine P. Roth's translation of Gregory of Nyssa's *On the Soul and the Resurrection*.

12. Gregory of Nazianzus, known for his eloquent defense of Nicene orthodoxy, emphasized the unity of the Trinity and the role of Christ in the process of theosis. He articulated the idea that Christ's incarnation enabled humanity to be reconciled with God and participate in the divine life. See Gregory of Nazianzus, *On God and Christ*, esp. oration 29.

2. *Athanasius of Alexandria (fourth century)*:

   a. Athanasius, a key figure in the Nicene controversy, defended Christ's divinity against the Arian heresy thereby establishing the foundations for the orthodox doctrine of the Trinity. Arianism was a heresy that claimed Jesus Christ was a created being, subordinate to God. Athanasius, along with other Christians, strongly opposed this view.

   b. Athanasius's defense of Christ's divinity was crucial in establishing the orthodox doctrine of the Trinity, which affirms the co-equal existence of the Father, Son, and Holy Spirit. His writings and leadership in the controversy had a lasting impact on the development of Christian theology.[13]

   c. In his work *On the Incarnation*, Athanasius expounds on the concept of theosis, teaching that through the incarnation, humanity is reconciled to God and enabled to partake in the divine life. He famously proclaimed, "God became man so that man might become god."[14]

   d. Athanasius emphasized the transformative power of Christ's salvific work, teaching that through his death and resurrection, humanity is freed from the bondage of sin and death, and empowered to live a life of holiness and communion with God.[15]

3. *Maximus the Confessor (seventh century)*:

   Maximus the Confessor, a prominent theologian and monk in the Eastern Christian tradition, made significant contributions to the development of theosis. He emphasized the union of the divine and human wills in Christ, teaching that through his incarnation, humanity is united with God and enabled to participate in the divine energies.

   He articulated the concept of "theosis by grace," wherein humanity is transformed by the uncreated energies of God, leading to a mystical union with the divine.[16] Maximus also emphasized the

---

13. Anatolios, *Early Development*.
14. Athanasius, *Incarnation*, 54.3. See also Russell, *Greek Patristic Tradition*.
15. Athanasius's emphasis on the transformative power of Christ's salvific work contributed to the development of theosis as a central theme within Christian theology, highlighting the intimate union between God and humanity.
16. Thunberg, *Microcosm and Mediator*. Maximus emphasized the dynamic nature

importance of asceticism and contemplative prayer in the process of theosis, teaching that through spiritual discipline and purification, believers can attain greater communion with God.[17]

The contributions of the Cappadocian Fathers, Athanasius of Alexandria, and Maximus the Confessor were instrumental in shaping the early Christian understanding of theosis. Their theological insights laid the foundation for the development of theosis as a central theme within Eastern Orthodox theology, emphasizing humanity's participation in the divine life and the transformative union with God. Through their writings and teachings, these theologians enriched the theological tradition of the church and continue to inspire theologians and believers alike in the pursuit of deification.

The Byzantine Era and Its Influence on Eastern Orthodox Theology

In the Byzantine era, the concept of theosis experienced significant development and became a central theme in Eastern Orthodox theology, particularly through the teachings of theologians such as Gregory Palamas. Here's how the concept of theosis evolved during this period and how it influenced Eastern Orthodox theology:

1. *Hesychasm and Gregory Palamas*:

    The fourteenth-century monk Gregory Palamas played a pivotal role in articulating the theology of theosis within the context of Hesychasm, a mystical tradition emphasizing contemplative prayer and the quest for divine union.[18] Gregory Palamas was a monk, a theologian, and was archbishop of Thessaloniki in the fourteenth-century Byzantine Empire. He lived during a time of significant theological debate within Eastern Christianity.

    Hesychasm is a mystical tradition within Eastern Orthodox Christianity, particularly associated with monks on Mount Athos

---

of theosis, portraying it as a continual process of spiritual growth and ascent towards union with God. He underscored the importance of human cooperation with divine grace in the journey towards deification.

17. Maximus also explored the implications of theosis for ethical and ascetical practices, emphasizing the transformative impact of participation in the divine life on human virtues and moral character.

18. Ware, *Jesus Prayer*.

in Greece. It emphasizes inner stillness, prayer, and contemplation as a means of experiencing God's presence and attaining theosis. The term "hesychasm" comes from the Greek word "hesychia," meaning inner quietness or stillness. At its core, hesychasm seeks union with God through a process of purification and illumination of the soul, leading to the vision of divine light. Practitioners engage in a variety of spiritual disciplines, including repetitive prayer, controlled breathing, and meditation on specific phrases or images, often referred to as the "prayer of the heart" or the "Jesus Prayer." This prayer typically involves the repetition of a short phrase such as "Lord Jesus Christ, Son of God, have mercy on me, a sinner," with deep concentration and devotion.[19]

Central to hesychastic practice is the cultivation of inner stillness or "nepsis," which involves quieting the mind and senses to create a space for encountering the divine presence. This inner stillness is believed to open the practitioner to the direct experience of God's energies or grace, which are understood to be distinct from God's essence.[20] The ultimate goal of hesychasm is theosis, or union with God, in which the individual becomes increasingly transformed by divine grace and likeness to Christ.

Hesychasm has had a significant influence on Eastern Orthodox spirituality, theology, and liturgy. It has produced a rich body of mystical literature, including the writings of notable figures such as Symeon the New Theologian and Gregory Palamas; the writings of both Symeon and Palamas, along with many others influenced by hesychasm, are featured in *The Philokalia*, a collection of spiritual texts compiled in the eighteenth century.[21]

However, hesychasm has also been the subject of controversy within the Eastern Orthodox Church, particularly in the fourteenth century during the Hesychast Controversy. This theological dispute centered on the nature of mystical experience and the relationship between God's essence and energies. Gregory Palamas defended the hesychastic tradition, arguing that it was possible for human beings to experience the uncreated energies of God, while

---

19. Hausherr, *Name of Jesus*.
20. Lossky, *Mystical Theology*.
21. Palmer, et al. *Philokalia*; Krivocheine, *Light of Christ*; Meyendorff, *Study of Palamas*.

critics accused hesychasts of advocating a form of mystical quietism or even heresy.[22]

Despite these controversies, hesychasm continues to be practiced and revered within Eastern Orthodox Christianity as a profound path to spiritual transformation and communion with the divine. Its emphasis on inner stillness, prayer, and contemplation remains a central aspect of Orthodox spirituality to this day.

Gregory Palamas played a pivotal role in articulating the theology of theosis within the context of Hesychasm, primarily through his defense of the Hesychasts against their critics. He championed the Hesychast practice of "hesychia," or inner stillness, combined with the repetitive utterance of the Jesus Prayer ("Lord Jesus Christ, Son of God, have mercy on me, a sinner") as a means of achieving union with God. Palamas argued that through these practices, Hesychasts could experience the divine energies of God directly. He distinguished between God's essence, which remains unknowable and inaccessible to humans, and his energies, through which he communicates and reveals himself.[23]

Palamas taught that while humans cannot know God's essence, they can experience his energies, and it is through these energies that theosis occurs. Palamas's teachings were not without controversy. He faced opposition from some theologians, most notably Barlaam of Calabria, who criticized Hesychasm as a form of mysticism that led to false spiritual experiences. In response, Palamas wrote several theological works defending the Hesychasts and their practices, most notably *The Triads* or *In Defense of the Holy Hesychasts*. Ultimately, Palamas's defense of Hesychasm and his articulation of the theology of theosis solidified these concepts within Eastern Orthodox theology.

His teachings continue to influence Eastern Christian spirituality to this day, emphasizing the importance of inner prayer, stillness, and the pursuit of union with God through his divine energies. Palamas distinguished between God's essence (*ousia*) and energies (*energeia*), teaching that while the essence of God

---

22. Meyendorff, *Study of Palamas*.

23. Palamas defended his teachings in a series of writings and theological treatises, emphasizing the importance of experiential knowledge of God in the Christian life. His ideas eventually gained acceptance within Eastern Orthodoxy, and he was later canonized as a saint; see van Rossum, "Deification in Palamas and Aquinas," 369.

remains unknowable and transcendent, his energies are accessible to humans and can be experienced directly through mystical prayer. Palamas emphasized the importance of hesychastic practices such as the Jesus Prayer and contemplative prayer in facilitating theosis, teaching that through these practices, believers can attain a direct experience of God's divine energies and participate in his life.[24]

2. *Conflict with Barlaam of Calabria*:

Palamas's teachings on theosis and hesychasm were met with opposition from Barlaam of Calabria, a Western theologian who rejected the idea of direct experience of God and criticized Palamas's distinction between essence and energies. Barlaam, influenced by Western Scholasticism, viewed God's essence as completely unknowable and argued against the possibility of experiencing him directly. He criticized Palamas's teachings as heretical, accusing him of advocating a form of pantheism or panentheism by suggesting that humans can participate in God's energies.[25]

This conflict, known as the Hesychast Controversy, led to theological debates within the Byzantine Empire and the eventual condemnation of Barlaam's views at the Fifth Council of Constantinople in 1351.[26]

3. *Synthesis of Eastern Orthodox Theology*:

Palamas's teachings on theosis and hesychasm became widely accepted within the Eastern Orthodox tradition, shaping the theological landscape of Byzantine Christianity. His teachings provided a synthesis of Eastern Christian spirituality, integrating elements of asceticism, mysticism, and theology into a cohesive framework for understanding theosis.

---

24. Palamas emphasized that theosis is not something that can be achieved through human effort alone but is a gift of God's grace. Through hesychasm and other ascetic practices, believers can prepare themselves to receive this gift; see Anastos, "Palamas' Radicalization," 335–36.

25. Meyendorff, *Palamas and Orthodox Spirituality*, 45–60.

26. Meyendorff, *Study of Palamas*. The controversy between Palamas and Barlaam came to be known as the Hesychast Controversy. It was not merely an abstract theological debate but also reflected deeper tensions between the Eastern and Western Christian traditions, particularly regarding the nature of mystical experience, the role of tradition, and the authority of theologians.

Palamas's emphasis on theosis as the goal of the Christian life and the importance of mystical experience in achieving union with God influenced subsequent generations of Eastern Orthodox theologians and mystics. Palamas's theology found widespread acceptance within the Eastern Orthodox Church for several reasons:

   a. *Doctrinal Continuity*: Palamas grounded his theology in the teachings of early church fathers, particularly those of the Eastern tradition, such as Athanasius the Great, Gregory of Nyssa, and Maximus the Confessor. By showing continuity with these revered figures, Palamas gained credibility among Orthodox theologians and clergy.

   b. *Experiential Authenticity*: Hesychasm provided a framework for direct, experiential encounters with God. The emphasis on prayer, stillness, and contemplation resonated with the mystical aspirations of many believers, offering a path to deeper spiritual intimacy with God.

   c. *Pastoral Relevance*: Theosis offered a compelling vision of the Christian life that spoke to the yearnings of ordinary believers. It emphasized not only salvation from sin but also the possibility of a transformative union with God, offering hope and inspiration in the midst of life's challenges.

   d. *Theological Coherence*: Palamas's theology provided a coherent framework for understanding the relationship between God and humanity, emphasizing both the transcendence and immanence of God. It addressed fundamental questions about the nature of God, the purpose of human existence, and the meaning of salvation in a way that resonated with Orthodox theological sensibilities.

4. *Legacy and Influence*:

   The theology of Gregory Palamas and the concept of theosis continue to exert a profound influence on Eastern Orthodox theology and spirituality to this day. Theosis remains a central theme in Eastern Orthodox theology, emphasizing humanity's participation in the divine life and the transformative union with God.[27] Palamas's

---

27. Further, theosis underscores the belief that salvation is not merely forgiveness of sins and moral improvement but also a profound union with God that transcends human nature. This union is understood as a participation in God's uncreated energies

teachings on hesychasm and theosis have inspired generations of Eastern Orthodox monks and mystics, contributing to the rich tradition of contemplative prayer and spiritual asceticism within the Eastern Christian tradition.

The concept of theosis evolved and flourished during the Byzantine era, particularly through the theological contributions of Gregory Palamas. His teachings on hesychasm and theosis continue to shape Eastern Orthodox theology and spirituality, emphasizing the transformative journey of union with God through prayer, asceticism, and mystical experience. Palamas taught that theosis involves a transformative process whereby believers participate in God's divine energies. This participation does not make humans divine by nature but allows them to experience and share in God's divine life and attributes. Through ascetic practices, prayer, and mystical experience, believers are gradually transformed and united with God.

Palamas's emphasis on direct mystical experience of God through prayer and asceticism has shaped Orthodox spirituality. His teachings support the idea that personal, experiential knowledge of God is central to the spiritual journey and the process of theosis. The doctrines formulated by Palamas have also influenced ecumenical discussions. Understanding theosis through the lens of uncreated energies and divine participation offers a perspective that can inform and enrich discussions with other Christian traditions about the nature of salvation and spiritual transformation.

Gregory Palamas remains a central figure in Orthodox theology. His writings are studied and revered for their depth and clarity regarding theosis. Modern Orthodox theologians continue to draw on his work to articulate and defend the Orthodox understanding of divine union and transformation. Palamas's teachings continue to inspire contemporary Orthodox spirituality. The emphasis on mystical prayer and ascetic practice resonates with modern seekers and practitioners who are exploring deeper dimensions of faith and spiritual experience.

---

rather than his essence, which allows for a real and transformative encounter with the divine.

Eastern Orthodox theology itself emphasizes humanity's participation in the divine life, facilitated through sacraments, prayer, ascetic practices, and the cultivation of virtues. Theosis involves a synergistic cooperation between God's grace and human response, where believers actively cooperate with God in their own sanctification and transformation.

Relevance in Daily Life

1. *Understanding and Experience of God*: The distinction between divine essence and divine energies proposed by the Cappadocian Fathers can help modern believers grasp how they can experience God in their lives. While the divine essence remains beyond human comprehension, the divine energies—the ways in which God interacts with the world—are accessible. In daily life, this means recognizing and experiencing God's presence through acts of love, grace, and beauty.

2. *Personal Spiritual Growth*: Theosis emphasizes transformation through participation in divine energies rather than direct contact with the divine essence. For individuals today, this means focusing on how daily practices like prayer, meditation, and ethical living allow them to experience and reflect divine qualities. It encourages a journey of personal growth where one seeks to embody virtues such as kindness, patience, and humility.

3. *Interfaith and Ecumenical Dialogue*: The modern relevance of theosis extends to interfaith dialogues and discussions about shared values. Understanding theosis can enrich conversations by highlighting how different traditions view the process of spiritual transformation and the divine-human relationship. This can foster mutual respect and deeper understanding among people of various faith backgrounds.

4. *Theological Education and Reflection*: In theological education, the concept of theosis helps frame discussions on how faith and spirituality are lived out. It provides a rich context for exploring how ancient teachings apply to contemporary issues, helping students and scholars alike understand the ongoing relevance of these ideas in today's world.

5. *Addressing Modern Challenges*: Theosis provides a framework for addressing modern existential and ethical challenges. For example, it can offer a perspective on how to approach issues like social justice, environmental stewardship, and personal well-being. By striving to align one's actions with divine energies, believers can address these challenges with a sense of purpose and divine guidance.

6. *Integration into Daily Life*: For everyday believers, theosis encourages a way of living that integrates spiritual growth with practical actions. It might inspire one to approach daily tasks with a sense of divine purpose, to seek continuous improvement in personal character, and to engage with others in ways that reflect God's love and grace.

7. *Cultural Relevance*: Modern Orthodox theologians continue to articulate theosis in ways that address contemporary cultural contexts. This means that the teachings are not static but are continually evolving to meet the needs of modern believers. For instance, exploring how theosis relates to contemporary issues like mental health, technology, and societal changes helps keep the concept relevant and impactful.

Chapter 5

The Biblical Foundations of Theosis

THE BIBLICAL FOUNDATIONS OF theosis, while not explicitly articulated as such in Scripture, can be inferred from various passages in both the Old and New Testaments. On the one hand, creation texts like Gen 1:26-27 suggest a clear connection between God and humanity (humanity is created in the image of God). God's appearances in bodily form, whether angelic (e.g., the burning bush in Exod 3) or truly human (as when Christ is said to have appeared under the old covenant).[1] God establishes unique fellowship with humans and makes sacred covenants (promises) about the future.

Jesus' incarnation manifests the potentiality inherent in the divine-human relationship for unity. Believers, who are given the right to become God's children (John 1:12), manifest a movement toward divinity. By virtue of our unity with Christ, the head of creation (Col 1:15-20; Eph 1), we can be united with the believers to whom Jesus spoke in John 14:10 and for whom he prayed, as God (Father, Son, and Spirit) speaks blessings over both males and females equally; we are called to be one with him. The teachings of Paul about being raised up with Christ indicate the attributes of the divine life are shared too (see Eph 2:4–7; Rom 6:4-5; Col 2:12-13). These scriptural references constitute a basis for theosis, which is humanity's love for and desire to have a relationship with God. They teach that God must elevate humanity into freedom in Godself, and when

---

1. Carson, *Difficult Doctrine*; Alexander and Rosner, *New Dictionary of Biblical Theology*.

he does, the assurance is that through faith, believers can share in God's divine nature, becoming coheirs with Christ and being progressively transformed into his likeness through the power of the Holy Spirit.

The Biblical Foundations of Theosis

1. *Genesis 1:26–27*: "Then God said, 'Let us make mankind in our image, in our likeness . . .'" (NIV). This passage establishes the foundational truth that humanity is created in the image and likeness of God. While the full implications of this image are not explicitly outlined, it suggests a deep connection and resemblance between humanity and their Creator, laying the groundwork for theosis.

    a. *"Let us make mankind in our image, in our likeness . . ."*: This phrase is significant for understanding the relationship between humans and God. The Hebrew word for "image" is "tselem," which conveys the idea of a representation or likeness. It suggests that humans are created to reflect God's nature, attributes, and character. The plural form used here ("our image" and "our likeness") has been interpreted by theologians as suggestive of the Trinity—the Father, Son, and Holy Spirit in communal creative action.[2]

    b. *"So that they may rule . . ."*: This part of the verse denotes not just dominion over the earth but also stewardship.[3] Humans are given authority over creation, which reflects God's own sovereignty. However, this dominion is not absolute but is to be exercised in harmony with God's will and purposes, reflecting God's own rule over creation.

    c. *"God created mankind in his own image . . ."*: The repetition emphasizes the significance of this act of creation. It underscores

---

2. The use of "us" and "our" suggests a divine conversation or consultation within the Godhead. This implies a shared will and purpose among the Father, Son, and Holy Spirit in the act of creation. Each person of the Trinity is involved in the creative process, emphasizing the unity and collaboration within the divine nature.

3. The Hebrew word *rada* (רָדָה) is used, which is often translated as "rule" or "have dominion" in English translations of the Bible. The command to "rule over" or "have dominion over" the rest of creation indicates that humanity is given stewardship over the earth and its creatures. This stewardship involves responsibility, care, and wise management of the natural world. It reflects God's intention for humans to exercise authority in accordance with his will and purposes. See Bruggeman, *Genesis*.

the inherent dignity and value of every human being as bearing the imprint of the divine. This concept is foundational to the idea of theosis—the journey of humans toward union with God, where they become more like him in character and conduct.[4]

d. The Hebrew word *kidmutenu*, which can be translated as "likeness" or "similarity," implies not just a physical resemblance but also a moral and spiritual likeness to God.[5] Theosis, in Christian theology, involves the transformation of the believer into the likeness of Christ, through the work of the Holy Spirit. Genesis 1:26–27 establishes the groundwork for this process. It suggests that from the very beginning, humans were created with the potential for communion and intimacy with God. The divine image in humanity serves as the starting point for theosis—the journey toward spiritual perfection and union with God. Therefore, these verses affirm that the desire for union with God is not a later development in religious thought but is intrinsic to the very nature of humanity as created by God. Theosis, then, is not just a lofty spiritual goal but a return to the original purpose for which humans were created—to reflect the image and likeness of God in all aspects of their being.

2. *Psalm 82:6*: "I said, 'You are gods; you are all sons of the Most High'" (NIV). Although this verse is often interpreted in various ways, it hints at humanity's potential to share in the divine nature as children of God. While humans are not ontologically gods, they are called to participate in the divine life and reflect the character of God. In this verse, the psalmist is speaking about human beings, addressing them as "gods" and "sons of the Most High." This language might seem startling or even blasphemous at first glance, but it holds a key to understanding theosis and the intimate relationship between humans and God.

The term *Elohim attem* in Hebrew, translated as "you are gods," is particularly significant. *Elohim* is a term often used in the Hebrew Bible to refer to God, but it can also be used more broadly

---

4. The idea of humanity being created in the image and likeness of God takes on profound significance in light of the Trinity. If God's communal nature is reflected in human beings, it suggests that our relational capacity, our ability to love, communicate, and collaborate, mirrors something fundamental about the nature of God himself.

5. Hamilton, *Book of Genesis*.

to refer to divine beings or judges.⁶ In this context, it's a reference to the divine potential within humanity. *Attem* means "you are" or "you have become." So, *Elohim Attem* suggests that humans have a divine aspect or potentiality within them. Psalm 82:6 can be interpreted as affirming this divine potentiality within humanity. It suggests that humans, by virtue of their relationship with the Most High, have the capacity to become like God, to embody divine qualities, and to participate in the divine life.

Furthermore, this verse emphasizes the intimate relationship between humans and God. The idea that humans are "sons of the Most High" underscores the familial bond between humanity and the divine. It speaks to a closeness, an intimacy, and a shared heritage between humans and their Creator. In essence, Ps 82:6, when interpreted in light of theosis and the significance of *Elohim Attem*, conveys the profound truth that humans are called to a divine destiny, invited to partake in the very life of God, and are intimately connected to their Creator from the beginning. It reminds us of our inherent dignity and potential as children of God.⁷

3. *Psalm 17:15*: "As for me, I will be vindicated and will see your face; when I awake, I will be satisfied with seeing your likeness" (NIV). This psalm expresses the longing for communion with God and the ultimate satisfaction that comes from being in his presence. It hints at the transformative nature of encountering God, wherein believers are conformed to his likeness. In understanding Ps 17:15 through the lens of theosis, we can discern several layers of meaning:

   a. *Beholding God's Face in Righteousness*: This signifies a longing for intimate communion with God, where righteousness is not just a moral state but also a state of being aligned with the divine will. The desire to behold God's face implies a deep yearning for closeness and intimacy with the divine.

   b. *Satisfaction in God's Likeness*: The satisfaction mentioned here is not merely earthly contentment but a profound spiritual fulfillment found in becoming like God. This likeness is not about

---

6. Bruggeman, *Message of the Psalms*.

7. Through the lens of theosis, Ps 82:6 implies that humans are not merely finite creatures but are invited into a transcendent relationship with God, called to partake in his very life. This divine destiny speaks to the profound potentiality within each individual to grow spiritually, to cultivate virtues, and to align their will with the divine will.

physical appearance but about acquiring God's attributes of love, holiness, and wisdom.

c. *Tamunateka*: The Hebrew word *tamunateka* in this verse adds depth to the concept of satisfaction. It can be interpreted as "when I am awake," implying a state of spiritual awakening or enlightenment. This awakening occurs as one becomes increasingly aware of and aligned with God's presence and purposes.[8]

d. *Created in Intimacy with God*: Psalm 17:15 hints at the divine purpose of humanity's creation. It suggests that from the beginning, humans were designed to experience intimate communion with God, to reflect his image, and to find ultimate satisfaction in union with him. Psalm 17:15, when viewed through the prism of theosis, portrays a profound spiritual journey towards intimacy with God, wherein the individual's longing for communion, righteousness, satisfaction, and awakening to the divine likeness converge in a beautiful expression of the human soul's deepest yearnings.[9]

4. *Isaiah 64:8*: "Yet you, LORD, are our Father. We are the clay, you are the potter; we are all the work of your hand" (NIV). This imagery of God as the potter and humanity as the clay underscores God's sovereignty and creative power in shaping and molding his people. It suggests a dynamic relationship wherein God continually works to transform and refine his creation. Let's delve deeper into the Hebrew words used in this verse:

a. *Hahomer* (הַחֹמֶר): This word translates to "the clay." It signifies the raw material, the substance from which something is formed. In the context of Isa 64:8, *hahomer* symbolizes humanity in its most basic form, pliable and malleable in the hands of God.[10]

b. *Yosarenu* (יֹצְרֵנוּ): This word means "our potter" or "our fashioner." It stems from the Hebrew root *yatzar*, which conveys the idea of forming, fashioning, or shaping something according to

---

8. MacDonald, *Believer's Bible*.

9. The phrase "I shall be satisfied" denotes a deep longing for fulfillment and contentment that can only be found in God. It reflects the recognition that true satisfaction comes from intimacy with the divine rather than from worldly pursuits or possessions. This echoes the teachings of theosis, which emphasize the ultimate fulfillment of human existence in union with God.

10. Oswalt, *Book of Isaiah*.

a predetermined plan or design. In this verse, *yosarenu* highlights God's role as the Creator who skillfully crafts and shapes humanity according to his divine purpose.[11]

c. *Context of Isaiah 64:8*: In the context of Isa 64:8, the imagery of God as the potter and humanity as the clay resonates deeply with the concept of theosis. Just as a potter molds and shapes clay according to his will, God forms and molds humanity according to his divine plan. Theosis entails allowing ourselves to be shaped and transformed by God, surrendering to his will and allowing his hands to mold us into vessels of his glory. This verse emphasizes the intimate relationship between God and humanity, portraying God as a loving Father who takes a personal interest in his creation. It invites us to embrace our identity as creatures fashioned by the hands of God and to cooperate with his transformative work in our lives, ultimately leading to a deeper union with him.

d. *Transformation in Isaiah 64:8*: Isaiah 64:8 presents a profound metaphor of God as the potter and humanity as the clay, illustrating the intimate relationship between Creator and creation. This relationship mirrors the concept of theosis, highlighting the process of spiritual transformation and union with God. As we yield ourselves to God's shaping hands, we participate in the divine work of becoming more like him.[12]

5. *Romans 8:29*: "For those God foreknew he also predestined to be conformed to the image of his Son, that he might be the firstborn among many brothers and sisters" (NIV). In this verse, Paul speaks of God's redemptive purpose for believers, which is to be conformed to the image of Christ. This process of conformity to Christ's likeness is central to theosis, as believers are progressively transformed into the image of the Son. A look at some of the Greek terms in this verse will help us understand this process of conformity:

---

11. Oswalt, *Book of Isaiah*.

12. In this metaphor, God is portrayed as the potter, the skilled artisan who molds and shapes the clay according to his will. Humanity is depicted as the clay, a substance that is malleable and receptive to the potter's touch. This imagery emphasizes the sovereignty of God as the Creator and the dependence of humanity upon him for its very existence.

a. *Foreknew (proōrisen)*: This term suggests more than mere knowledge beforehand; it implies an intimate, predetermined relationship. It speaks to God's intimate knowledge and relationship with humanity even before creation.

b. *Conformed (symmorphous)*: This word implies a transformation or molding into a similar form. It signifies the process of becoming like Christ, aligning with his character and nature.

c. *Image (eikōnos)*: Refers to the likeness or representation. In this context, it pertains to the likeness of Christ, suggesting that humans are meant to reflect his character and attributes.

d. *Firstborn (huiou)*: This denotes priority, preeminence, and inheritance. Christ is the firstborn, not in a temporal sense, but in terms of rank and importance. The phrase implies that Christ's divine nature and relationship with the Father are to be shared by believers.[13]

e. *Interpreting Romans 8:29*: Interpreting this verse in light of theosis, we see that God's plan from the beginning was for humans to be intimately connected with him, to share in his likeness and participate in his divine nature. This process involves a transformation, where believers are molded into the image of Christ, reflecting his character and attributes. This transformation is not just a superficial change but a deep, inward renewal of the individual, leading to union with God. Thus, Rom 8:29 emphasizes the intimate relationship between God and humanity, highlighting God's desire for humans to share in his divine nature through the process of theosis, ultimately resulting in conformity to the image of Christ. This verse underscores the profound depth of God's love and his ultimate plan for humanity's restoration and union with him.[14]

6. *Second Corinthians 3:18*: "And we all, who with unveiled faces contemplate the Lord's glory, are being transformed into his image with ever-increasing glory, which comes from the Lord, who is the Spirit" (NIV). This verse speaks of the ongoing transformation of believers

---

13. Moo, *Letter to the Romans*.

14. By emphasizing that God predestined believers to be conformed to the image of his Son, Rom 8:29 underscores the divine initiative in the process of theosis. It is God who initiates and sustains this transformative work in the lives of believers, drawing them closer to himself and shaping them according to his divine purpose.

into the image of Christ through the work of the Holy Spirit. It highlights the dynamic nature of theosis as a process of spiritual growth and maturation. Let's break down the key terms:

a. *Autēn (αὐτὴν)*: This refers to "the same" or "that same."[15] In this context, it likely denotes the image or glory of the Lord mentioned earlier in the verse.

b. *Eikona (εἰκόνα)*: This word translates to "image" or "likeness." It is used in the New Testament to denote the resemblance of one thing to another.[16]

c. *Metamorphoumetha (μεταμορφούμεθα)*: This is where we get the English word "metamorphosis" from. It means to undergo a transformation or a change in form.[17]

d. *Doxēs eis doxan (δόξης εἰς δόξαν)*: This phrase translates to "from glory to glory." It signifies a progression or advancement from one state of glory to another.[18]

In this verse, Paul is presenting a profound theological concept regarding the transformative nature of the Christian life. He speaks of believers being transformed into the image of the Lord, from glory to glory. Here, the idea of theosis, which is the process of becoming like God, can be inferred. The phrase "the same image" or "that same image" (*autēn eikona*) points to the image of God in which humanity was created. This harkens back to the Genesis account where it's stated that humanity was created in the image and likeness of God. However, due to sin, this image was marred. Through Christ and the work of the Holy Spirit, believers are being restored to this original image.

The term *metamorphosis metha* suggests a radical transformation, akin to a caterpillar metamorphosing into a butterfly. It implies a deep, inward change that affects every aspect of one's being. This transformation is not instantaneous but is a continual process, reflecting the ongoing work of the Holy Spirit in the believer's life.

---

15. Hays, *2 Corinthians*.
16. Powell, *New Testmanet*.
17. Blue Letter Bible, s.v. "μεταμορφόω."
18. Barnett, *Second Epistle to the Corinthians*, 174–76.

The phrase "from glory to glory" (*doxēs eis doxan*) highlights the progressive nature of this transformation. As believers grow in their relationship with God, they experience increasing measures of his glory in their lives. This journey towards greater conformity to the image of Christ is marked by various stages of spiritual growth and maturity. The verse 2 Cor 3:18 underscores the intimate relationship between God and humanity, wherein believers are being continually transformed into the likeness of Christ through the work of the Holy Spirit. It speaks to the inherent potential and destiny of humanity to participate in the divine nature, reflecting the profound truth that God has always intended for us to be in communion with him, sharing in his glory.[19]

7. *Second Peter 1:4*: The phrase *theias koinonia physeōs*, "partakers of the divine nature" in English,[20] is a rich theological concept that reveals the profound relationship between God and believers, highlighting both the privilege and the transformation inherent in the Christian faith.

   a. *Partakers*: The word "partakers" (*koinonoi*) implies active participation and sharing in something. In this context, believers are not passive recipients but actively engaged participants in the divine nature.

   b. *Divine nature*: The phrase "divine nature" (*theias physeōs*) refers to the essential attributes and qualities of God himself. It encompasses his holiness, righteousness, love, wisdom, and all other divine characteristics that distinguish God from creation.

   c. *Significance and Meaning*:

      i. *Union with Christ*: Through faith in Jesus Christ, believers are united with him spiritually. This union is so intimate that believers share in his nature—his holiness and righteousness become our own through the indwelling of the Holy Spirit.

---

19. This transformation is not self-generated but comes from the Lord who is the Spirit. It is the Holy Spirit who empowers and enables believers to undergo this process of transformation, working within them to conform them to the image of Christ. Thus, the believer's transformation is not a product of human effort or striving but is the fruit of the Spirit's work within them.

20. Davids, *2 Peter*.

ii. *Transformation*: The concept of being partakers of the divine nature signifies a profound transformation in the believer's life. It means that as we grow in our relationship with God; his character increasingly shapes our thoughts, desires, and actions. We begin to reflect his love, kindness, forgiveness, and justice in our lives.

iii. *Holiness and Sanctification*: Partaking in the divine nature involves a process of sanctification where the Holy Spirit works within us to conform us to the image of Christ (Rom 8:29). This process involves the renewal of our minds (Rom 12:2), the crucifixion of our old self (Gal 2:20), and the cultivation of virtues such as love, joy, peace, patience, kindness, goodness, faithfulness, gentleness, and self-control (Gal 5:22–23).

d. *Implications for Christian Living*:

i. *Identity*: Understanding ourselves as partakers of the divine nature shapes our identity. We are no longer defined solely by our earthly characteristics or limitations but by our spiritual union with Christ and the transformative power of his Spirit.

ii. *Purpose*: It gives us a clear purpose—to live in a manner that reflects God's character and brings glory to him. Our lives become a testimony to his grace and power at work within us.

iii. *Hope and Assurance*: Knowing that we are partakers of the divine nature gives us hope and assurance in our journey of faith. It reminds us that God is actively working in us to complete the good work he has begun (Phil 1:6).

In conclusion, 2 Pet 1:4 reveals the profound truth that believers are not merely recipients of God's blessings but active participants in his divine nature. It speaks to the transformative power of God's grace and the sanctifying work of the Holy Spirit in the lives of believers, shaping them to reflect the image of Christ in the world. This truth calls us to live holy, loving, and righteous lives, empowered by our union with Christ and motivated by our desire to honor and glorify God in all that we do.

These biblical references, among others, provide a foundation for theosis by highlighting humanity's divine calling, the transformative work of God, and the ultimate destiny of believers to be conformed to the image of Christ. While the term theosis may not be explicitly used in Scripture, its theological themes and implications are deeply rooted in the biblical narrative.

8. *First John 3:2*: "Dear friends, now we are children of God, and what we will be has not yet been made known. But we know that when Christ appears, we shall be like him, for we shall see him as he is." John anticipates the future fulfillment of theosis when believers will be fully transformed into the likeness of Christ. This transformation will occur at the eschatological culmination of God's redemptive plan.

   a. *Ephanerōthē* (ἐφανερώθη): This is the aorist passive form of the verb *phaneroó* (φανερόω), meaning "to manifest" or "to make known." It implies a revelation or unveiling, suggesting that something previously hidden has now become visible or known.[21]

   b. *Hoti* (ὅτι): This is a conjunction that can mean "because," "since," or "that." It introduces a clause explaining the reason or cause of something.

   c. *Homoioi* (ὁμοίοι): This is an adjective meaning "like," "similar," or "of the same nature." It's used to describe the relationship between believers and Christ.

   d. *Esometha* (ἐσόμεθα): This is the future tense form of the verb *eimí* (εἰμί), meaning "to be." It indicates a future state or condition.

   e. *Opsometha* (ὀψόμεθα): This is the future tense form of the verb *horáō* (ὁράω), meaning "to see" or "to perceive." It suggests a future event of seeing or perceiving.[22]

   In 1 John 3:8, the verse speaks of the purpose of the Son of God's manifestation (ἐφανερώθη), which is to destroy the works of the devil. This implies a transformative act, where the revelation of the Son brings about a change in the state of affairs, shifting from darkness (the domain of the devil) to light (the domain of God). The clause introduced by *hoti* (ὅτι), meaning "that" or "because," elucidates the reason for the Son's manifestation. It suggests that the

---

21. Marshall, *Letters of John*.
22. Marshall, *Letters of John*.

Son came into the world because the devil has been sinning from the beginning. This highlights the cosmic battle between good and evil and underscores the salvific mission of Christ to overcome the power of sin and darkness.

The future tense verbs *homoioi* (ὅμοιοι), *esometha* (ἐσόμεθα), and *opsometha* (ὀψόμεθα) point towards a future reality for believers. The term *homoioi* (ὅμοιοι) emphasizes the likeness or similarity between believers and Christ. This echoes the concept of theosis, wherein believers are transformed into the likeness of Christ, partaking in his divine nature.[23]

The future tense verbs *esometha* (ἐσόμεθα) and *opsometha* (ὀψόμεθα) indicate a future state or condition where believers will be like Christ and will see him as he is. This suggests a process of transformation and a future realization of the intimate relationship between humans and God, culminating in the vision of God's glory. The verse 1 John 3:8 offers a profound insight into the transformative work of Christ, the cosmic battle between good and evil, and the future hope of believers to be like Christ and behold him in all his glory, ultimately fulfilling the concept of theosis and the intimate communion between humans and God.

The term theosis (θέωσις) in Greek carries rich linguistic and theological nuances that have profound implications for Christian theology. Understanding these nuances is essential for grasping the depth and significance of theosis within the Christian tradition.

Linguistic and Theological Nuances

1. *Linguistic Nuances*:

    a. *Etymology*: The term *theosis* is derived from the Greek word *theos*, meaning "God."

    b. *Theological Contexts*: In theological contexts, theosis refers to the transformative process by which a person becomes united with God, sharing in his divine nature. This does not mean becoming

---

23. The term *homoioi* (ὅμοιοι) emphasizes the concept of likeness or similarity. In the context of theosis, believers are understood to be transformed spiritually, morally, and ethically into the likeness of Christ. This transformation is not merely external but involves the renewal of the inner person to reflect the virtues, character, and holiness of Christ.

God in essence but participating in the divine nature and experiencing a profound union with God. Theosis conveys the idea of being united with God in a way that reflects his divine attributes and nature. It emphasizes a mystical and transformative relationship where believers grow into a divine likeness through God's grace. As such, theosis conveys the idea of becoming like God or being united with God.[24]

c. *Verbal Noun*: Theosis is a verbal noun derived from the verb *theou*, which means "to become divine" or "to be deified."[25] The use of a verbal noun emphasizes that theosis is not a one-time event but an ongoing process. It involves continuous spiritual growth, purification, and transformation as believers participate more fully in the divine nature.

Theosis is understood as a journey of becoming more like God through divine grace. This journey involves active engagement in practices such as prayer, asceticism, and mystical experiences, which facilitate the process of transformation. The dynamic aspect of theosis reflects the belief that spiritual development is progressive. Believers gradually move toward greater union with God, reflecting his attributes more fully as they advance in their spiritual journey. This linguistic construction emphasizes the dynamic and ongoing nature of theosis as a process of transformation rather than a static state.[26]

2. *Theological Nuances*:

a. *Divine Likeness*: Theosis involves the participation of humans in the divine nature and the attainment of divine likeness. It implies a deep communion with God, wherein humans reflect the attributes and qualities of God in their own lives.

---

24. The term theosis underscores the dynamic and relational nature of humanity's relationship with God. It signifies a journey of spiritual growth and maturation, wherein individuals are continually drawn closer to God and are gradually transformed into his likeness.

25. Ware, *Orthodox Way*; Meyendorff, *Palamas and Orthodox Spirituality*.

26. Framing theosis as a verbal noun emphasizes its ongoing nature. It suggests that the process of becoming like God is not something that is ever fully completed in this life but is a continual striving towards greater conformity to the divine image. It speaks to the idea of spiritual growth and transformation as a lifelong journey, characterized by perseverance, humility, and a deepening relationship with God.

b. *Union with God*: Theosis signifies a mystical union with God, wherein humans are united with the triune God in love and communion. It involves the integration of human will with the divine will and the sharing of life with God.

c. *Salvation and Sanctification*: Theosis is intricately connected to the process of salvation and sanctification in Christian theology. It encompasses not only the forgiveness of sins but also the transformation of human nature into conformity with Christ.

d. *Transformation and Transfiguration*: Theosis entails a radical transformation of the human person, both inwardly and outwardly. It involves the purification of the soul, the illumination of the mind, and the transfiguration of the body, reflecting the glory of God.

e. *Eschatological Fulfillment*: Theosis points towards the eschatological fulfillment of God's plan for creation, wherein humanity will be fully transformed and united with God for eternity. It anticipates the ultimate restoration and renewal of all things in Christ.

Implications for Christian Theology

1. *Divine-Human Interaction*: Theosis, then, brings to light the living and loving character of the divine-human interaction wherein humans are invited into common union with God. Theosis highlights that the encounter between God and humanity is an event. This is not a fixed or once and for all occurrence but an ongoing progression and development. These efforts help us enter into a richer relationship with God, which includes prayer and worship, sacraments, and spiritual practice. Theosis is not about believing the right things or performing some rituals; it's receiving God by faith and letting him work on us to become like him.

   At the heart of this insight is human participation in divine life. In other words, it is not just ideas or statements but rather a way of getting into a relationship with God. It is one in which love, intimacy, and communion (connectedness) are normal. Theosis is really not much more than being united with God, where the trajectory of residing in flesh to residing in divinity merges and where

THE BIBLICAL FOUNDATIONS OF THEOSIS 71

an individual becomes one heart, mind, and spirit joined together increasingly into the fullness of life found in him.

It emphasizes the transformative potential of the Christian life, wherein believers are called to grow in holiness and become more like Christ. At its core, the notion of the transformative potential of the Christian life in theosis encapsulates the belief that embracing the teachings of Christ can lead to profound personal and spiritual growth. It suggests that Christianity is not merely a set of doctrines to be intellectually assented to, but rather a dynamic and ongoing journey of inner renewal and outward manifestation of one's faith.

2. *Holiness*: Holiness is a core principle in this understanding, involving alignment with biblical, moral, and ethical standards. This encompasses pursuing inner purity, ethical behavior, and a deeper connection with God. Rather than being fixed, holiness is viewed as an ongoing process of improvement, characterized by contrition, mercy, and the Holy Spirit's empowering influence. The aspiration to become Christlike is fundamental to Christian spirituality. Jesus is regarded as the ideal manifestation of divine love, empathy, and virtue, with followers urged to mirror his example. This goes beyond merely copying his actions to embracing his mindset, principles, and qualities such as modesty, benevolence, and altruism. The transformative power of Christian faith extends beyond individuals to impact communities and society at large. As people are changed through their relationship with Christ, they are encouraged to engage in advancing God's kingdom. This involves promoting fairness, unity, and the well-being of all creation.[27]

3. *Human Dignity*: Theosis is a powerful means of conveying the dignity and worth of all human beings as participants in divine life, made according to God's image. At the very core of it all is a foundational belief in the dignity and worth of every individual person. It means that the human race was made in God's image, with attributes like rationality, creativity, moral awareness, and the ability to know love and be loved. This suggests that humans should strive to embody divine attributes like love, justice, creativity, and wisdom

27. Holiness is not a fixed state but an ongoing process of improvement, characterized by contrition, mercy, and the Holy Spirit's influence. The aspiration to become like Christ is fundamental to Christian spirituality. This involves embracing his mindset, principles, and qualities. The transformative power of Christian faith extends beyond individuals to impact communities and society at large.

in their actions and relationships. This implies that humans have an inherent capacity for goodness, rationality, and moral behavior. It suggests we should aim to cultivate and express these qualities in our lives. This aligns with many spiritual and philosophical traditions that emphasize the importance of personal growth and its impact on others. It suggests that by developing our own "divine" qualities, we naturally become beacons for others. This indicates a belief that human purpose extends beyond material concerns, aiming for a higher state of being or consciousness. This perspective presents a deeply purposeful view of human existence. It suggests that by cultivating our highest potentials, we not only fulfill our own nature but also contribute to the spiritual and moral evolution of humanity as a whole.

Additionally, theosis is a description of the change of heart for human beings striving to attain union with God. In this way, it connotes a progressive spiritual development, purification, and sanctification in which Christians are transformed into the likeness of Christ. It is a path of synergy between us and God as we cooperate with him in faith, repentance, prayer, and reception of the sacraments.

Theosis also underscores the ultimate destiny of humanity, which is to be fully united with God in eternal communion. This eschatological hope inspires believers to pursue holiness and perfection, striving to become "partakers of the divine nature" (2 Pet 1:4) and to attain theosis in its fullest expression. The concept of theosis underscores the dignity and value of human beings by affirming their divine potential and calling them to participate in the life of God. It emphasizes the transformative journey towards union with God, rooted in the belief that humans are created in the image and likeness of God and destined for eternal communion with him.

4. *Forgiveness of Sins*: Salvation, in its essence, encompasses the profound concept of the forgiveness of sins. This forgiveness refers to the divine act of absolving or not holding individuals accountable for their transgressions in the eyes of God. It is a cornerstone of many world religions, where followers are encouraged to seek reconciliation with the divine through sincere repentance and the subsequent receipt of forgiveness.

However, salvation extends beyond mere forgiveness. It initiates a profound inner transformation of the individual as they progress in their faith journey. This transformation, often referred to as sanctification or character development, is a crucial aspect of the salvific process.

The concept of being transformed addresses the question, How does an individual's conduct and character evolve after experiencing such deep and beautiful forgiveness as described? This transformation is not instantaneous but a gradual process whereby the forgiven person, in response to divine grace, begins to align their thoughts, actions, and overall character with the divine will.

Thus, salvation emerges as a multifaceted concept encompassing several key elements:

a. *Justification*: The act of being declared righteous before God, often through faith.

b. *Forgiveness*: The divine pardon for sins, removing the guilt and punishment associated with transgressions.

c. *Character Transformation*: The ongoing process of inner change, leading to a life that increasingly reflects divine values and virtues.

This holistic view presents salvation not as a single event but as a comprehensive experience that touches every aspect of a person's being. It begins with forgiveness but extends to a lifelong journey of growth and transformation. This understanding of salvation resonates deeply within the heart of each person who professes faith in Christ, offering not just hope for eternity but a path to a transformed life in the present. The interplay between forgiveness and character transformation underscores the dynamic nature of salvation. It is not merely about escaping divine judgment but about entering into a new way of being that reflects the character of the divine. This perspective on salvation offers a rich, multidimensional understanding that addresses both the immediate need for forgiveness and the long-term process of becoming more aligned with the divine nature.

5. Theosis invites Christians to cultivate a deep spirituality marked by prayer, sacramental participation, and ethical living as they journey towards union with God. Theosis is about the transformation of

the human person, both spiritually and morally, into the likeness of God. This transformation involves a journey that encompasses various dimensions of the Christian life:

a. *Prayer*: Central to theosis is the cultivation of a life of prayer. Through prayer, individuals open themselves to communion with God, seeking to deepen their relationship with him. This can take many forms, including personal prayer, liturgical prayer, and contemplative prayer. By engaging in regular prayer, Christians seek to align their will with God's will and to be receptive to the transformative work of the Holy Spirit in their lives.

b. *Sacramental Participation*: The sacraments play a vital role in the Christian life and are seen as means of grace through which God's presence and power are experienced. By actively participating in the sacramental life of the church—such as through the Eucharist, baptism, confession, and confirmation—Christians receive the spiritual nourishment necessary for their journey towards theosis. The sacraments are understood as encounters with the living God, moments of divine presence that contribute to the ongoing transformation of the believer.

c. *Ethical Living*: Integral to the process of theosis is ethical living guided by the teachings of Jesus Christ. This involves not only adhering to moral principles but also embodying the virtues of Christ—such as love, humility, compassion, and forgiveness—in everyday life. Ethical living is not merely about following rules but about cultivating a disposition of the heart that reflects the character of God. Through acts of charity, service, and justice, Christians participate in God's redemptive work in the world and grow in likeness to him. The journey of theosis is ongoing and lifelong, characterized by continual growth and transformation. It is a process in which individuals cooperate with the grace of God, responding to his invitation to share in his divine life. Ultimately, the goal of theosis is union with God, where the believer becomes fully conformed to the image of Christ and experiences the fullness of divine love, joy, and peace.

In conclusion, the concept of "theosis" embodies a rich tapestry of linguistic and theological nuances that profoundly shape its understanding and implications within Christian thought. This term, deeply rooted in Eastern Christian traditions but increasingly recognized in Western theology, encapsulates a transformative journey that lies at the heart of Christian spirituality and anthropology. Theosis speaks to the profound calling of humanity—a calling that transcends mere moral improvement or religious observance. It describes a process of deep, ontological transformation whereby human beings, through divine grace and their cooperative efforts, gradually become more like God. This concept is not about humans becoming divine in essence, but rather about participating more fully in the divine nature, as alluded to in 2 Pet 1:4.

The journey of theosis invites believers into an ever-deepening communion with the triune God. It suggests that the ultimate purpose of human existence is not just to know about God but to know God intimately and to be known by him. This intimate knowing involves a progressive conformation to the image of Christ, who is understood as the perfect image of God in human form.

Furthermore, theosis points to the fulfillment of humanity's ultimate destiny in Christ. It suggests that human beings were created not just to be servants or subjects of God but to be partners in divine life—to become, in the words of the church fathers, "gods by grace."[28] This destiny is both a present reality, unfolding in the lives of believers through faith, sacraments, and spiritual disciplines, and an eschatological hope, finding its complete fulfillment in the age to come. The concept of theosis also carries significant implications for how we understand salvation. Rather than seeing salvation merely as rescue from sin or punishment, theosis presents it as a positive movement towards fullness of life and being. It encompasses justification, sanctification, and glorification in a holistic vision of human transformation and divine-human communion.

In embracing the concept of theosis, Christian theology affirms the incredible dignity and potential of human nature. It declares that humans, created in God's image, are capable of reflecting divine attributes such as love, wisdom, and creativity. At the same time, it maintains a proper distinction between Creator and creature, emphasizing that this divinization is always by grace, never by nature. Thus, "theosis" stands as a powerful theological concept that enriches our understanding of human purpose, divine-human relationship, and the nature of salvation itself. It offers a vision of Christian life that is dynamic, transformative,

---

28. Russell, *Greek Patristic Tradition*, loc. 423.

and ultimately oriented towards the fullest possible union with God in Christ through the Holy Spirit.

Relevance in Daily Life

1. *Understanding Human Dignity and Potential*:

    a. *Teaching*: Theosis teaches that humans are not just servants of God but partners in divine life, capable of reflecting divine attributes like love, wisdom, and creativity. This perspective can elevate one's sense of self-worth and purpose. In daily life, this means striving to live in ways that reflect these divine attributes, such as showing love and compassion in relationships, exercising wisdom in decision making, and pursuing creative and meaningful endeavors.

    b. *Practical Application*: One might, for example, see work in professional settings as an opportunity to manifest divine attributes, which can encourage ethical behavior, creativity, and excellence. In personal relationships, understanding one's potential to reflect divine love can foster deeper connections and more empathetic interactions.

2. *A Holistic View of Salvation*:

    a. *Teaching*: Theosis frames salvation not merely as escape from sin or punishment but as a transformative journey towards fullness of life and being. This perspective invites believers to view their spiritual journey as an ongoing process of growth and transformation rather than a static state.

    b. *Practical Application*: In practice, this means embracing spiritual disciplines such as prayer, fasting, and community service not just as duties but as means of personal and communal transformation. For instance, regular participation in these practices can help one grow in virtue and deepen one's relationship with God and others.

3. *The Present and Future Dimensions of Theosis*:

    a. *Teaching*: Theosis is both a present reality and an eschatological hope. This means that while believers work towards this divine

THE BIBLICAL FOUNDATIONS OF THEOSIS

union now, they also look forward to its complete fulfillment in the future. This dual aspect can provide motivation and perspective in daily life.

    b. *Practical Application*: Knowing that the transformative process is ongoing can encourage persistence and patience in spiritual growth. For instance, when faced with challenges or setbacks, remembering that these are part of the transformative journey can help maintain hope and perseverance.

4. *Distinction Between Creator and Creature*:

    a. *Teaching*: Theosis underscores that while humans are called to become "gods by grace," this divinization is always by God's grace and not through human effort alone. This maintains humility and acknowledges the distinction between Creator and creature.

    b. *Practical Application*: This understanding can shape a balanced approach to spiritual growth. Believers might work diligently towards spiritual goals while recognizing that ultimate transformation comes from divine grace. This balance can prevent pride and foster a spirit of gratitude and dependence on God.

5. *Transformative Vision of Christian Life*:

    a. *Teaching*: Theosis provides a dynamic and transformative vision of Christian life, encouraging believers to view their journey as one of continual growth towards union with God. This vision can make everyday actions and decisions more purposeful.

    b. *Practical Application*: Embracing this transformative vision can lead to a more intentional and purposeful life. For instance, engaging in acts of charity, pursuing personal spiritual development, and working towards personal goals with a sense of divine partnership can all be seen as steps towards achieving theosis.

Chapter 6

Transfiguration of Christ as a Theosis Event

THE TRANSFIGURATION OF CHRIST, as depicted in the Synoptic Gospels, indeed represents a profound theological event that captures the essence of Christ's divine nature and mission. The transfiguration is a critical moment where Jesus' divine nature is momentarily revealed in a visible and spectacular way. His face shining like the sun and his garments becoming white as light serve as a powerful affirmation of his divinity. This event underscores the belief that, while Jesus lived a human life, his divine nature was always present, albeit often hidden. The transfiguration allows the disciples to glimpse this divine glory, reinforcing the Christian doctrine of Christ's dual nature—fully human and fully divine.

The transfiguration is also a theophany, a visible manifestation of God's presence. This is reminiscent of earlier Old Testament theophanies, such as Moses' encounter with God on Mount Sinai. It signifies a direct encounter with the divine and a moment of profound spiritual revelation. The event is not only a glimpse of divine glory but also a foretaste of the future kingdom of God. It hints at the ultimate glorification that awaits believers and the coming of God's kingdom in its fullness. This eschatological aspect provides a hopeful vision of the future and encourages believers to live in anticipation of the kingdom of God.

The transfiguration invites deep theological reflection on the nature of Christ and the transformative power of divine encounters. It challenges believers to consider the mystery of Christ's dual nature and the implications of such a profound encounter with divine glory. The event prompts reflection on how such encounters can transform our understanding and experience of faith.

The mountaintop setting of the transfiguration symbolizes a spiritual ascent. It suggests that significant spiritual insights often come through striving and elevation in faith. The transfiguration, therefore, becomes a metaphor for the spiritual journey that requires perseverance and faith to reach higher understanding and transformation.

The transfiguration occurs in the context of Jesus' impending suffering and crucifixion. This juxtaposition of glory and suffering highlights the Christian understanding that divine glory does not negate the reality of suffering but rather provides hope and assurance of ultimate victory and transformation.

The transfiguration of Christ is a rich and multidimensional event in Christian theology, providing a profound insight into Christ's divine nature, his mission, and the transformative potential of divine encounters. It continues to inspire believers, inviting them to a deeper understanding of their faith and a commitment to spiritual transformation.

The Mystery of Christ's Personhood

This transformation symbolizes the revelation of his true nature as the Son of God. The transfiguration of Jesus on Mount Tabor is a deeply symbolic and pivotal event in the Gospels; it is recorded in Matt 17:1–9, Mark 9:2–8, and Luke 9:28–36.

The transfiguration is often seen as a pivotal event where Jesus revealed his divine glory to Peter, James, and John on Mount Tabor. His appearance changed: his face was shining like the sun and his clothes had become dazzling white. This event is significant not only for its narrative impact but also for its profound theological implications regarding Jesus' identity and mission.

   a. *Revelation of Divine Glory*: The transfiguration is often interpreted as a moment where Jesus reveals his divine glory to his closest disciples, Peter, James, and John. His appearance changes dramatically: his face shines like the sun, and his clothes become dazzling white (Matt 17:2). This transformation symbolizes the revelation of his true nature as the Son of God, pointing to his divine essence and prefiguring his resurrection glory.[1]

b. *Confirmation of Jesus' Identity*: The voice from the cloud, identified as God the Father, declares, "This is my Son, whom I love; with him I am well pleased. Listen to him!" (Matt 17:5 NIV). This declaration echoes the similar proclamation at Jesus' baptism (Matt 3:17), affirming Jesus' identity as the beloved Son of God. The transfiguration thus serves as a divine endorsement of Jesus' authority and mission, reinforcing his role as the fulfillment of Old Testament prophecies and the bearer of salvation for humanity.[2]

c. *Connections with Old Testament Figures*: The presence of Moses and Elijah conversing with Jesus during the transfiguration is significant. Moses represents the Law and Elijah represents the Prophets, symbolizing the continuity and fulfillment found in Jesus Christ. Their presence underscores Jesus' role as the culmination of God's redemptive plan, bringing together the Law and the Prophets in himself (Matt 5:17).[3]

d. *Foreshadowing the Resurrection*: The dazzling white garments and radiant appearance of Jesus anticipate his resurrection glory. This transformative moment on Mount Tabor offers a glimpse into the future glory of Christ after his death and resurrection, affirming the continuity of his divine nature and highlighting the ultimate victory over sin and death through his sacrificial death.[4]

---

1. The transfiguration serves as a glimpse into Jesus' true identity as the Son of God. By revealing his glory to Peter, James, and John, Jesus affirms his unique relationship with the Father and establishes his authority as the divine Son. This moment of revelation strengthens the disciples' faith and prepares them for the challenges ahead, particularly Jesus' approaching suffering and death, which they must comprehend in light of his divinity.

2. The transfiguration underscores the continuity and fulfillment of divine promises found in the Old Testament. In the Hebrew Bible, the presence of God often manifested in brightness and glory, as seen in the accounts of Moses on Mount Sinai or in the temple visions of Isaiah and Ezekiel. Similarly, Jesus' radiant transformation signifies the presence of God with humanity, fulfilling the prophetic expectation of the messiah who would bring divine revelation and redemption.

3. The presence of Moses and Elijah at the transfiguration highlights the continuity of God's redemptive plan across history. It demonstrates that Jesus is the pinnacle of God's revelation and the fulfillment of all previous revelations. He is the culmination of God's promises and the ultimate mediator between God and humanity.

4. The transfiguration anticipates and foreshadows Jesus' resurrection. The dazzling appearance of Jesus signifies the glory that will be fully revealed after his death and

e. *Implications for Discipleship*: The transfiguration is not only a revelation of Jesus' identity but also a call to discipleship and faith. The disciples' response to this event underscores the importance of recognizing Jesus' true nature and authority, listening to his teachings, and following him faithfully even amidst challenges and uncertainties.[5]

The presence of Moses and Elijah conversing with Jesus underscores the continuity between the Law (represented by Moses) and the Prophets (represented by Elijah) with Jesus as the fulfillment of both.

1. *Moses and the Law*: Moses is a central figure in Jewish tradition, revered as the lawgiver who received the Torah (Law) from God on Mount Sinai. The Law given through Moses encompassed moral, ethical, ceremonial, and civil regulations that governed the life of Israel. It represented God's covenant relationship with his people and outlined the standards of righteousness and holiness.

2. *Elijah and the Prophets*: Elijah, on the other hand, was one of the greatest prophets in Israelite history, known for his zeal for God and his fearless confrontation of idolatry and injustice. He symbolizes the prophetic tradition, through which God communicated his word and revealed his will to the people of Israel. The prophets called the people to repentance, proclaimed God's judgment and mercy, and anticipated the coming of the messiah.

3. *Fulfillment in Jesus Christ*: The presence of Moses and Elijah conversing with Jesus at the transfiguration signifies their recognition of Jesus as the fulfillment of both the Law and the Prophets. Jesus himself affirmed this continuity in Matt 5:17, saying, "Do not think that I have come to abolish the Law or the Prophets; I have not come to abolish them but to fulfill them."

---

resurrection. It serves as a glimpse into the future state of Jesus' glorified body, which his disciples would later witness after the events of his passion and crucifixion. This anticipatory glimpse reassures the disciples and strengthens their faith, preparing them for the upcoming trials and challenges.

5. The transfiguration serves as a preparation for the disciples to face the challenges and uncertainties that lie ahead, particularly Jesus' impending suffering and crucifixion. Seeing Jesus in his glorified state strengthens their faith and provides them with a glimpse of the ultimate victory that Jesus will achieve through his death and resurrection. It encourages them to trust in Jesus' teachings, even when those teachings include predictions of suffering and persecution for themselves as his followers.

Jesus embodies the essence and purpose of the Law. He fulfills its moral demands perfectly (Matt 5:17–48), teaches its true meaning (Matt 22:34–40), and establishes a new covenant that fulfills and surpasses the old (Heb 8:6–13). In him, the Law finds its ultimate fulfillment as he embodies perfect righteousness and becomes the mediator of a new covenant based on grace and forgiveness.

4. *Prophetic Fulfillment*: Likewise, Jesus fulfills the prophetic expectations of Israel. He is the ultimate Prophet who speaks God's word with divine authority (John 12:49–50). The prophecies concerning the suffering messiah (Isa 53) and the establishment of God's kingdom (Dan 7:13–14) find their fulfillment in Jesus' life, death, and resurrection.

Elijah's presence at the transfiguration is particularly significant because Elijah was expected to return before the messiah's coming (Malachi 4:5–6). The appearance of Elijah with Jesus affirms Jesus' identity as the long-awaited Messiah and the fulfillment of all prophetic promises.

5. *Implications for Christian Faith*: The presence of Moses and Elijah at the transfiguration underscores the unity and continuity of God's redemptive plan throughout history, culminating in Jesus Christ. It affirms Jesus' authority to interpret and fulfill the Scriptures, demonstrating that he is the focal point of God's revelation and the centerpiece of salvation history.

For Christians, understanding Jesus as the fulfillment of the Law and the Prophets reinforces the importance of embracing his teachings, following his example of love and obedience, and recognizing him as the source of eternal life and reconciliation with God.

In essence, the presence of Moses and Elijah conversing with Jesus at the transfiguration signifies Jesus' role as the fulfillment of God's promises and the embodiment of divine truth. It invites believers to recognize Jesus' authority, to deepen their understanding of God's redemptive plan, and to embrace the transformative power of his life and teachings.

Theophany and Divine Revelation

The transfiguration is viewed as a theophany—a tangible manifestation of the divine. It underscores God's presence and affirms Jesus' godly nature. This divine disclosure not only bolsters the disciples' belief but also readies them for impending trials, especially Jesus' forthcoming suffering and demise. This moment carries profound theological weight in validating Jesus' divine essence and equipping his followers for the hardships and ultimate goal of his mission.

The manifestation of divine glory in Jesus strengthens the understanding and belief in his divine nature. It's a clear sign that Jesus is not just a great teacher or prophet but is indeed divine. By revealing his divine essence in a powerful way, Jesus prepares and strengthens his disciples for the upcoming trials. Knowing that Jesus has divine authority helps them remain steadfast and encouraged even as they face significant challenges. This event serves as a profound theological statement about who Jesus is. It validates his divine essence and the significance of his mission, emphasizing that his suffering and death are part of a greater divine plan.

1. Confirming Jesus' Divine Identity

   a. *Theophany and Divine Presence*: A theophany is a direct manifestation of God to humans, where the divine presence becomes tangible and visible. In the transfiguration, God's glory shines forth as Jesus' appearance changes dramatically—his face shines like the sun, and his clothes become dazzling white (Matt 17:2). This radiant transformation serves as a powerful affirmation of Jesus' divine nature. It echoes Old Testament theophanies like the burning bush (Exod 3) and the cloud on Mount Sinai (Exod 24), where God's presence was similarly revealed in awe-inspiring ways.

   b. *Confirmation of Jesus' Divine Identity*: The voice from the cloud during the transfiguration declares, "This is my Son, whom I love; with him I am well pleased. Listen to him!" (Matt 17:5 NIV). This divine declaration echoes the words spoken at Jesus' baptism (Matt 3:17), affirming Jesus' unique relationship with God as the beloved Son. The transfiguration thus serves as a pivotal moment of revelation, confirming Jesus' divine identity before his disciples and reinforcing the truth of his messianic mission.

   c. *Strengthening of Disciples' Faith*: Witnessing the transfiguration profoundly impacts Peter, James, and John, the disciples present on Mount Tabor. It strengthens their faith by providing them with a direct encounter with the divine glory of Jesus. This experience deepens their understanding of who Jesus truly is—the Son of God—and solidifies their commitment to follow him despite the challenges and uncertainties ahead.

d. *Preparation for Jesus' Passion and Death*: The transfiguration also serves as a preparation for the disciples to comprehend the significance of Jesus' impending suffering, death, and resurrection. Moses and Elijah, representing the Law and the Prophets, respectively, appear with Jesus and speak about his departure (Luke 9:31). This conversation likely refers to Jesus' upcoming passion in Jerusalem, emphasizing the necessity and fulfillment of his sacrificial mission.

e. *Application to Christian Life*: For believers, the transfiguration offers profound lessons and implications. It invites reflection on the reality of God's presence in Jesus Christ, reinforcing the foundational truth of Christian faith. It challenges disciples to listen to Jesus' teachings attentively, to embrace the revelation of his divine identity, and to trust in his redemptive work, even amid trials and suffering.

The transfiguration, as a divine manifestation, highlights the visible revelation of God's splendor through Jesus, validating his godly nature and readying his followers for the significant trials and core purpose of his mission. This event serves as a crucial turning point in the Gospel narratives, encouraging believers to strengthen their faith, accept the revelation of God's presence in Jesus, and adhere to his teachings in their daily lives.

2. Spiritual Transformation

The transfiguration serves as a model of spiritual transformation for believers. It highlights the potential for humans to be transformed by the divine presence and to participate in the divine nature (2 Pet 1:4). The dazzling white garments of Jesus symbolize purity and the transfiguration of the human spirit in God's presence. The transfiguration of Jesus not only reveals his divine glory but also serves as a profound model of spiritual transformation for believers, highlighting the potential for humans to be transformed by encountering the divine presence and participating in the divine nature.

a. *Symbolism of Dazzling White Garments*: The dazzling white garments that Jesus wears during the transfiguration symbolize purity, holiness, and divine radiance. In the biblical context, white garments often represent spiritual purity and righteousness (Rev 19:8). Jesus' transfigured appearance with these radiant clothes signifies his perfect holiness and his role as the embodiment of divine purity.

b. *Transformation in God's Presence*: The transfiguration illustrates the transformative power of being in God's presence. As Jesus is transfigured before Peter, James, and John on Mount Tabor, his appearance changes to reveal his divine glory. This transformation is not merely physical but spiritual, indicating the potential for humans to be transformed and renewed in their inner beings through encountering God's glory.

c. *Participation in Divine Nature*: The apostle Peter later reflects on this transformative potential in 2 Pet 1:4, where he writes about believers becoming "partakers of the divine nature" through God's promises and grace. The transfiguration of Jesus exemplifies this concept by showing that through Christ, humans can be united with God in a profound way, sharing in his holiness and reflecting his glory.

d. *Spiritual Transformation for Believers*: For believers, the transfiguration serves as a model and encouragement for their own spiritual journey. It invites them to seek moments of divine encounter through prayer, worship, and meditation on Scripture. These encounters with God's presence have the power to transform their hearts, minds, and spirits, conforming them more closely to the image of Christ (Rom 8:29).

e. *Implications for Christian Life*: The transfiguration challenges believers to pursue holiness and spiritual transformation actively. It calls them to embrace God's presence in their lives, allowing his Spirit to work within them to purify their motives, thoughts, and actions. By participating in the divine nature through faith in Jesus Christ, believers can experience genuine growth in spiritual maturity and reflect God's glory to the world.

The transfiguration of Jesus is a profound symbol of spiritual transformation and a reminder of the potential for humans to be changed by encountering God's presence. It underscores the call for believers to pursue holiness, embrace their identity as children of God, and actively participate in the ongoing work of transformation that God desires for all who follow Christ.

Temporal and Eternal Perspectives

The experience of the disciples on Mount Tabor exposes limited perspectives with eternal truths. The idea of shelters reveals Peter's desire to keep the divine encounter from ending. But God's voice from the cloud stresses Jesus is his beloved Son and to listen to him. This especially requires seeking Jesus' teachings and mission rather than holding onto transient experiences. The expression of Peter wanting to build shelters for Jesus, Moses, and Elijah is a very human response to the divine. It expresses a desire to save and savor the incredible meeting of his divine majesty. We might be excused for this inclination. In our human skin, we become awed at the sheer immanence of God—all too often not so much a burning bush as an almost corporeal but very elusive flame; we find ourselves flailing to hold onto that moment and make it manifest.

However, God's response disrupts this impulse. From the cloud that overshadowed them, God's voice declares, "This is my beloved Son, with whom I am well pleased; listen to him" (Matt 17:5 ESV). This declaration serves several purposes that guide the disciples—and us—towards a deeper understanding:

1. *Jesus as the Beloved Son*: God's affirmation of Jesus as his beloved Son is a central proclamation of Jesus' divine nature and authority. It reinforces that Jesus is not merely a prophet like Moses or Elijah but the Son of God himself.

2. *Instruction to Listen to Him*: This directive is crucial. It redirects the disciples' focus from the spectacular moment on the mountain to the teachings and mission of Jesus. It emphasizes that the true significance lies not in the transitory experiences of divine manifestation but in the enduring truth and wisdom communicated through Jesus' words and actions.

3. *The Transient Versus the Eternal*: Peter's instinct to build shelters reflects humanity's tendency to cling to the fleeting experiences of divine presence. However, the divine command redirects attention towards the eternal truths that Jesus embodies—truths that transcend the momentary epiphany on Mount Tabor. Thus, this event

should lead us to reflect upon our own spiritual lives. It helps us to consider whether we are looking for God in the extreme moments of experience or listening to Jesus faithfully on common days. It calls us to put the way of Jesus—his call for love, forgiveness, justice, and mercy—at the forefront in a world that often confuses means and ends.

The transfiguration points to the New Testament as being a successor and continuation of the Old Testament (Moses and Elijah). It represents Jesus as the realization of God's great redemptive scheme for man that commenced during Old Testament times with the Law and the Prophets. Mount Tabor and the experience of the disciples serve as a poignant analogy for our own struggle against temporal fancies for the sake of eternal truths. Its challenge to us is to stop seeking temporary spiritual highs and establish ourselves in Jesus' truth and mission. The transfiguration calls us to consider our journey of faith. It motivates us to look for times of divine experience in prayer, reflection, and praise. We are called to establish ourselves in Jesus' truth and mission and to put his truth and mission first in all aspects of life.

Witnesses of Transformative Power in the World

Becoming a true disciple of Christ is difficult; we must bind ourselves—both individually and as a community—seriously to this calling, because what awaits us is nothing less than collective conversion. It calls for blending spiritual values into the way we live, changing ourselves, and becoming an inspiration to others. This is truly an invitation to the interconnection of things, which provides impetus for us all as we start down new spiritual paths with fresh determination, living our lives more meaningfully and improving according to God's will. It challenges us to put on the teachings of Christ in our everyday lives and be vessels for his transformative power on earth. A loaded but rich prompt—recast as multifaceted nudge—is to reflect on what each of us might do differently to give people space and encouragement. Space, particularly, beckons one away from spiritual lassitude or hitching onto someone else's predigested journey.

Theosis asks people to live every second of their lives with the instructions provided by Christ. With such vigilance, the opportunities literally assault you on all sides. It requires the manifestation of love, forgiveness, humility, and the just execution of justice in practical realities, displaying the transformation brought about by Christ. To be effective witnesses, individuals must undergo personal transformation themselves. This involves allowing Christ's teachings to reshape their values, behaviors, and relationships, thereby embodying his divine nature and grace.

1. *Seeking Divine Encounter*: The transfiguration invites believers to actively seek moments of divine encounter in their lives. Just as Peter, James, and John were privileged to witness the radiant glory of Jesus on Mount Tabor, so too are believers encouraged to cultivate spaces for prayer, meditation, and worship where they can experience the presence of God. These moments of encounter serve to deepen one's faith, strengthen spiritual resolve, and provide clarity amidst life's challenges.

2. *Embodying Christ's Teachings*: Beyond seeking moments of divine encounter, the transfiguration challenges believers to embody the teachings of Christ in their daily lives. Jesus, transfigured before his disciples, exemplifies the fullness of divine glory and authority. His teachings—of love, compassion, justice, and forgiveness—are not merely theoretical principles but practical mandates for living out one's faith authentically. Thus, the transfiguration prompts believers to reflect on how they can more fully align their lives with the transformative message of Christ.

3. *Living as Witnesses*: The transfiguration also calls believers to live as witnesses of Christ's transformative power in the world. The disciples, having witnessed the glory of Jesus on the mountain, were commissioned to bear witness to this revelation among others. Similarly, believers are entrusted with the task of sharing the gospel through their words, actions, and lifestyles. They are called to be beacons of light in a world often marked by darkness, demonstrating the hope and redemption found in Christ.

The transfiguration underscores the continuity of heaven and earth. It connects the temporal with that which is eternal; it emphasizes that the believer's spiritual walk on this earth does not end in our realm but rather enters into eternity where those who love God are forever united with him. Essentially, the transfiguration urges believers to live out their faith much more consciously. It challenges them to rediscover and pursue divine encounters, walk as Christ walked, live daily lives that are believable witnesses to his resurrection power. It encourages reflection on how you can deepen your spiritual journey and live more closely to the way Jesus lived. The transfiguration functions to act as a constant reminder and guide, lighting the way toward a brighter, fuller relationship with God, along with greater participation in everything else.

Theosis and Participation in Divine Life

Theosis is related to the transfiguration in that it involves transforming human nature with divine grace. In the radiant appearance of Jesus before his disciples, heaven invites us to experience a deeper perception of communion with God, offering us a glimpse of the divine that we earnestly seek. This moment reveals the profound nature of a divine encounter, which is essential to the process of theosis or divinization. The first Sunday of Lent beautifully illustrates how divine revelation and human transformation are intertwined, encapsulating this sacred union in the singular event of the Transfiguration, where the glory of God is revealed and the disciples are invited into a deeper relationship with the divine, becoming partakers of his divine nature. This hints to the powerful nature of divine encounter, which is essential for theosis. The first Sunday in Lent beautifully demonstrates how divine revelation and human transformation are intertwined, particularly as they relate to the themes of spiritual struggle and renewal. This is encapsulated in the event of the Transfiguration, which is commemorated later in the liturgical calendar. It is an epiphany of the divine glory, which appears so far away and beyond reach, but in Jesus shows itself in a visible, radiant shape—one into which people are invited. The confession of the Eastern Orthodox tradition is that we do not participate in this radiance with a passive participation but with an active and transformative one, through our deification as humans.

Thus the transfiguration can be interpreted as a turning point where Jesus shows us that he is divine and invites humanity to share in his life. Showcasing the ways in which revelation, transformation, and deification are interconnected brings out how meeting Christ reveals God's glory far more deeply than we might expect. However, the Transfiguration of Christ is not just a magnificent explosion of divine power; it is an invitation. It reveals Christ paves a way for humanity to share the divine life. The appearance of Moses and Elijah speaking with Jesus serves as a link to the Law (Moses) and Prophets (Elijah), indicating that God's design for salvation is being realized in him. Time and space are pushed aside when this divine meeting takes place, a meeting that brings the heavenly realm to earth, showing us a glimpse of God's kingdom.

One of the main themes that helps us to understand how important this transfiguration was is the theme of transformation. As Jesus' face is transfigured from its earthly form into a heavenly glow, we receive a glimpse of the resurrection glory, which not only foreshadows what Jesus himself will look like, risen from death and in all-consuming splendor, but joined with Christ as one body through faith alone it also guarantees for us a glimmering preview of what awaits every believer. It bespeaks the awesome influence that is wrought upon humanity from contact with the divine glory seen in Jesus Christ—from darkness into light, and out of mortality to immortality.

The transfiguration points towards the broader theme of transformation that extends beyond Jesus himself. It signifies the potential for humanity to undergo spiritual transformation by encountering the divine presence revealed in Christ. This transformation is depicted as a movement from darkness to light, from mortality to immortality. It highlights the transformative power of encountering God's glory, which has the capacity to renew and transfigure individuals spiritually, morally, and even physically.[6]

For believers, the transfiguration offers a glimpse into the ultimate destiny of those united with Christ. It anticipates a future transformation where believers will share in Christ's glory and be transformed into his likeness. This transformation is not just a future hope but a present reality for those who are in communion with Christ through faith.[7]

In interpreting the transfiguration through the lens of theosis, several key theological reflections emerge:

---

6. The transfiguration hints at the transformation from mortality to immortality. Jesus' transfigured appearance prefigures his resurrection glory. It anticipates the victory over death that Jesus would achieve through his sacrificial death and subsequent resurrection. This victory over death offers hope for humanity, pointing towards the possibility of eternal life and spiritual renewal for those who believe in Jesus Christ.

7. The theme of transformation in the transfiguration underscores the universal call to discipleship and spiritual growth. It challenges individuals to continually seek a deeper relationship with God and to allow the Holy Spirit to work within them, bringing about spiritual fruit and maturity. Just as Jesus' disciples were transformed by witnessing his glory, believers are invited to open themselves to the transforming power of God's presence in their lives.

1. *Accessibility of God's Glory*: The radiant glory of Christ on the mountaintop signifies that the divine glory, which is typically beyond human comprehension and access due to sin and separation becomes accessible through Christ. This accessibility is not just for Christ himself but is extended to believers who are united with him. It speaks to the transformative power of God's presence that can elevate human beings to share in his glory.

2. *Transformative Union*: Theosis emphasizes that the union with God is not merely a legal or positional status but a transformative participation in the divine nature. This participation begins in the present life of believers through faith in Christ and continues into eternity. The transfiguration serves as a visible representation of this transformative union, where the disciples witness Jesus' glorified state and are thereby given a glimpse of their own potential destiny in Christ.

3. *Present Reality and Future Hope*: The event also underscores that union with God is both a present reality and a future hope. Through faith in Jesus Christ, believers are already participants in the divine life, experiencing God's transformative power in their lives. At the same time, the fullness of this union will be fully realized in the future, in the heavenly kingdom where believers will share completely in the glory of God.

4. *Invitation to Participation*: The transfiguration invites believers into a deeper participation in the life of Christ. It challenges them to be transformed by the renewing of their minds (Rom 12:2), to seek after holiness (Heb 12:14), and to grow in conformity to the image of Christ (Rom 8:29). Theosis, therefore, is not passive but active—a journey of continual transformation and sanctification empowered by the Holy Spirit.

The transfiguration resonates deeply with the concept of theosis or deification by illustrating God's invitation for humanity to participate in his divine nature through Jesus Christ. It affirms that God's glory is accessible and transformative for those who believe in him, highlighting that union with God is not only a future hope but a present reality experienced through faith and active participation in the life of Christ.[8]

---

8. While the transfiguration demonstrates a glimpse of the future glory that believers will fully experience in eternity, it also emphasizes that the process of theosis begins

As believers contemplate the transfiguration, they are reminded of their high calling to share in the divine life and to pursue holiness and transformation in communion with God.[9]

In conclusion, the transfiguration of Jesus is a pivotal event that reveals his divine nature, opens a path for humanity to partake in divine life, and embodies themes of revelation, transformation, and theosis. It invites believers to contemplate the profound implications of encountering the glory of God as revealed in Jesus Christ—a transformative encounter that illuminates the path to eternal life and communion with God.

Hope and Assurance

The power to rise from the dead was part of Jesus' divine authority over death and his ability as God in flesh to overcome sin on our behalf. It serves as proof of his claims about himself, such as being the Son of God and that he is the Messiah prophesied in the Old Testament. For Orthodox Christianity, the resurrection of Christ is essential for deification because it opens up a pathway by which human beings can participate in God's divine life. Through his resurrection, Jesus defeated sin and death, freeing humanity from bondage to both by making amends for their injustice before God.

This justification before God, which is through faith in Jesus' resurrection from the dead (Rom 4:25), issues when believers are granted eternal life as a free gift of grace; it is here that believers enter immediately into regeneration and sanctification, the ongoing process by which they are increasingly made to be more like Jesus Christ. The resurrection serves as hope to believers, in that, if Christ is risen from the dead, then their future lies in the arms of God where they too can be with him forever. Jesus' rising from the grave is not simply for a chosen few, but universal in effect, for all of mankind. It is redemptive and offers theosis to all who trust in Jesus Christ as Lord and Savior. God has

---

in the present life. Through the indwelling Holy Spirit and the sacramental life of the church, believers are empowered to grow spiritually, deepen their communion with God, and participate in his divine nature.

9. The transfiguration encourages believers to recognize their high calling to share in the divine life. Just as Jesus' disciples witnessed his transfigured glory, believers are called to behold and reflect the glory of God in their lives. This involves pursuing holiness and transformation, conforming more and more to the image of Christ through the renewing work of the Holy Spirit. It is a journey of spiritual growth and maturation where believers increasingly reflect God's love, grace, and righteousness to the world.

shown and demonstrated his grace through the resurrection of Christ for all humanity. It is not based on race, nationality, or anything that divides us as humans (Gal 3:28; Eph 2:8–9) For now God the Father in heaven is reconciling everything! Did you know that? Believers are brought to life increasingly in spiritual newness, transformation, and eventual sanctification by faith in the relationship with Jesus Christ our Lord (Rom 6:4; Col 3:1–4).

The message of the resurrection extends to all people without exception. It is inclusive, welcoming anyone who responds in faith to the gospel message of salvation through Jesus Christ (Acts 10:34–35; Rom 10:12–13). Jesus commissioned his followers to proclaim the gospel to all nations, inviting everyone to repentance and faith in him (Matt 28:18–20; Acts 1:8). This underscores the universal scope of Christ's redemptive work. The resurrection assures believers of eternal life with God. Just as Jesus was raised from the dead, so too will those who belong to him experience resurrection and share in his glory (1 Cor 15:20–23; Phil 3:20–21).

The resurrection of Jesus Christ indeed inaugurates a new creation where believers are made new in Christ, participating in God's ongoing work of renewal and restoration. The concept of Jesus as the "first fruits" of the new creation, as found in 1 Cor 15:20–22, highlights the transformative power of his resurrection and its implications for both individual believers and the cosmos. This theological concept is supported by several biblical passages and theological reflections:

1. *New Creation*:
    - *Scriptural Basis*: The resurrection is seen as the beginning of the new creation. Jesus is described as the "firstborn from among the dead" (Col. 1:18; Rev. 1:5) and the "new Adam" of the new creation (Rom 5:12–21).
    - *Theological Reflection*: The resurrection marks the termination of the old creation and the germination of the new creation. Believers are no longer part of the old creation but are now part of the new creation, which is characterized by divine life and a new relationship with God.
2. *Participation in God's Work*:
    - *Second Corinthians 5:17*: "Therefore, if anyone is in Christ, he is a new creation. The old has passed away; behold, the new has come" (NIV). This passage emphasizes that believers are part of

this new creation, where the old things have passed away and the new things have come .

- *Revelation 21:5*: "Behold, I am making all things new" (NASB). This verse underscores God's promise to renew and restore creation, which is already underway through Christ's resurrection.

3. *Attainment of Theosis*:
   - *Theosis*: Theosis refers to the transformative process where believers are united with God, participate in his divine nature, and grow in holiness and likeness to Christ .
   - *Empowerment by the Holy Spirit*: Through Christ's victory over sin and death, believers are restored in their relationship with God and empowered by the Holy Spirit to live out their faith in communion with him.

4. *Impact on Human Destiny and Spiritual Flourishing*:
   - *Christ's Victory*: Christ's resurrection signifies his victory over sin and death, which opens the way for believers to attain theosis and live a life of spiritual flourishing.
   - *Ongoing Work of Renewal and Restoration*: The resurrection inaugurates an ongoing process of renewal and restoration, where believers are continually transformed and empowered to live in communion with God.

The resurrection inaugurates a new creation where believers are made new in Christ and participate in God's ongoing work of renewal and restoration (2 Cor 5:17; Rev 21:5). Therefore, the resurrection of Jesus Christ opens the way for all humanity with faith to attain theosis—a transformative process where believers are united with God, participate in his divine nature, and grow in holiness and likeness to Christ.[10] Through Christ's victory over sin and death, believers are restored in their relationship with God and empowered by the Holy Spirit to live out their faith in communion with him. This theological concept underscores the profound impact of Christ's resurrection on human destiny and spiritual flourishing.[11]

---

10. The invitation to theosis through faith in Christ is extended to all humanity. It is not restricted by race, ethnicity, or social status but is available to anyone who responds in faith to the gospel (Acts 10:34–35; Rom 10:12–13).

11. The transformative power of the resurrection is universal, impacting individuals

Relevance in Daily Life

The transfiguration reveals the constant presence of Christ's divine nature, even during his human life. This teaches us that the divine is always near, even in ordinary moments or difficult times. Believers can find solace in knowing they're never truly alone, with divine support always available, though sometimes hidden. The event's timing, just before Christ's suffering, offers hope in the face of adversity. It reminds us that our own struggles are part of a greater divine plan and that pain is not the end of the story. Victory and transformation are promised, encouraging us to persevere through hardships.

Set on a mountaintop, the transfiguration symbolizes spiritual elevation and insight. This metaphor inspires us to pursue deeper understanding and growth in our faith through practices like prayer and meditation. It suggests that moments of clarity often come after dedicated spiritual effort.

The transfiguration also highlights how divine encounters can reshape our faith. It encourages us to be receptive to spiritual insights that might alter our worldview, priorities, and actions. This promotes an active approach to seeking experiences that enrich our spiritual lives.

Lastly, the event offers a glimpse of God's coming kingdom. This vision can guide our daily conduct, inspiring us to embody values like love, justice, and compassion. It encourages purposeful living, aligning our actions with a broader spiritual perspective.

In essence, the transfiguration serves as a powerful illustration of divine presence, hope in suffering, potential for spiritual growth, and the transformative nature of divine encounters. It challenges believers to weave these insights into their everyday lives, nurturing a more profound and resilient faith.

---

and communities across cultures and generations. It transcends geographical boundaries, affirming the universal relevance of Christ's redemptive work (Rev 7:9–10).

Chapter 7

Theosis in Catholic and Protestant Theology

THE CONCEPT OF THEOSIS, or the transformation of humans into a divine nature, is most prominently expressed in Eastern Orthodox Christianity. However, it also appears, though less frequently, in Catholic and Protestant traditions. While the terminology and focus may vary, the core idea of human participation in divine life resonates across these Western Christian traditions.

In Catholic theology, especially within the mystical tradition, there are similarities to the Eastern Orthodox view of deification. Although the term *unio mystica* (mystical union) is not as commonly used in Catholic contexts, figures such as St. Teresa of Ávila and St. John of the Cross describe profound experiences of union with God, wherein their souls are transformed into a divine likeness. Additionally, the Catholic understanding of grace aligns with the concept of theosis. Grace is seen as a supernatural gift that imbues the soul with divine life, allowing it to share in God's existence and thus partake in a form of deification through grace.

While Protestant theology may not emphasize theosis as strongly or focus as much on ecstatic experiences as the Eastern Orthodox tradition does, it still incorporates elements of the concept. The doctrine of justification by faith, a central tenet in Protestantism, suggests that a transformation occurs within individuals as they relate to God. Though not always explicitly labeled as deification, this transformation signifies a fundamental change in a person's nature and their relationship with God. Protestant theologians like Karl Barth have also engaged with this idea. Barth discusses the concept of the "Man as Child," through whom God becomes incarnate in believers, resulting in a union wherein the human and the divine meet.[1] In this way, one can view this union as a form of theosis, wherein the believer experiences divine life through faith.

Although theosis is not typically a central or explicitly stated concept in Catholic and Protestant theology, the broader idea of human involvement in divine life is present across various themes. In the Catholic mystical tradition, in the Protestant focus on justification by faith, and in aspects of panentheism, there are suggestions that humans undergo transformation through their relationship with God. While the term theosis may not be used and the emphasis might differ, the fundamental concept of transformation and participation in divine life remains a significant theme in Western Christian theology.

1. **Divinization in Catholic Theology**

In Catholic theology, the idea of human transformation into the divine is often referred to as "divinization" or "deification," as seen in concepts like Mysterium Magnum.[2] However, among Protestant theologians, Karl Barth was notably critical of the idea of theosis. Despite this, both Catholic and Protestant views emphasize that humans are intended to participate in divine life. This participation is made possible through Jesus Christ, who, as the visible, incarnate Son of God, bridges the gap between humanity and the divine. Through the grace provided by the Holy Spirit, and through a lifelong process of spiritual growth and participation in the sacraments, humanity is invited to experience unity with God.

In Eastern Orthodox theology, God's vision for humanity extends beyond simply saving us from sin. Salvation is viewed as a deep journey of renewal and transformation rather than just forgiveness. This perspective suggests that humans have inherent divine qualities that are waiting to be developed. It emphasizes a restoration of our essential nature, aiming to return to a state of profound connection with the divine similar to humanity's original condition before the fall. This process of transformation, called divinization, begins

---

1. Barth, *Church Dogmatics* IV/1, 151–70.
2. Böhme, *Mysterium Magnum*.

with the sacrament of baptism and continues throughout a person's life. Baptism is seen not merely as a ritual but as a true union with Christ and an integration into the divine reality. This process ignites an inner divine spark, catalyzing a deep-seated transformation that surpasses external changes in behavior or status.

The journey of theosis acknowledges life's trials and tribulations as integral to spiritual growth. It emphasizes the importance of persistently nurturing one's relationship with God. This relational aspect underscores that theosis isn't solely about individual betterment but about deepening one's divine connection. This theological framework paints an inspiring picture of human potential and the interplay between the human and divine. It proposes that humanity's calling extends beyond moral refinement to a form of participation in divinity itself. Such a perspective offers profound insights into the nature of human existence, life's purpose, and the essence of salvation. It presents Christianity as a path of continuous spiritual evolution, culminating in the ultimate glorification of human nature.

The grace of the Holy Spirit is active in human participation in this process, as it is he who indwells believers to help them grow in holiness and become increasingly more like Christ. Through the work of the Spirit believers are being lead closer to God, their minds enlightened to understand spiritual truths and their wills strengthened against temptation, while he purges them from sin, sanctifying them through Christ our Savior. Thus theosis is not something merited by human beings but a divine gift that God offers to any who are open and willing to pursue this path.

The sacraments were defined by Christ to be real, which means they are tangible signs of God's grace for Christians. Believers are sustained, strengthened, and healed on the journey to union with God through the sacraments themselves (particularly the Eucharist and reconciliation). The Eucharist, in particular, is considered the source and summit of the Christian life, as it is the sacrament in which Christ himself becomes present, offering his very self for the nourishment and transformation of the faithful.[3]

---

3. *Catechism of the Catholic Church*, para. 1324. Theosis is made possible by God's grace, which is freely given to humanity. Through baptism, believers are initiated into the Christian life and receive sanctifying grace, which enables them to grow in holiness and participate more fully in the divine life. The sacraments, particularly the Eucharist

Theosis is also characterized by a deep sense of union and communion with God. It is not merely a matter of intellectual assent to doctrinal truths but a lived experience of intimacy with the divine. Through prayer, worship, and contemplation, believers enter into communion with God, experiencing his presence and love in their lives. This communion with God is not only vertical but also horizontal, as believers are called to love and serve one another in imitation of Christ.

Furthermore, theosis entails the pursuit of holiness, which involves the transformation of the whole person—body, mind, and soul—into the likeness of Christ. This process of sanctification requires self-denial, repentance, and the cultivation of virtues such as love, humility, and compassion. It is a lifelong journey of spiritual growth and maturation, in which believers strive to become more like God in thought, word, and deed.

Within Catholic theology, the concept of theosis represents the profound truth that humanity is called to participate in the divine life through Christ, facilitated by the grace of the Holy Spirit and realized through the sacraments and the ongoing journey of spiritual transformation. It is a dynamic process of becoming more like God, characterized by union, communion, and the pursuit of holiness.

The Catechism of the Catholic Church (*CCC*) teaches that "the Son of God became man so that we might become God,"[4] reflecting the idea of divinization. This idea is deeply ingrained in Catholic theology and has its origins in the early teachings of the church fathers, particularly in the Eastern Christian tradition.

a. *Biblical Foundation*: The concept of divinization finds its roots in various passages of the Bible. For instance, 2 Pet 1:4 speaks of believers becoming "partakers of the divine nature," while John 1:12–13 speaks of those who receive Christ and are given the power to become children of God. Additionally, Jesus himself prayed for the unity of believers with God in John 17:21–23.

b. *Incarnation*: At the heart of divinization lies the doctrine of the incarnation—the belief that the eternal Son of God took on human nature in the person of Jesus Christ. Through the

---

and reconciliation, are means through which God's grace continues to nourish and transform believers on their journey towards union with God.

4. *Catechism of the Catholic Church*, para. 460.

incarnation, God bridged the gap between divinity and humanity, making it possible for humans to be united with God.

c. *Union with Christ*: Divinization involves a profound union with Christ. Through baptism and faith in Christ, believers are incorporated into his mystical body, becoming one with him. This union allows believers to share in Christ's divine life and participate in his redemptive work.

d. *Grace and Transformation*: Divinization is not merely a metaphorical concept; it involves a real and transformative union with God. Through the grace of God, believers are sanctified and transformed, becoming more like Christ in their thoughts, desires, and actions.

e. *Cooperation and Participation*: While divinization is initiated by God's grace, it also requires the active cooperation of believers. Through prayer, the sacraments, moral living, and participation in the life of the church, believers open themselves to the transforming work of the Holy Spirit.

f. *The Beatific Vision*: Divinization reaches its culmination in the beatific vision—the direct, intuitive knowledge of God enjoyed by the blessed in heaven.[5] In the beatific vision, believers behold God face to face and experience the fullness of divine love and joy for eternity.

g. *Early Christian Witness*: The concept of divinization was articulated by early Christian theologians, particularly in the Eastern Christian tradition. Figures such as Athanasius, Gregory of Nyssa, and Maximus the Confessor emphasized the transformative union between God and humanity through the incarnation.

The statement from the CCC underscores the profound mystery of divinization, wherein humanity is elevated to share in the divine life through the incarnation of Christ. It highlights the ultimate goal of human existence—union with God—and the transformative power of God's grace in the lives of believers. Grace is understood as the free and unmerited favor of God that

---

5. *Catechism of the Catholic Church*, para. 1023: "By virtue of our apostolic faith, we believe that those who die in God's grace and friendship and are perfectly purified live forever with Christ. They are like God for all eternity, for they 'see him as he is' (1 John 3:2), face to face."

transforms and elevates the human soul. It is through this grace that individuals are able to participate in divine life. The transformative power of grace changes believers, making them more like Christ and more aligned with God's will.

Divinization in Catholic theology emphasizes how Christians share in the divine life through grace, particularly through the sacraments. The sacraments play a pivotal role in this process of divinization. Each sacrament is considered to be an encounter with the living Christ, through which believers receive sanctifying grace.[6] For example, in the sacrament of baptism, the individual is not only cleansed from sin but also incorporated into the body of Christ, becoming a partaker of his divine life. Similarly, in the Eucharist, Catholics believe they receive the true body and blood of Christ, thereby deepening their union with him and with one another.

While the ultimate realization of theosis may be reserved for the afterlife, it is not a merely future event. It is a present process that begins in this life. As believers grow in their relationship with God, they are progressively transformed into the likeness of Christ. This transformation involves a deepening of their faith, love, and holiness.

1. *Living Out a Heavenly Purpose on Earth*: Theosis is intimately connected to the believer's calling to live a holy life. By striving for holiness, believers are participating in the divine life and preparing themselves for the ultimate union with God. This involves a conscious effort to conform their lives to the teachings and example of Christ.

2. *The Role of Prayer and Sacraments*: Prayer and sacraments play a crucial role in the process of theosis. Prayer is a means of communication with God, through which believers can deepen their relationship with him and receive the grace necessary for transformation. Sacraments, such as baptism and the Eucharist, are channels of divine grace that confer spiritual blessings and unite believers to Christ.

---

6. The ultimate goal of divinization is for humans to be transformed into the likeness of Christ and to share in the inner life of the Trinity. This transformation is ongoing throughout the believer's life, aided by the sacraments and the cooperation of the individual with God's grace. It implies a journey of holiness, where the virtues of faith, hope, and charity are cultivated, and where the believer's actions increasingly reflect the love and truth of God.

3. *Rethinking Divinity and Humanity*: The concept of theosis challenges our traditional notions of divinity and humanity. It reminds us that God is not distant or aloof but intimately involved in the lives of his creation. It also affirms the inherent dignity and potential of every human being, created in the image of God for union with him.

4. *The Church as the Body of Christ*: Theosis is also closely related to the church. The church is the body of Christ, and its members are called to participate in the divine life through their union with him. The church provides the means of grace, instruction, and community that are essential for theosis. Theosis is a dynamic process that begins in this life and culminates in the afterlife. It involves a transformation of the believer's nature and a deepening of their relationship with God. By living a holy life, participating in the sacraments, and growing in their union with Christ believers can experience theosis as a present reality and prepare themselves for the ultimate union with God in heaven.

Divinization is a profound and transformative reality in Catholic theology, highlighting the invitation for humanity to share in the divine life through grace, especially through the sacraments. It calls believers to a deeper understanding of their identity and destiny, and to a life of holiness and love in communion with God and one another.[7]

In fact, the imitation of Christ's virtues is an essential part of divinization. In Christianity, Jesus Christ is the perfect incarnation of God, manifesting virtues such as love, humility, compassion, and self-sacrifice, which unite humanity to his divine nature. Catholics believe we get drawn into the divine life through imitating Christ and thereby becoming more like him. That is, it's not a matter of an impostor wearing a mask and pretending to be something they are not (although that will always happen). But genuine imitation, as counterfeits, are revealed for what they truly are—beautifully exposed by the grace of God at work in one who believes.

---

7. Divinization in Catholic theology is the profound process by which humans, through the grace of God and particularly through the sacraments of the church, are elevated to share in God's divine life. It underscores the transformative power of God's grace, the centrality of Christ in this process, and the sacraments as pivotal encounters where believers receive and grow in sanctifying grace.

Another important dimension of divinization is participation in the redemptive work of Christ. Specifically, Catholics think that Jesus' life, death, and resurrection brought about the salvation of humanity, reuniting us to God with an opportunity for eternal life. It is not a one-time event in the past but an ongoing reality that believers are invited to live into, participating with God's redemptive work. Catholics regard themselves as cooperating with Christ to exercise his role in the salvation of souls and the renewal of the world through their prayers, sacrifices, almsgiving, and acts of love.

Theosis involves not merely intellectual assent to Christ's teachings or outward imitation of his behavior. It entails a profound and transformative conformity to Christ's image, a radical reformation of the entire self to align with his will and desires. This transformation is not something that individuals can achieve on their own. It is the work of divine grace, which operates through the sacraments and other means of spiritual nourishment. The sacraments, in particular, are channels of grace that unite believers to Christ and feed them on their pilgrimage as disciples.

Sacramental grace plays a pivotal role in this process. Through the sacraments, believers receive the divine life of Christ, which empowers them to conform their lives to his image. Baptism, for example, initiates believers into the life of Christ and cleanses them from original sin. The Eucharist nourishes believers with the body and blood of Christ, strengthening them for their spiritual journey. Grace is not merely an external force that acts upon believers. It is a divine gift that infuses the human soul with supernatural qualities, enabling it to participate in the divine life.

Grace empowers believers to love God with all their heart, soul, and mind, and to love their neighbors as themselves. It also enables them to resist temptation and persevere in their faith. Theosis is a transformative process that involves a radical conformity to Christ's image. This transformation is the work of divine grace, which operates through the sacraments and other means of spiritual nourishment. By receiving the grace of Christ through the sacraments and cooperating with his grace in their lives, believers can experience theosis as a present reality and prepare themselves for the ultimate union with God in heaven.

To think theologically about what it means for participation in Christ's life to be central to the process of divinization is to embrace this interpretation of ecclesial presence. Indeed, for believers, this invites some very radical implications. It calls them to a discipleship that is more than mental acquiescence or assent to Christian dogma but, instead, one in which they actively imitate Christ and participate in his mission of redemption as he transforms their lives. It demands a willingness to yield fully and completely to God, allowing his grace to move in them for the sake of the kingdom.

Catholic theology emphasizes participation in the life of Christ as central to divinization. Believers are called to imitate Christ's virtues, participate in his redemptive work, and be conformed to his image as they journey toward union with God. This process of participation in Christ's life is not passive but requires active cooperation with the grace of God, leading to a transformation of the entire person and ultimately to a sharing in the divine life.

2. Divination in Protestant Theology

Protestant theology has tended to stress the idea of being in some way united with (or towards) Christ as a central theme such that there are significant similarities between Protestant systems and what Eastern Orthodoxy calls participation or deification. The shared emphasis only points to a deep spiritual connection of the true believers in Christ being united with him constitutionally by faith unto a transforming and saving union. Theology is built upon this realization that mankind, due to our fallen state, can never save ourselves. Rather, salvation is a free gift of grace from God that comes to people through trusting in the death and resurrection of Jesus Christ. In faith, they are joined to Christ who clothes them in his righteousness and makes them joint heirs with him.

This union with Christ is so deep and spiritual that believers meet God as they are reconciled to him through their transformation into the image of his Son. This is a progressive transformation that happens from the inside out, and it has been called sanctification, which is how believers are made more holy or—in official language—how they are sanctified by God through Jesus Christ, his Son, on behalf of the center point where we meet tomorrow.[8]

---

8. *Catechism of the Catholic Church*, para. 1999: "The grace of Christ is the first and the last word of Christian life. This grace is given by the Holy Spirit through the Church. It is the gift of God's love, which gives believers the strength to live a life in Christ. Christians are sanctified by the action of the Holy Spirit, who gives them the power to

This means that union with Christ is not a one time legal act but an ongoing and living relationship that informs all aspects of the believer's life.

One of the key distinctions in Protestant theology is the principle of *sola fide*, or faith alone. This principle emphasizes that salvation is received through faith in Christ alone, apart from any merit or works on the part of the individual. While good works are considered important as evidence of genuine faith and as a response to God's grace, they are not the basis for salvation. Instead, salvation is solely by grace through faith in Christ.[9]

The concept of union with Christ, therefore, serves as the theological framework through which Protestant theology understands the relationship between faith and works. Believers are not saved by their works but are saved for good works, which flow naturally from their union with Christ. This understanding aligns with the apostle Paul's teaching in Eph 2:8-10, where he emphasizes that salvation is by grace through faith, and that believers are created in Christ Jesus for good works.[10]

In reflecting on this theological framework, Protestants often find resonance with the Eastern Orthodox concept of theosis, albeit with some distinct theological emphases. Both traditions affirm the transformative nature of salvation, wherein believers are united with Christ and participate in his divine life. However, Protestant

---

participate in the divine life of God." See also *Catechism of the Catholic Church*, para. 1695: "Justification is the work of God's grace and is the beginning of the new life in Christ. It is through this grace that we are united to Christ and his Church, and it is through the sacraments and the gift of the Holy Spirit that we are continually sanctified and conformed to Christ."

9. During the Reformation, figures like Martin Luther, John Calvin, and others emphasized the primacy of faith in salvation as they sought to reform perceived abuses and deviations from biblical teachings within the Roman Catholic Church. See Calvin, *Institutes*, 3.2.9: "We are justified by faith alone, and not by works; yet, to show that the true faith always produces good works, we must teach that good works, which follow after justification, are the natural fruit of the union of faith and Christ." Central to their theological position was the conviction that salvation is a free gift of God's grace, received through faith in Jesus Christ alone, rather than being earned through human effort or merit.

10. *Sola fide* stands as a foundational principle in Protestant theology, affirming that salvation is received through faith in Jesus Christ alone, apart from any works or merit of the individual. It highlights the centrality of God's grace in the process of justification and emphasizes the role of faith as the instrumental means by which individuals are reconciled to God.

theology tends to emphasize the forensic aspects of salvation—such as justification by faith alone—while also acknowledging the transformative and relational dimensions of union with Christ.

The doctrine of union with Christ stands as a central and richly textured theme in Protestant theology, highlighting the profound mystery of God's grace and the intimate communion between believers and their Savior. It invites believers to continually deepen their understanding of and participation in this union, as they journey towards greater conformity to the image of Christ and the fulfillment of God's purposes in their lives.

   a. *Sanctification and Christian Growth*: The centrality of this view in Protestant theology is necessarily connected to a number of particular beliefs about salvation, God, and the Holy Spirit as well. Although sanctification is not explicitly cast in terms of divinization, as it is in some branches and instances within Christian theology, the idea that Christians are being progressively transformed into the image of Christ, through which we embrace love for our neighbour, outstrips such a humanist core. Central to Protestant theology is the doctrine of justification by faith alone, meaning that individuals are justified or declared righteous before God on account of their faith in Christ finished work at Calvary. Holiness—often seen as the next step in a believer's relationship with God—is ushered in by this initial act of justification.

   Sanctification, then, can be understood as the ongoing work of God in the life of the believer, whereby they are progressively transformed into the likeness of Christ. This transformation is made possible by the indwelling presence of the Holy Spirit, who empowers believers to grow in grace, knowledge, and obedience to God's will. The process of sanctification involves various elements:

   i. First, it involves a growing awareness of one's own sinfulness and the continual need for repentance and dependence on God's grace. As believers come to recognize the depth of God's love for and forgiveness of them, they are motivated to live lives that are pleasing to him.

   ii. Second, sanctification involves the renewing of the mind through study and meditation on God's word, who speaks to us through Scripture. As believers immerse themselves in Scripture, they are transformed by the renewing of their minds, gaining a deeper understanding of God's character and purposes and learning to think and act in accordance with his will.

iii. Third, sanctification is manifest in obedience to God's commands and the cultivation of the fruit of the Spirit in one's life. As believers yield themselves to the leading of the Holy Spirit, they begin to exhibit the virtues of love, joy, peace, patience, kindness, goodness, faithfulness, gentleness, and self-control, which are the marks of Christlikeness (Gal 5:22–23 NIV)

iv. Fourth, sanctification involves participation in the life of the church and the practice of spiritual disciplines such as prayer, worship, fellowship, and service. As believers engage in these activities, they are strengthened and nourished in their faith and are equipped to live lives that reflect the character of Christ to the world.

v. Fifth, sanctification, which is central to Protestant theology, deals with the process of becoming Christlike through his Spirit at work in the believer. This metamorphosis includes an increased awareness of one's sinful nature, a transformation of the mind through the study of Scripture, and following and doing what God says to do, as well as involvement with church life and spiritual exercises. In the end, sanctification is simply God working in a believer to help them grow in the grace and knowledge of our Lord Jesus Christ that they might reflect his character more fully in every area of life.

b. *Eschatological Hope*: At the heart of Christian theology, across various denominations, including Protestantism, Catholicism, and Orthodoxy, lies the profound anticipation of believers' future glorification and participation in the fullness of God's kingdom. This shared hope is deeply rooted in the Christian understanding of salvation, eschatology, and the nature of God himself.

Salvation in Christian theology is not merely a past event or a present reality but also a future hope. It encompasses the idea of being saved from the power and consequences of sin, being reconciled to God, and ultimately being transformed into the likeness of Christ. This transformation is not limited to the spiritual realm but extends to the physical realm as well, including the resurrection and glorification of believers' bodies.

The anticipation of resurrection and glorification is firmly grounded in the belief in the bodily resurrection of Jesus Christ. In all Christian traditions, the resurrection of Jesus is seen as the pivotal event in human history, demonstrating God's victory over sin and death. Jesus' resurrection serves as a prototype or guarantee of the future resurrection of believers. As the apostle Paul writes in 1 Cor 15:20–23, "But Christ has indeed been raised from the dead, the firstfruits of those who have fallen asleep."[11]

This future resurrection and glorification entail the complete renewal and transformation of believers' bodies. They will be raised imperishable, glorious, powerful, and spiritual (1 Cor 15:42–44). This transformation is not just a physical one but also a moral and spiritual one, as believers will be fully conformed to the image of Christ (Rom 8:29).

The anticipation of future glorification also underscores the Christian belief in the consummation of God's kingdom. In Protestant, Catholic, and Orthodox theology, there is a shared understanding of the kingdom of God as both a present reality and a future hope. While believers already experience the reign of God in their lives through faith in Jesus Christ, they await the ultimate fulfillment of God's kingdom when Christ returns in glory. This future kingdom will be characterized by perfect justice, peace, and the full manifestation of God's glory.

The hope of future glorification underlines a salvation process that is relationship based. At the final restoration of God's kingdom, believers will experience an ethereal friendship with a beloved deity. This communion mirrors the triune God in himself, Father, Son, and Holy Spirit communing perfectly between one another. So our hope of glory, then, is not simply

---

11. The anticipation of resurrection and glorification in Christian theology finds its foundation in the bodily resurrection of Jesus Christ. This event stands as the pivotal moment in history, demonstrating God's victory over sin and death and serving as a guarantee of the future resurrection of all believers. It offers hope, assurance, and the promise of eternal life in communion with God, reflecting the profound significance of Jesus' resurrection in Christian faith and practice.

for individual redemption but also that all the other members of his body may be saved.

Aspects of this eschatological hope—particularly as they pertain to the resurrection, the redemption of believers' bodies, and even future fellowship with God himself—are common across Protestantism (or at least in the theology associated with it), Roman Catholic teachings, and Orthodox beliefs. This commonality extends to other core covenantal elements, all of which ultimately point back to Christ. It is what keeps believers going and it gives them the hope to continue on till they see God's promises fulfilled.

c. *Implication in Life and Spirituality*: The concept of believers being united with Christ in his death and resurrection is a foundational aspect of Christian theology with profound implications for believers' identity, assurance of salvation, and spiritual growth.

Firstly, this concept stems from various passages in the New Testament, particularly in the writings of the apostle Paul. In Rom 6:3-4 Paul writes, "Or don't you know that all of us who were baptized into Christ Jesus were baptized into his death? We were therefore buried with him through baptism into death in order that, just as Christ was raised from the dead through the glory of the Father, we too may live a new life" (NIV). This union with Christ in his death and resurrection is also emphasized in Gal 2:20, where Paul states, "I have been crucified with Christ and I no longer live, but Christ lives in me" (NIV).

The theological significance of this union is profound. It speaks to the believer's identification with Christ in his redemptive work. Through faith, believers are united with Christ in such a way that his death becomes their death and his resurrection becomes their resurrection. This union is not merely symbolic or metaphorical but is understood to be a spiritual reality through the work of the Holy Spirit.

One aspect of this union is liberation from the power of sin and death. In Rom 6:6, Paul declares, "For we know that our old self was crucified with him so that the body ruled by sin might be done away with, that we should no longer be slaves to sin" (NIV). This means that believers are no longer under the dominion of sin, but rather empowered by the indwelling Spirit to live a life of righteousness and holiness.

This union provides believers with assurance of salvation. Since their identity is now rooted in Christ and his finished work on the cross, believers can rest assured that their salvation is secure. As Paul writes in Rom 8:1, "Therefore, there is now no condemnation for those who are in Christ Jesus" (NIV). This assurance is not based on their own merit or performance but on the faithfulness of Christ.

Furthermore, this union serves as the foundation for the believer's Christian faith and spiritual growth. It reminds believers of their new identity in Christ and their participation in his ongoing work of redemption in the world. It motivates them to live lives that are pleasing to God, knowing that they are empowered by the same Spirit that raised Christ from the dead (Rom 8:11).

The believer's union with Christ in his death and resurrection is a central theme in Christian theology with profound implications for their identity, assurance of salvation, and spiritual growth. It is a reality that shapes the way believers view themselves, their relationship with God, and their mission in the world.

d. *Vocation and Purpose of Life*: Union with Christ is a profound theological concept that lies at the heart of Christian faith and practice. It refers to the spiritual union between believers and Jesus Christ, whereby believers are intimately connected to Christ in a way that transcends mere intellectual assent or adherence to a set of beliefs. This union is not merely a metaphorical or symbolic idea but a profound reality that shapes the identity, vocation, and purpose of every believer.

At its core, union with Christ emphasizes the relational aspect of salvation. Through faith in Christ, believers are united with him in his death, burial, and resurrection (Rom 6:3–5). This union signifies not only a legal standing before God as forgiven sinners but also a living, dynamic relationship with Christ. Just as branches are united with the vine and draw life from it (John 15:1–5), believers are united with Christ and derive their spiritual life, strength, and sustenance from him.

This union profoundly shapes believers' understanding of their vocation and purpose in life. As members of the body of Christ, believers are called to live in communion with him and to reflect his character and mission in the world. The apostle Paul captures this truth eloquently when he writes, "I have been crucified with Christ. It is no longer I who live, but Christ who lives in me" (Gal 2:20 NIV). This union implies a profound transformation whereby believers become conformed to the image of Christ (Rom 8:29) and participate in his redemptive mission to reconcile all things to himself (2 Cor 5:18–20).

The intimacy and communion that comes from being in union with Christ is profound. It is less of a head knowledge and more than just following the motions. It is a love relationship with trust and intimate fellowship. By spending time in prayer, reading Scripture, and the administration of the sacraments, believers nurture an intimate relationship with their Savior, through which they experience strength, direction, and well-being—qualities that can sustain a person through difficult times.

i. *Prayer as Communion*: Prayer is not simply a ritual but the mode of fellowship with him through whom we live and move. Prayer is a conversation, an exchange where two hearts share. Brothers and sisters offer prayers to show their love and gratitude and to request the things they want God to give them—for example, his help and peace.

ii. *Scripture as Encounter*: The reading of Scripture is not just an intellectual activity, it is a meeting with the word of God living. When a believer goes to read the Bible, it is not just another literary piece they are studying. Instead of considering the knowledge and wisdom of an author who passed thousands of years ago, God speaks directly through his word. Its pages show us the nature and love of God, his promises, and his designs in salvation.

iii. *Reminders of Union in the Sacraments*: Fellowship in the sacraments, especially communion, stands as a form of material reintegration Christ and his people are undergo while they remain on this earth. In the body and blood of Christ offered in the Eucharist, believers commune with Christ's death and resurrection. By this sacrament they are married to Christ. After the manner of Christ's everlasting nuptials, this relationally refers to Christ living within them by the Holy Spirit, so that they might live as his disciples.

iv. *The Basis of the Christian Life*: Christ the center gives union with himself as a base of operations for all Christian living. It provides identity, vocation, and purpose for believers. Their close relationship with Christ reflects his character and mission; through this, they participate in salvation and become light to the world. They are equipped to love their neighbors, meet the needs of those in need, and share testimonies through their good works.

3. **Fostering Ecumenical Dialogue: Catholic and Protestant**

Ecumenical dialogue about theosis spirituality between Catholics and Protestants involves delving into various dimensions—including historical, theological, scriptural, and practical dimensions—and navigating challenges and opportunities. Let's break down each aspect:

a. *Historical Contexts*: Understanding the historical development of theosis in both Catholic and Protestant traditions is crucial. While the concept has deep roots in Eastern Orthodox theology, elements of it can be found in Western Christian thought as well. Exploring how different theological traditions have interpreted and engaged with theosis throughout history provides insights into the diversity of Christian perspectives on spiritual transformation.[12]

b. *Theological Foundations*: Examining the theological foundations of theosis in Catholic and Protestant theology helps to identify commonalities and differences. While Catholics may emphasize the role of sacraments and the communion of saints in the process of divinization, Protestants may focus more on justification by faith and the indwelling of the Holy Spirit. Recognizing the

---

12. Understanding these historical developments provides insights into how theological diversity within Christianity enriches the understanding of spiritual transformation and the ultimate goal of union with God. It also underscores the common goal across Christian traditions: the transformation of believers into the image of Christ and their participation in the divine life through grace.

THEOSIS IN CATHOLIC AND PROTESTANT THEOLOGY   113

theological richness of both traditions allows for a more nuanced understanding of theosis spirituality.[13]

c. *Reflecting on Scripture*: Scripture serves as a primary source for understanding theosis spirituality. Both Catholics and Protestants can engage in fruitful dialogue by exploring biblical passages that speak to the theme of union with God and likeness to Christ. Reflecting on these texts together can deepen mutual understanding and appreciation of each other's theological perspectives.[14]

d. *Considering Practical Implications*: Ecumenical dialogue about theosis spirituality should not remain theoretical but should also consider practical implications for Christian life and practice. This may involve exploring how theosis shapes one's understanding of prayer, worship, ethics, and spiritual disciplines. By sharing insights and experiences, Catholics and Protestants can learn from one another and grow in their spiritual journeys.

e. *Navigating Challenges and Opportunities*: Engaging in ecumenical dialogue about theosis spirituality inevitably involves facing challenges such as doctrinal differences, historical divisions, and theological misunderstandings. However, it also presents opportunities for mutual learning, reconciliation, and cooperation in areas of common concern. By approaching these challenges with humility, openness, and a commitment to dialogue, Christians from diverse traditions can work towards greater unity in the body of Christ.

The dialogue on the spirituality of theosis between Catholics and Protestants provides a fruitful ground for mutual learning and

---

13. Recognizing the theological richness of both Catholic and Protestant traditions allows for a nuanced understanding of theosis spirituality within Christianity. It acknowledges the diversity of theological perspectives and practices while highlighting the shared commitment to spiritual transformation and union with God. This nuanced understanding invites dialogue and mutual enrichment between traditions, fostering a deeper appreciation of the multifaceted ways in which Christians seek to grow in likeness to Christ and participate in the divine life.

14. Scripture serves as a primary and unifying source for both Catholics and Protestants in exploring theosis spirituality. By engaging in dialogue grounded in biblical texts that speak to union with God and likeness to Christ, both traditions can deepen their mutual understanding and appreciation of one another's theological perspectives, ultimately enriching the broader Christian understanding of spiritual transformation and the pursuit of divine life.

gaining new insights into Christianity. By contemplating whether humans can share in this divine transformation without becoming gods, Christians can gain a profound understanding from their distinct traditions. In this way, it seems imperative for those seeking meaningful dialogical engagement to also take into account the historical matrix as well as the theological pillars of tradition that hold up a spirituality centered on deification not only in Protestantism but in all traditions grappling with Lutheran tenets. Though the term theosis may be chiefly Eastern Orthodox, both Western traditions also see a concept of union with or transformation in God. Christians can thus better appreciate the historical development of these ideas in their own traditions and see how much nuance they share even across widely differing applications.

The New Testament, along with the broader biblical text, provides numerous passages that support the concept of theosis, or divine transformation. This idea is grounded in scriptural themes of divine adoption, transformation, and participation in the nature of God, which are explicitly and implicitly found throughout both the Old and New Testaments. By examining these passages together, Christians can understand the biblical basis for theosis and its significance.

Practically, theosis spirituality encourages believers to live in accordance with Christ's teachings, pursue holiness, and participate in divine life. Observing how theosis is practiced can offer Christians valuable insights into what it means to genuinely follow God. Although advancing a dialogical theology on theosis can be challenging due to theological terminology, historical context, and cultural perspectives, these challenges also present opportunities for growth and meaningful communication. Christians can navigate these discussions successfully by approaching them with openness, respect, and a willingness to learn, allowing Christ to help break down barriers to deeper connection.

So the other side of this coin is an ecumenical dialogue about spirituality centered on theosis that could invigorate and enhance spiritual life among both Catholics and Protestants. Through dialogue, Christians will grow in their understanding of the faith and foster relationships, witnessing both their unity in Christ and the differences that enrich it.

4. **Relevance in Daily Life**
    a. *Diverse Approaches*: Catholics and Protestants have distinct views on divine transformation. Catholics focus on theosis through sacraments and church mediation, while Protestants emphasize a personal relationship with God and scriptural faith. Understanding these differences can enrich one's spiritual journey by showcasing various paths to divine union. Practical application involves incorporating elements from different traditions into personal practice. For instance, Catholics might deepen their faith through a Protestant emphasis on Scripture, while Protestants could explore the communal aspects of Catholic spirituality.
    b. *Historical and Theological Context*: Grasping the historical and theological backgrounds of theosis can deepen appreciation for one's own tradition and the traditions of others. This understanding fosters respect and openness in interfaith dialogue and personal spirituality. Studying the development of theosis across traditions can enhance one's faith journey and promote thoughtful, respectful spiritual conversations.
    c. *Exploring Union with God Across Traditions*: While theosis is often associated with Eastern Orthodoxy, the concept of divine union exists in Catholicism and Protestantism too. Examining these similarities and differences can broaden our understanding of how each tradition seeks divine communion. Believers can reflect on how their tradition's concept of union with God shapes daily spiritual practices, enhancing personal growth and spiritual routines.
    d. *Engaging in Dialogue*: Meaningful interfaith dialogue can lead to mutual learning and growth, fostering appreciation for Christian diversity and deepening understanding of one's own faith. Christians can seek opportunities for interfaith dialogue through study groups, lectures, or discussion forums addressing theosis and divine transformation.
    e. *Navigating Nuances and Commonalities*: Recognizing both differences and shared aspects in views on divine transformation can lead to more nuanced and respectful interfaith relationships. Approaching faith discussions with an open mind can enrich personal spiritual journeys and contribute to harmonious interfaith relationships.

Chapter 8

Compare Theosis in Many Denominations

CATHOLICISM EMPHASIZES *UNIO MYSTICA*,[1] a deep communion with God that highlights the union believers can achieve through spiritual practices and views grace as a transformative force that elevates the soul to a state of divine likeness, facilitating spiritual growth. Grace enables believers to participate in the divine life through communion with God, fostering a deep spiritual connection. Grace is understood as a divine gift that enables spiritual transformation, facilitating the believer's journey towards God. Theosis is seen as a future hope, to be fully realized in the afterlife, where believers will attain complete union with God.

Protestantism emphasizes that the idea of divine union is present in concepts like justification by faith and sanctification, which involve a union with Christ. Sanctification involves a progressive transformation of the believer into the image of Christ, reflecting a continuous process of spiritual development. Justification by faith and sanctification involve participation in the divine life through union with Christ,

---

1. *Unio mystica* is a Latin term that translates to "mystical union." It refers to a state of profound spiritual union or oneness with God or a higher power. This state is often characterized by (a) ecstasy (a feeling of intense joy, bliss, or rapture), (b) transcendence (a sense of being beyond the limitations of the physical world), and (c) unity (a deep sense of oneness with God or a higher power). In various spiritual traditions, *unio mystica* is often associated with (a) mystical experiences (direct, personal experiences of the divine), (b) contemplation (a state of deep meditation or contemplation), and (c) enlightenment (a state of spiritual awakening or realization).

allowing believers to experience God's presence. Grace is necessary for salvation and sanctification, providing the means for believers to live a holy life. Theosis is often understood as a future hope but may also be experienced in part in the present life, reflecting both an ongoing process and an ultimate goal.

For Orthodoxy, theosis is a core doctrinal concept that emphasizes the ultimate deification or divinization of human nature, where believers become like God through a real union with him. Theosis is a gradual process of transformation, leading to holiness and union with God. Theosis involves a direct participation in the divine life and nature, where believers are united with God's energies while his essence remains beyond their comprehension. Grace is the means through which theosis is accomplished, enabling believers to achieve union with God. Theosis is understood as both a present process and a future hope, emphasizing that the journey toward union with God begins in this life and continues into eternity, culminating in the ultimate transformation and deification of the believer.

While the terminology and emphasis may differ, these commonalities demonstrate the shared theological heritage of Catholic, Protestant, and Orthodox Christianity. The concept of theosis, though emphasized to varying degrees in various contexts, remains a central theme in all three traditions, pointing to the ultimate goal of human existence: union with God. This shared understanding underscores the profound significance of theosis across different Christian denominations. Here I find some commonalities or similarities in how the concept of theosis is understood among Catholic, Protestant, and Orthodox traditions.[2]

Despite differences in terminology and theological emphasis, Catholic, Protestant, and Orthodox traditions share significant commonalities in their understanding of divine transformation and union with God. All three traditions affirm the transformative power of divine grace, the importance of participating in the divine life, and the impact of spiritual practices on ethical living. These shared elements underscore a common theological heritage while allowing for a rich diversity of expressions and interpretations across Christian traditions.

2. While there are nuanced differences in how the concept of theosis is understood and practiced among Catholic, Protestant, and Orthodox Christians, these differences do not obscure the profound shared belief in humanity's potential for union with God and transformation into his likeness. This theological unity underscores the richness of Christian tradition and its ongoing dialogue on the nature of salvation and the divine-human relationship.

The Main Emphasis

1. Ultimate Goal

All three traditions affirm that the ultimate goal of the Christian life is union with God, often expressed as theosis, divinization, or union with Christ. This involves participation in the divine nature and conformity to the image of Christ.[3] Theosis, a term particularly prominent in Eastern Orthodox theology, encapsulates the idea of becoming more like God, not in the sense of acquiring divine attributes, but in developing virtues, such as love, humility, and holiness, that reflect the character of God. It involves a journey of spiritual ascent, where the individual gradually becomes more united with God through prayer, sacraments, and the cultivation of virtues.

Similarly, within Catholic theology, the concept of divinization or deification underscores the idea that through grace, humans are elevated to share in God's divine life. This notion finds expression in the Catholic understanding of the sacraments, especially in the Eucharist, where believers partake in the body and blood of Christ, thus entering into deeper communion with God.

In Protestant theology, while the language of theosis or divinization may not be explicitly used, the concept of union with Christ is central to many Protestant traditions. The Protestant emphasis on justification by faith is often seen as the starting point of this union, where believers are declared righteous before God through Christ's atoning sacrifice. This declaration of righteousness, however, is not merely legal but initiates a process of transformation, where believers are progressively conformed to the image of Christ through the work of the Holy Spirit.

The ultimate goal of union with God, therefore, involves both an initial declaration of righteousness and an ongoing process of sanctification. It is a journey marked by communion with God, participation in the life of Christ, and the cultivation of virtues that reflect the character of God. This union is not only a future hope

---

3. There are theological distinctions among Eastern Orthodox, Catholic, and Protestant traditions; all affirm that the ultimate goal of the Christian life is union with God. This union, expressed as theosis, divinization, or union with Christ, involves participation in the divine nature and conformity to the image of Christ—a journey of spiritual transformation and communion with God that spans the believer's earthly life and extends into eternity.

but a present reality for believers who are called to live in intimate relationship with God and to bear witness to his transformative power in the world.

From a theological perspective, the concept of union with God speaks to the profound mystery of God's love and grace, which seeks to draw humanity into communion with himself. It reflects the biblical narrative of God's desire to dwell among his people and to share his life with them. It also highlights the significance of Christ's incarnation, death, and resurrection as the means by which this union is made possible, bridging the gap between humanity and divinity.

The goal of union with God is not merely individual salvation but the restoration of all creation to its intended purpose and the fulfillment of God's redemptive plan. It is a vision of reconciliation, transformation, and ultimate communion with the triune God, in whom all things find their truest fulfillment and joy.

2. **Scriptural Basis**

Each tradition finds support for the concept of theosis in Scripture, particularly in passages such as 2 Pet 1:4. In this verse, the author (traditionally attributed to Peter) speaks of believers as "partakers of the divine nature." This phrase underscores the transformative nature of salvation, indicating that through Christ and the promises of God, believers are enabled to share in God's own nature. This participation is not understood as a mere imitation of God's attributes but as a genuine sharing in his life and character.[4]

From a Catholic perspective, this passage aligns with the theology of grace and sanctification. Catholics interpret theosis as the process by which believers are progressively transformed by God's grace, becoming more like Christ and growing in holiness. The participation in the divine nature is seen as a result of the indwelling of the Holy Spirit, who enables believers to share in the life of the Trinity through the sacraments and the practice of the Christian virtues.

---

4. The verse from 2 Pet 1:4 provides a foundational scriptural basis for the concept of theosis, illustrating how believers are invited into a profound union with God through Christ. This union is transformative, involving a genuine participation in God's divine nature rather than a superficial imitation. Across Catholic, Protestant, and Orthodox traditions, this understanding of theosis underscores a shared theological heritage focused on the transformative power of God's grace, the centrality of Christ in salvation, and the ultimate goal of human existence: union with God in holiness and communion.

In the Protestant tradition, this verse speaks to the concept of union with Christ and the believer's identity in him. Protestants emphasize the imputed righteousness of Christ, whereby believers are declared righteous before God through faith in Christ's atoning sacrifice.[5] The participation in the divine nature is understood as a consequence of this union, wherein believers are united with Christ and empowered by the Holy Spirit to live transformed lives, bearing fruit that reflects their new identity in Christ.

In the Orthodox tradition, 2 Pet 1:4 is often cited in support of the doctrine of theosis. Orthodox theologians interpret this passage as affirming the potential for humans to be united with God in a profound and intimate way. Theosis is understood as the ultimate goal of the Christian life, wherein believers are deified or divinized through their union with Christ. This participation in the divine nature involves the purification of the soul, the illumination of the mind, and the transformation of the whole person to reflect the image of Christ.

Across all three traditions, 2 Pet 1:4 serves as a foundational text that underscores the transformative nature of salvation and the believer's union with God. It speaks to the mystery of God's grace, which enables humanity to share in his divine life and to be conformed to the image of Christ. As believers participate in this divine nature, they are called to live lives of holiness, love, and service, bearing witness to the transformative power of God's grace in the world.

3. **Importance of Grace**

All three traditions emphasize the centrality of grace in the process of theosis. Whether it's through sacraments (Catholic), divine energies (Orthodox), or the work of the Holy Spirit (Protestant), believers rely on God's grace for transformation.[6]

---

5. Calvin, *Institutes*; Luther, *Commentary on Galatians*.

6. Across all traditions, there is a recognition that theosis is initiated by God's grace. It is God who takes the initiative to draw humanity into union with himself, and it is his grace that empowers believers in their journey of transformation. While the emphasis on grace is universal, there are differences in how each tradition views the role of human response. Catholics emphasize cooperative synergy with grace, Orthodox stress participation in divine energies, and Protestants highlight faith as the response that receives and trusts in God's transforming grace.

In Catholicism, grace is understood as the supernatural gift of God's love, freely given to humanity to enable them to partake in divine life. This grace is mediated through the sacraments, particularly baptism and the Eucharist. Through these sacraments, Catholics believe that individuals are infused with grace, enabling them to grow in holiness and participate in the process of theosis. Grace is seen as transformative, empowering believers to live out their faith in daily life and to grow in virtue.

In Eastern Orthodoxy, the concept of grace is closely tied to the idea of divine energies. Orthodox theology teaches that God's energies are the uncreated expressions of his divine nature, through which he interacts with and sustains the created world. These energies are made accessible to humanity through the incarnation of Christ and the work of the Holy Spirit. Through participation in the sacraments, prayer, and ascetic practices, Orthodox Christians seek to open themselves to the divine energies, allowing God's grace to transform them and bring them into union with him.

In Protestantism, particularly in Reformed and evangelical traditions, grace is often emphasized as God's unmerited favor extended to sinful humanity. It is through the work of the Holy Spirit that individuals are convicted of sin, come to faith in Christ, and are regenerated or "born again." This grace is received through faith alone, apart from any merit or works on the part of the believer. However, it is also understood as transformative, leading to a life of obedience and discipleship as believers grow in their relationship with God.

Theological reflection on the importance of grace in the process of theosis highlights several key points.

a. First, grace is essential for human transformation and spiritual growth. Regardless of theological differences, all three traditions affirm that it is through God's grace that believers are enabled to become more like him.

b. Second, grace is understood as a gift freely given by God, not something that can be earned or merited through human effort. This underscores the unconditional nature of God's love and the dependence of humanity on his grace for salvation and sanctification.

c. Third, the means by which grace is received and experienced may vary across traditions, but the ultimate source remains the same: God himself. Whether through sacraments, divine energies, or the work of the Holy Spirit, believers rely on God's grace for transformation.

d. Fourth, the importance of grace emphasizes the centrality of God in the process of theosis. It is God who initiates, sustains, and brings to completion the work of transformation in the lives of believers. As such, grace invites believers into a deeper relationship with God, inviting them to cooperate with his grace as they journey towards union with him.

4. **The Role of Christ**

Christ plays a central role in theosis in all three traditions. Whether it's through his incarnation, death, and resurrection (Catholic and Orthodox) or through union with him by faith (Protestant), believers are united with Christ in their journey towards union with God.[7]

a. *Incarnation*: The incarnation of Christ, the belief that God took on human flesh in the person of Jesus Christ, is central to Christian theology. In the Catholic and Orthodox traditions, Christ's incarnation represents God's profound closeness to humanity. By taking on human nature, Christ sanctified human existence and provided the means for humanity to participate in the divine life. Theosis, therefore, begins with the incarnation, as it establishes the possibility of union between the divine and the human.[8]

b. *Death and Resurrection*: Christ's death and resurrection are pivotal events in Christian soteriology. In both Catholic and Orthodox traditions, Christ's death on the cross is seen as the ultimate act of sacrificial love; through this sacrificial act humanity's sins are forgiven and reconciliation with God is made possible. His

---

7. Christ's central role in theosis across Catholic, Protestant, and Orthodox traditions underscores his unique position as the mediator between God and humanity. Believers are united with Christ in their journey towards union with God, experiencing transformation and participating in the divine life through his redemptive work.

8. The incarnation of Christ, which holds that God became human in the person of Jesus Christ, is a fundamental element of Christian theology. In both Catholic and Orthodox traditions, this belief signifies God's deep intimacy with humanity. By assuming human nature, Christ sanctified human existence and created a path for humanity to share in divine life. Consequently, theosis starts with the incarnation, as the incarnation makes possible the union between the divine and human realms.

resurrection signifies victory over sin and death, offering believers the hope of new life and participation in Christ's divine nature. Through baptism and the Eucharist, believers are united with Christ in his death and resurrection, symbolizing their own journey towards theosis.

c. *Union with Christ by Faith*: In Protestant theology, theosis is often understood in terms of union with Christ by faith. Through faith in Christ, believers are united with him spiritually, becoming partakers of his divine nature (2 Pet 1:4). This union is not based on human effort or merit but on God's grace received through faith. Through the indwelling of the Holy Spirit, believers are transformed from glory to glory, conforming more closely to the image of Christ (2 Cor 3:18).

Theological reflection on the role of Christ in theosis emphasizes the centrality of Christ in the Christian life. Whether through his incarnation, death, and resurrection, or through union with him by faith, Christ is the mediator through whom believers are united with God and participate in the divine life. Theosis, then, is not merely a moral or ethical transformation but a profound ontological change, whereby believers are transformed into the likeness of Christ and share in his divine nature.

Differences

There are also differences in emphasis and terminology regarding the concept of theosis. Eastern Orthodoxy places a strong emphasis on theosis as the goal of the Christian life; Catholicism emphasizes divine filiation and sanctification; and Protestantism focuses on justification and sanctification, often without the language of theosis.

1. **Theological Framework**
   a. *Catholicism*: Theosis is often framed within the broader context of sacramental theology, emphasizing the role of the church, sacraments, and grace in facilitating the process of divinization.[9]

---

9. In Catholic theology, theosis is intricately connected to sacramental theology, which highlights the role of the church and sacraments as channels through which God's grace is communicated to believers. Through the reception of sacraments and cooperation with divine grace, Catholics believe that individuals are transformed and sanctified, gradually becoming more like Christ and participating in the divine life. The emphasis on sacramental theology underscores the communal and ritualistic aspects of

i. *The Church*: The Catholic Church is seen as the mystical body of Christ, through which the grace of God is mediated to believers. In the context of theosis, the church serves as the community of believers who support and encourage one another in the journey towards union with God. It provides the necessary spiritual nourishment, guidance, and fellowship that enable individuals to grow in holiness and participate more fully in the divine life.

ii. *Sacraments*: The sacraments are outward signs instituted by Christ to give grace. They are channels through which God's grace is communicated to believers, enabling them to participate in the divine life more fully. Each sacrament confers a specific grace relevant to the particular stage of the Christian journey. For example, baptism initiates believers into the life of Christ, making them adopted children of God and heirs to the kingdom. The Eucharist nourishes and sustains believers by uniting them with the body and blood of Christ. Through the sacrament of reconciliation, believers are reconciled with God and one another, restoring them to a state of grace. These sacraments, along with others such as confirmation, matrimony, holy orders, and anointing of the sick, play a vital role in the process of theosis by continually imparting divine grace and sanctifying believers.

iii. *Grace*: At the heart of theosis is the concept of grace, understood as God's free and unmerited gift of divine life to human beings. Grace is what enables individuals to grow in holiness, overcome sin, and become more like God. It is through the working of grace in the soul that theosis takes place. This grace is communicated primarily through the sacraments, but it can also be experienced through prayer, studying Scripture, acts of charity, and other spiritual practices.

The Catholic understanding of theosis emphasizes the transformative journey of individuals towards union with God, facilitated by the church, sacraments, and grace. Through active participation in the life of the church, reception of the sacraments, and openness to the working of

---

the Catholic faith; the church's sacramental life plays a pivotal role in nurturing believers' spiritual growth and facilitating their journey towards union with God.

grace, believers are called to become more like God and ultimately to share in the divine life for all eternity. This process of divinization is not merely an individual endeavor but a communal journey, rooted in the mystical body of Christ and sustained by the grace of God.

b. *Orthodoxy*: Theosis is articulated within the framework of divine energies, emphasizing the distinction between God's essence and energies and the transformative union with God that transpires through prayer and ascetic practices. The essence of God refers to his innermost being, which is utterly transcendent and incomprehensible to human understanding. On the other hand, God's energies refer to the manifestations of his divine power, grace, and presence in the world. These energies are accessible to humans and are the means by which they can experience communion with God.[10]

This distinction between essence and energies is crucial for understanding theosis. While humans cannot directly participate in God's essence, they can partake in his energies.[11] Through prayer, worship, and ascetic practices, individuals open themselves to the transformative presence of God's energies in their lives. This process leads to a gradual and profound change in the person, as they are increasingly filled with God's grace and are conformed more closely to his image.

Theosis involves both an ontological transformation and a relational union with God. Ontologically, theosis entails a change in the very nature of the human person, as they are sanctified and purified by the divine energies.[12] This transformation involves the healing of human nature from the effects of sin and the restoration of the image and likeness of God within each individual.

---

10. The distinction between the essence and energies of God in Orthodox theology underscores the mystery of God's transcendence and his immanence. While God's essence remains incomprehensible and beyond human reach, his energies are accessible and enable believers to experience communion with him, participate in his divine life, and ultimately, attain union with him through theosis.

11. Zizioulas, *Being as Communion*. Zizioulas explores the distinction between essence and energies in Orthodox thought, particularly in the context of theosis and how the believer can participate in God's energies without directly partaking in his essence.

12. Ware, *Orthodox Church*.

At the same time, theosis involves a deepening of the relationship between the human person and God. Through theosis, individuals enter into a dynamic communion with the triune God, participating in the divine life and sharing in the love, joy, and glory of the Trinity. This union with God is not static union but is a continual process of growth and deepening intimacy.

Theosis is not only an individual journey but also a communal and ecclesial reality within the Orthodox tradition. The church, as the body of Christ, plays a vital role in facilitating theosis through its sacramental life, liturgical worship, and spiritual guidance. The community of believers supports and nurtures individuals in their journeys towards union with God, providing them with the spiritual resources and companionship they need along the way.

The concept of theosis within Orthodox theology offers a profound vision of human destiny and the nature of salvation. It emphasizes the possibility of transformative union with God through participation in his divine energies, leading to the deification of humanity and the fulfillment of God's eternal purposes for his creation.

c. *Protestantism*: Theosis is understood through the lens of union with Christ, emphasizing the believer's spiritual union with Christ by faith and the indwelling of the Holy Spirit for sanctification. At the heart of Protestant theology lies the doctrine of justification by faith alone. This doctrine teaches that humans are justified, or made right with God, not by their own works or merits but solely through faith in the finished work of Christ on the cross. This understanding of justification is closely tied to the Protestant view of union with Christ.[13]

Union with Christ is a central theme in the New Testament, particularly in the writings of the apostle Paul. It refers to the mystical, spiritual union between believers and Christ, which is established at the moment of salvation. This union encompasses

---

13. The doctrine of justification by faith alone is foundational in Protestant theology, highlighting that salvation is a gift of God received through faith in Christ's atoning work. This understanding emphasizes God's grace and the exclusivity of Christ's sacrificial death for human salvation. Union with Christ deepens this relationship, portraying believers as participants in Christ's redemptive work and beneficiaries of his righteousness. Together, these doctrines emphasize the centrality of Christ in salvation and the transformative power of faith in the Christian life.

several aspects, including identification with Christ in his death and resurrection, participation in his righteousness, and sharing in his life and inheritance.

Through faith, believers are united to Christ, and as a result, they share in his righteousness and are declared justified before God. This union also has ongoing implications for the believer's sanctification, or the process of becoming more like Christ. The indwelling of the Holy Spirit plays a crucial role in this process, as the Spirit works within believers to conform them to the image of Christ and produce the fruit of righteousness in their lives.

In Protestant theology, sanctification is understood as both a definitive act that occurs at the moment of salvation and an ongoing process that continues throughout the believer's life. The believer is positionally sanctified, meaning they are set apart as holy in God's sight through their union with Christ. However, they are also progressively sanctified as they grow in grace and conformity to Christ through the work of the Holy Spirit.

Theosis, then, can be understood within the Protestant tradition as the ongoing process of becoming more like Christ through union with him by faith and the indwelling presence of the Holy Spirit. This process involves the transformation of the believer's character, desires, and affections to reflect those of Christ. While Protestants may not use the term "theosis" explicitly, the concept is nevertheless integral to their understanding of salvation and sanctification.

From a theological perspective, this emphasis on union with Christ and the role of faith and the Holy Spirit in the believer's sanctification underscores the importance of grace in the Christian life. Salvation is not merely a one-time event but an ongoing relationship with Christ in which believers are continually being transformed into his likeness. This understanding also emphasizes the trinitarian nature of salvation, as it involves the work of the Father, Son, and Holy Spirit in bringing about the believer's union with Christ and their conformity to his image.

Protestant theology offers a rich understanding of theosis through the lens of union with Christ, highlighting the transformative nature of salvation and sanctification through faith and the indwelling of the Holy Spirit. This perspective emphasizes the ongoing nature of the believer's relationship with Christ and underscores the centrality of grace in the Christian life.

2. **Sacramental Emphasis:**

   a. *Catholicism*: Sacraments, particularly baptism and the Eucharist, are central to the Catholic understanding of theosis, serving as channels of grace and the means of participation in the divine life.

   Baptism, the first sacrament of initiation, is often regarded as the gateway to the other sacraments. Through baptism, an individual is cleansed of original sin and initiated into the body of Christ, the church. This sacrament incorporates the baptized into the paschal mystery of Christ—his death and resurrection—thereby initiating the process of theosis. In baptism, one is united with Christ and becomes a new creation (2 Cor 5:17), adopted as a child of God and made a member of the mystical body of Christ. This incorporation into Christ enables the baptized to participate in the divine life, sharing in God's own holiness and becoming heirs of the kingdom.

   The Eucharist, often referred to as the "source and summit" of the Christian life, is another sacrament central to the Catholic understanding of theosis. In the Eucharist, Catholics believe that the bread and wine truly become the body and blood of Christ through the process of transubstantiation. When the faithful receive the Eucharist, they partake in the real presence of Christ, entering into communion with him in a profound way. This communion is not merely symbolic but is a participation in the very life of God. Through the reception of the Eucharist, Catholics are nourished spiritually, strengthened in their journey towards theosis, and united more closely with Christ and with one another in the mystical body of the church.

   Both baptism and the Eucharist are seen as channels of grace, through which God's divine life is communicated to believers. They are not merely symbolic rituals but effective signs of God's presence and action in the world. Through these sacraments, Catholics believe they are empowered by the Holy Spirit to live out their Christian vocation, growing in holiness and conformity to the image of Christ.

The Catholic understanding of theosis through the sacraments emphasizes the transformative power of God's grace in the lives of believers. By participating in these sacred mysteries, Catholics are drawn into ever-deeper communion with God, becoming more like him in love, righteousness, and holiness. This process of divinization is ongoing and lifelong, culminating in the ultimate union with God in the beatific vision, where believers will behold God face to face and share in his eternal glory.

b. *Orthodoxy*: While sacraments are important in Eastern Orthodox theology, theosis is often more closely associated with hesychastic practices, such as contemplative prayer and asceticism, which facilitate the experience of God's divine energies. However, sacraments do hold a significant place within Orthodox theology as the means through which God's grace is imparted to believers. They are tangible encounters with the divine, wherein the faithful participate in the mysteries of the church; they include baptism, chrismation, Eucharist, confession, marriage, ordination, and unction. Through these sacraments, Orthodox Christians are initiated into the life of Christ and are continually nourished on their journey towards theosis.

However, while sacraments are vital channels of divine grace, theosis finds its deeper resonance in hesychastic practices. Hesychasm, rooted in the Greek word "hesychia" meaning inner stillness or quiet, encompasses various ascetic and contemplative disciplines aimed at cultivating a deep, unceasing prayerful communion with God. Central to hesychasm is the practice of the Jesus Prayer: "Lord Jesus Christ, Son of God, have mercy on me, a sinner."[14] Through repetition of this prayer with focused attention and inner quietude, practitioners seek to purify their hearts and minds, inviting the presence of God to dwell within them.

Theosis, therefore, becomes intimately intertwined with the hesychastic tradition. Through the disciplined practice of hesychasm, believers open themselves to the transformative work of

---

14. See *Way of a Pilgrim*. This classic work of Russian Orthodox spirituality is a foundational text on the practice of the Jesus Prayer. It describes the journey of a pilgrim who seeks to understand and practice continuous prayer (the Jesus Prayer) and illustrates how it purifies the heart and leads to divine union. See also Palmer et al., *Philokalia*.

the Holy Spirit, who gradually illumines their souls and elevates them towards union with God. This union, however, is not one of absorption into the divine essence but rather a participation in the divine energies of God. As Gregory Palamas, a prominent figure in hesychasm, elucidates, believers are granted a share in God's uncreated energies, experiencing his presence and power in a manner that transcends human understanding.[15]

The theological significance of theosis lies in its affirmation of the dynamic relationship between God and humanity. It underscores the belief that God became human so that humans might become like God—a concept encapsulated in the early Christian dictum of "divinization" or "deification." Through theosis, humanity is invited into a journey of continual growth and transformation, wherein individuals are restored to the image and likeness of God, which was marred by sin.

In essence, theosis represents the ultimate goal of the Christian life—an ever-deepening communion with God that transcends the limitations of the created order. While sacraments serve as crucial milestones on this journey, hesychastic practices offer a path towards the intimate encounter with God's divine energies, leading to the realization of humanity's true potential as children of God. Thus, theosis stands as a profound testament to the transformative power of God's grace and the enduring call to communion with the divine.

c. *Protestantism*: While Protestant traditions acknowledge sacraments like baptism and the Lord's Supper, the emphasis is less on sacramental participation and more on faith and the work of the Holy Spirit in the believer's life. Protestant traditions generally hold a different view of sacraments, emphasizing the role of faith and the work of the Holy Spirit in the believer's life. While they do acknowledge sacraments such as baptism and the Lord's Supper, their significance is often interpreted more symbolically, as acts of obedience and remembrance rather than channels of grace *ex opere operato* (Latin for "from the work worked").[16] This means that the efficacy of the sacraments

---

15 Palamas, *Triads*. This foundational text by Gregory Palamas elaborates on his teachings about theosis, the nature of God's uncreated energies, and how believers participate in the divine life through grace.

16. Horton, *Better Way*. This book outlines how sacraments are viewed symbolically

is not inherent in the ritual itself but is contingent upon the faith and disposition of the believer.

For Protestants, salvation is understood primarily as a personal and individual experience of faith in Jesus Christ as Lord and Savior. The Holy Spirit is seen as the agent of transformation in the believer's life, working through faith rather than sacramental participation. This emphasis on faith alone (*sola fide*) as the means of justification, alongside other Protestant principles like *sola scriptura* (Scripture alone) and *sola gratia* (grace alone), underscores the centrality of personal relationship with God through Christ.[17]

The Protestant perspective on sacraments reflects a broader theological framework that prioritizes the direct relationship between the believer and God, without the need for intermediary structures or rituals. This does not diminish the importance of sacraments in Protestant worship and theology but rather redefines their significance within a framework of faith and grace. Thus, while Protestants may participate in sacraments such as baptism and communion, their focus remains on the inward transformation wrought by the Holy Spirit through faith in Christ rather than on the outward ritual itself.

3. **Ecclesial Authority:**

   a. *Catholicism*: The Catholic Church, with its hierarchical structure and magisterial authority, plays a significant role in guiding believers on the path of theosis through its teaching authority and administration of sacraments. At the heart of the Catholic Church's guidance towards theosis is its hierarchical structure and magisterial authority. The church's hierarchy, headed by the pope and consisting of bishops, priests, and deacons, serves as a visible representation of Christ's authority on earth.[18] This

---

within the Reformed tradition and stresses their role in remembering and obedience, rather than as automatic channels of grace.

17. McGrath, *Christian Theology*. This comprehensive textbook provides an overview of key Protestant theological principles, including *sola fide*, *sola scriptura*, and *sola gratia*, and their significance in the context of the Protestant Reformation and the centrality of the believer's relationship with God.

18. Congar, *Meaning of Tradition*. Yves Congar, a prominent theologian, discusses the nature of the church's hierarchy and its role as a visible sign of Christ's authority and presence in this work. He elaborates on how the church is the "sacrament" of Christ's continuing presence in the world.

hierarchical structure ensures the continuity and unity of the church, providing believers with guidance and direction in their spiritual journey.

Central to the church's role in guiding believers towards theosis is its teaching authority, known as the magisterium. The magisterium, composed of the pope and the bishops in communion with him, is tasked with preserving, interpreting, and teaching the deposit of faith entrusted to the church. Through the magisterium, the Catholic Church offers authoritative guidance on matters of faith and morals, providing believers with a reliable source of truth and guidance in their quest for union with God.[19]

Additionally, the Catholic Church administers the sacraments, which are visible signs of God's grace instituted by Christ himself. The sacraments are essential channels through which believers participate in the divine life of God and progress towards theosis. Through the sacraments of initiation (baptism, confirmation, and the Eucharist), believers are incorporated into the body of Christ and receive the grace necessary for their journey towards union with God. The sacraments of healing (reconciliation and anointing of the sick) restore and strengthen believers on their spiritual journey, while the sacraments of vocation (matrimony and holy orders) provide grace for specific states in life and ministries within the church.[20]

Furthermore, the Catholic Church offers believers a rich spiritual tradition that includes prayer, contemplation, and the pursuit of holiness. Through practices such as liturgical worship, spiritual direction, and devotion to the saints, believers are supported in their quest for union with God and the attainment of theosis.

The hierarchical structure and magisterial authority of the Catholic Church can be understood as essential components of

---

19. The magisterium of the Catholic Church serves as the authoritative and reliable guide for believers in their quest for union with God (theosis). Through its teaching authority, the magisterium preserves and interprets the deposit of faith, offers moral and doctrinal guidance, and administers sacraments that nourish and sustain believers on their spiritual journey. It is seen as a foundational element in Catholic theology and practice, ensuring fidelity to Christ's teachings and unity within the church. See the *Catechism of the Catholic Church*, para. 2032–40.

20. *Catechism of the Catholic Church*, sec. 2.

God's plan for guiding humanity towards union with him. By entrusting the church with authority and teaching, God provides believers with a reliable and authoritative guide on their spiritual journey. The administration of sacraments further reinforces this guidance, providing believers with tangible encounters with God's grace as they progress towards theosis.

Ultimately, the Catholic Church's role in guiding believers towards theosis reflects its mission to proclaim the gospel and lead all people to salvation. Through its teaching authority, administration of sacraments, and rich spiritual tradition, the church accompanies believers on their journey towards union with God, inviting them to participate fully in the divine life and ultimately to attain eternal communion with him.

b. *Orthodoxy*: The Eastern Orthodox Church, with its emphasis on apostolic succession and conciliar tradition, provides guidance and spiritual direction to believers in their pursuit of theosis. Central to Orthodox theology is the concept of apostolic succession, which asserts that the authority and teachings of the apostles have been faithfully transmitted through an unbroken line of bishops, starting from the apostolic era and continue up to the present day.[21] This lineage ensures the continuity and authenticity of the church's teachings and sacraments. By tracing its origins back to the apostles, the Orthodox Church emphasizes its connection to the early Christian community and the teachings of Jesus Christ himself. This continuity provides believers with a sense of grounding and assurance that they are participating in a tradition that stretches back to the very origins of Christianity

The Orthodox Church places a strong emphasis on the conciliar tradition, or conciliarity, meaning that major decisions regarding doctrine and governance are made collectively through councils involving bishops, clergy, and laity representatives. This conciliar approach is exemplified by the seven ecumenical councils, where crucial theological matters were deliberated and resolved through consensus.[22] These councils, such as the First

---

21. Ware, *Orthodox Church*.

22. Conciliarity in the Orthodox Church embodies the principle of collective decision making through councils, particularly through the ecumenical councils that have shaped Orthodox doctrine and practice. This approach reflects a commitment to unity, consensus, and the guidance of the Holy Spirit in addressing theological, doctrinal, and

Council of Nicaea and the Second Council of Constantinople, played a vital role in shaping Orthodox doctrine and preserving orthodoxy against heresy. The conciliar tradition underscores the communal nature of the church, highlighting the importance of unity and consensus in discerning the will of God.

A central tenet of Orthodox spirituality is the idea of theosis, which can be understood as "becoming divine" or "godlike." Theosis describes the process through which humans are transformed and joined with God, sharing in his divine essence. This transformative journey involves cleansing the soul, developing virtues, and nurturing a profound, intimate connection with God through prayer, worship, and involvement in the church's sacramental practices. Theosis is not just an abstract idea but a lived experience, where followers aim to embody Christlike qualities in their thoughts, words, and actions. It's an ongoing path of spiritual development and maturation, informed by church teachings and inspired by the examples set by saints throughout history.

Orthodox Christianity offers believers a comprehensive framework for spiritual growth and transformation. Through its emphasis on apostolic succession, conciliar tradition, and theosis, the Orthodox Church provides guidance and direction for believers seeking to deepen their relationship with God and live out their faith in the world. In Vladimir Kharlamov's "*Theosis* in Patristic Thought," he states, "There are no conciliar decisions that affirmed a certain doctrine of theosis, nor were there any dogmatic controversies in the patristic period concerning this issue. Modern Eastern Orthodox consensus on theosis, or at least the idea of such consensus, is rather a speculative synthesis of the final phase of Byzantine theology than an accurate historical representation of this concept's development."[23]

c. *Protestantism*: Protestant theology, with its emphasis on individual interpretation of Scripture and the priesthood of all believers, allows for greater diversity in theological perspectives on theosis and less reliance on ecclesial authority. Unlike in

---

pastoral issues that impact the life of the church and its faithful. See Ware, *Orthodox Church*.

23. Kharlamov, "Patristic Thought," 161.

hierarchical ecclesiastical structures, where theological interpretation is often centralized and regulated by ecclesial authorities, Protestantism grants individuals the freedom to engage directly with Scripture and formulate their own understandings of theological concepts such as theosis. This freedom fosters theological diversity within the Protestant tradition, as various theologians and denominations may interpret the biblical texts differently and offer distinct theological insights on theosis.

Moreover, the priesthood of all believers, another key Protestant doctrine, affirms that every believer has direct access to God through Jesus Christ and is called to participate in the ministry and mission of the church. This priesthood empowers individuals to engage in theological reflection and discernment and not rely solely on ecclesial authorities for theological guidance.[24] Consequently, Protestant theologians are encouraged to explore theological concepts like theosis through personal study, prayer, and dialogue within the community of believers, rather than simply accepting authoritative pronouncements from ecclesial hierarchies.

The emphasis on individual interpretation and the priesthood of all believers does not diminish the importance of tradition or communal discernment within Protestantism. Rather, it shifts the locus of authority from ecclesial structures to the community of believers as a whole. The Protestant understanding of the church as a gathered community of believers, rather than a hierarchical institution, allows for a more dynamic and decentralized approach to theological inquiry.

Protestant theology, with its emphasis on individual interpretation of Scripture and the priesthood of all believers, provides a fertile ground for diverse perspectives on theological concepts such as theosis. This emphasis on individual engagement with Scripture and communal discernment fosters theological exploration and dialogue within the Protestant

---

24. The priesthood of all believers in Protestant theology emphasizes the direct access of every believer to God, their active participation in the ministry and mission of the church, and their capacity for theological reflection and discernment. This doctrine affirms the dignity and responsibility of all believers in living out their faith and serving God's purposes in the world.

tradition, allowing for a rich tapestry of theological perspectives to emerge.[25]

While Catholic, Eastern Orthodox, and Protestant theologies share the common goal of theosis or union with God, their approaches differ according to the individual theological framework, sacramental emphasis, and church authority. These differences shape how each tradition understands theosis and the methods believers use to pursue it.

All three traditions agree that the ultimate purpose of Christian life is to achieve a transformative union with God. This process involves aligning oneself more closely with God's nature and experiencing his divine grace.

Despite their theological, liturgical, and doctrinal differences, these Christian traditions share a unified vision of attaining union with God. Each offers a unique perspective on this transformative journey, reflecting their distinct emphases and interpretations. Nevertheless, the central aim of becoming one with God and experiencing his transformative grace remains a common thread that unites these diverse Christian traditions.

Relevance In Daily Life

In Catholic theology, the path to theosis (union with God) is closely tied to the church and its sacraments. Catholics view sacramental participation as a direct conduit for divine grace. The church's role is central in this spiritual journey. For Catholic believers, integrating sacraments into daily life is crucial. This often involves frequent Mass attendance, frequent reception of Communion, and regular confession. While personal devotion and prayer are valued, they're typically understood within the framework of church doctrine and traditions. The sacraments of Eucharist, confession, and confirmation are particularly emphasized as means of receiving God's grace. These rituals are seen as more than symbolic—they're considered active channels through which believers can draw closer to the divine. In essence, Catholic spiritual life intertwines personal faith with communal religious practices, with the church and its sacraments serving as the primary structure for pursuing union with God.

---

25. "The neo-Protestantism of post-Kantian theology in Europe and America shied away from the idea [of theosis] as too metaphysical (if not physical) and mystical to fit in with the project of moralizing dogma. Karl Barth scoffed at the idea of deification as a real ontological transformation of persons through participation in God. Emil Brunner considered it mystical and therefore useless to the emphasis he wished to place on the I-Thou encounter between God and the individual" (Olson, "Deification," 342–44).

Eastern Orthodox theology centers on a mystical approach to union with God (theosis), emphasizing deep, contemplative spiritual practices. The path to theosis is viewed as an intimate, experiential journey rather than a purely intellectual one. The church's rich liturgical tradition forms a cornerstone of this spiritual quest. Equally important is the practice of the Jesus Prayer, a short, repetitive invocation that serves as a focal point for meditation and communion with the divine. In their daily lives, Orthodox believers often engage in frequent prayer, with the Jesus Prayer ("Lord Jesus Christ, Son of God, have mercy on me, a sinner") playing a key role. Regular participation in the Divine Liturgy and other church services is also crucial to their spiritual routine. Orthodox spirituality draws significant inspiration from monastic traditions. As such, even lay believers often incorporate ascetic practices into their lives as a means of pursuing theosis. These might include fasting, extended periods of prayer, or other forms of self-discipline. Overall, the Eastern Orthodox approach to theosis blends communal worship, personal devotion, and ascetic practices, all aimed at fostering a profound, transformative relationship with God.

Protestant views on theosis (union with God) are diverse but share common threads. Central to most Protestant approaches is the emphasis on cultivating a direct, personal connection with God. This relationship is primarily nurtured through faith in Jesus Christ and reliance on Scripture as the authoritative guide for spiritual life. Unlike Catholic and Orthodox traditions, Protestant theology generally places less emphasis on sacraments as channels of divine grace. Instead, the focus is often on individual spiritual practices and personal faith development. In daily life, Protestants typically engage in activities that foster their personal relationship with God. These often include (a) regular Bible study, emphasizing individual interpretation and application of Scripture; (b) personal prayer, viewed as direct communication with God; and (c) participation in communal worship services.

For many Protestants, the concept of theosis may be understood more abstractly. Rather than a mystical union, it's often framed in terms of spiritual growth and character development. The goal is typically to become more Christlike in thought and action, with an emphasis on ethical living and putting faith into practice. Overall, Protestant spirituality tends to be highly individualized, with believers encouraged to actively pursue their own spiritual maturity through personal study, prayer, and lived faith.

Chapter 9

Theosis in Contemporary Christian Spirituality and Ethics

THE CALL TO THEOSIS, or divinization is still a key topic in contemporary Christian spirituality and morals. It also functions as a powerful framework for those who want to understand the Christian journey and be led toward increased holiness and moral integrity. In this chapter, we will discuss the impact of theosis on modern Christian spirituality and morality.

Theosis offers one of the most powerful—and potentially liberating—paradigms for interpreting Christian living. It is the belief that we are all on a journey towards God and becoming more like him, living with his life overflowing through us. This vision of spiritual development and transformation encourages Christians to strive for holiness and live in obedience to God. Theosis also emphasizes spiritual practices such as prayer, meditation, and sacramental living. Just as with the early Quakers (not to mention what Jesus preached), silence, attention to Scripture, and worship in community are seen as vital for walking closely and being disciplined by grace; all are essential disciplines of Christian spiritual formation. Through practicing these disciplines, believers can align themselves with the divine and move towards deification.

Theosis is intimately tied to the life of virtue. Virtues are personality traits that evoke the nature of God and ultimately help us to live according to his law. Love, humility, compassion, and the pursuit of justice are all essential virtues for theosis. Through these virtues, the believer is formed further into Christlikeness and participates more in the divine nature. Similarly, theosis has a practical or ethical dimension. It calls believers to mirror the love, mercy, and justice of God in their relationships and their use of creation. Theosis encourages believers in two important ways: to exercise compassion for their neighbors and to work towards the common good. By embracing the ethical implications of deification, believers can contribute to transforming society by bearing witness to the love of God.

The idea of theosis remains relevant in modern Christian spiritual and theological scholarship. It provides a deep way to meditate on an understanding of the walk with Christ, as it encourages living lives that strive for holiness and communion with God while actively making decisions toward virtuous behavior. Christians who practice theosis draw closer to God, participate in society more than ever before with greater effect, and partake of divine life. This involves the ongoing process of sanctification, where Christians seek to align their lives with God's will and character. The pursuit of godliness is expressed through ethical living and the cultivation of virtues.

1. **Spiritual Growth and Transformation**

    a. Theosis provides a compelling vision of spiritual growth and transformation, inviting believers into a dynamic and intimate relationship with God. In contemporary Christian spirituality, theosis serves as a reminder of the ultimate goal of the Christian life: to become like Christ and participate fully in the divine life. Theosis acknowledges the inherent potential within each individual to reflect the image of God and to grow into union with him.

        i. *Dynamic Relationship with God*: At the heart of spiritual growth and transformation is a dynamic relationship with the divine. This relationship is not static but evolves over time, deepening through prayer, contemplation, study of Scripture, participation in the sacraments, and acts of love and service. It is a journey marked by both moments of profound connection and periods of struggle and doubt, yet always guided by the steadfast love and grace of God.

        ii. *Becoming Like Christ (Imitatio Christi)*: Central to the concept of theosis is the aspiration to become like Christ. Christ, as the perfect image of God, serves as the archetype for human transformation. Through imitating Christ's virtues, embodying his teachings, and surrendering to his will, individuals participate in the process of divinization. This transformation involves the renewal of the mind, heart, and will to align with the values of the kingdom of God.

iii. *Participation in Divine Life*: Spiritual growth and transformation culminate in the participation of the believer in the divine life. This participation entails not only experiencing God's presence and grace but also sharing in his mission of reconciliation, justice, and love in the world. The transformed individual becomes a conduit of God's mercy and compassion, reflecting his light and love to others.

iv. *Ultimate Goal of Christian Life*: In contemporary Christian spirituality, theosis serves as a poignant reminder of the ultimate goal of the Christian life. Beyond mere moral improvement or religious observance, the Christian journey is about being transformed into the likeness of Christ and entering into full communion with the triune God. It is an ongoing process that extends beyond earthly life, culminating in the beatific vision and eternal union with God in the heavenly realm.

Spiritual growth and transformation, as articulated through the concept of theosis, invite believers into a profound and transformative journey of communion with God. It is a journey characterized by intimacy, renewal, and alignment with the divine will, ultimately leading to the fulfillment of the deepest longings of the human soul and the realization of God's redemptive purpose for creation. It suggests that, through this journey, people aim to fulfill their profound desires and understand their role within the grander scheme of creation, as guided by their belief in a redemptive divine plan.

b. Believers are encouraged to cultivate practices such as prayer, meditation, study of Scripture, and participation in the sacraments to deepen their union with God and experience spiritual renewal.[1]

---

1. The cultivation of practices such as prayer, meditation, study of Scripture, and participation in the sacraments is central to Christian spirituality. These practices are essential for believers seeking to deepen their union with God, experience spiritual

i. *Prayer*: Prayer is essentially communication with God. It's not merely reciting words but engaging in a dialogue with the divine. Through prayer, believers express their adoration, confession, thanksgiving, and supplication to God. Jesus, in the Gospels, frequently retreated to pray, emphasizing its importance as a means of communion with the Father. The theological reflection on prayer underscores its role in fostering intimacy with God, aligning our will with his, and seeking guidance, strength, and comfort from him.

ii. *Meditation*: Christian meditation involves contemplating the truths of God's word, reflecting on his character, and pondering his works. It's a deliberate focusing of the mind and heart on spiritual realities. Biblical meditation involves not emptying the mind but filling it with God's truth. Psalm 1 speaks of the blessedness of the one who meditates on God's law day and night. Through meditation, believers deepen their understanding of God, his will, and his ways, allowing his truth to transform their lives.

iii. *Study of Scripture*: The Bible is considered the inspired word of God and the primary source of divine revelation. Studying Scripture involves not only reading it but also interpreting and applying its teachings. Through the study of Scripture, believers gain insight into God's character, his plan of redemption, and his expectations for his people. Theological reflection on the study of Scripture emphasizes its role in shaping believers' beliefs, values, and behaviors according to God's will.

iv. *Participation in the Sacraments*: In many Christian traditions, sacraments such as baptism and the Lord's Supper (or Eucharist) are significant. These sacraments are seen as visible signs of God's invisible grace. Baptism symbolizes initiation into the Christian faith and the washing away of sin, while the Lord's Supper commemorates Christ's

---

renewal, and grow in their faith journey. By engaging in these disciplines with sincerity and consistency, Christians open themselves to God's transformative work and align themselves more closely with his will and purposes. Thus, these practices are not merely religious obligations but essential means by which believers nurture their relationship with God and live out their faith in daily life.

sacrifice on the cross and nourishes believers spiritually. Participating in the sacraments not only strengthens believers' faith but also fosters a sense of community among believers as they partake together.

Theological reflection on these practices underscores their role in deepening believers' union with God and fostering spiritual renewal. Through prayer, believers commune with God; through meditation, they internalize his truth; through the study of Scripture, they gain insight into his will; and through participation in the sacraments, they experience his grace in tangible ways. These practices are not ends in themselves but means through which believers grow in their relationship with God and are transformed into his likeness.

2. **Ethical Living and Social Justice**

   a. Theosis has significant implications for ethical living and social justice, as believers are called to reflect the character of Christ in their attitudes and actions. This transformative process is not one of self-assertion or self-exaltation but rather a journey of humility, obedience, and self-emptying, mirroring the kenotic nature of Christ as described in Phil 2:5–8.

      Ethical living and social justice naturally emerge as significant implications of theosis because they reflect the outworking of this transformative journey. As believers grow in their likeness to Christ, they increasingly exhibit virtues such as love, compassion, justice, mercy, and humility. These virtues are not simply moral principles to adhere to but are intrinsic aspects of God's character, which the believer is called to embody.

      Ethical living, therefore, becomes more than a set of rules or guidelines; it becomes a natural expression of one's union with God. In this state of union, believers are empowered by the Holy Spirit to discern right from wrong and to act justly in their interactions with others.[2] This ethical framework is not based

---

2. Ethical living in Christian spirituality is deeply intertwined with the believer's union with God through the Holy Spirit. It involves a transformation of the inner being that shapes outward actions and attitudes. Rather than a rigid adherence to rules, ethical living becomes a natural expression of one's relationship with God; one is empowered by the Holy Spirit to discern right from wrong and to act justly in all circumstances. This holistic approach to ethics emphasizes love for God and neighbor as the guiding principles for navigating moral complexities and advancing God's kingdom of justice

solely on external laws but is grounded in the internal transformation of the heart, where love for God and love for neighbor become the guiding principles of one's actions.

Theosis has profound implications for social justice because it challenges believers to see the inherent dignity and worth of every human being, to see each person as created in the image of God. This recognition of the divine image in others compels believers to advocate for the rights and well-being of the marginalized, oppressed, and vulnerable in society. It fosters a commitment to systemic change and the pursuit of justice, not merely as a social obligation but as a reflection of God's concern for the downtrodden and the oppressed.

In essence, theosis transforms ethics from a legalistic framework into a dynamic expression of divine love and justice. It calls believers to a higher standard of living, where their attitudes and actions are shaped by their intimate union with God and their participation in the divine nature. As believers increasingly reflect the character of Christ, they become agents of transformation in the world, working towards the establishment of God's kingdom of justice, mercy, and love.

b. Contemporary Christian ethics emphasizes the importance of virtues such as love, compassion, justice, and humility, which are cultivated through the process of theosis.

   i. *Love*: In Christian ethics, love transcends mere emotion or sentimentality. It is seen as the foundational virtue upon which all others are built. Contemporary Christian ethicists emphasize the concept of agape, a selfless, sacrificial love that seeks the good of others above oneself. This love reflects the very nature of God, who is described as love itself in Christian theology. Through the process of theosis, individuals are called to grow in their capacity to love God and neighbor, aligning their will with the divine will and embodying love in their actions.[3]

---

and righteousness in the world.

3. Theosis calls believers to embody love in their actions towards God and neighbor. Love, in this context, is not merely a sentiment but a dynamic force that compels selflessness, compassion, justice, and forgiveness. It motivates believers to care for the marginalized, to advocate for justice, and to extend mercy and grace to others.

ii. *Compassion*: Compassion flows naturally from love. It is the empathy and concern for the suffering of others, leading to a desire to alleviate that suffering. In the Christian ethical framework, compassion is not just a feeling but a call to action. Jesus Christ, the central figure of Christianity, exemplified this virtue throughout his ministry, showing mercy to the marginalized, healing the sick, and comforting the brokenhearted. Through the process of theosis, Christians are called to cultivate a compassionate heart, reflecting God's own compassion for humanity.[4]

iii. *Justice*: Justice is another essential virtue emphasized in contemporary Christian ethics. It involves giving each person their due, upholding fairness, equality, and righteousness. In the Christian tradition, justice is intimately tied to the concept of shalom, which encompasses peace, wholeness, and harmony in all relationships.[5] The pursuit of justice is not only a social imperative but also a spiritual one, as it reflects God's concern for the oppressed and marginalized. Through the process of theosis, individuals are called to advocate for justice by standing up against injustice and working towards the establishment of God's kingdom on earth.[6]

iv. *Humility*: Humility is the virtue that acknowledges one's own limitations and dependence on God. It is the recognition that all gifts and talents come from God and are to be used for the service of others. Jesus Christ, in his earthly life, exemplified perfect humility, taking on the form of a servant and readily submitting to the will of the Father. In the process of theosis, individuals are called to cultivate humility

---

4. Cultivating a compassionate heart through theosis significantly impacts how Christians live out their faith. It transforms ethical living from a legalistic adherence to rules into a heartfelt response of love and compassion towards others. Compassionate living becomes a natural expression of one's union with God and alignment with his will.

5. Bruggeman, *Peace*; Sider, *Scandal*.

6. Advocating for justice through theosis transforms how Christians live out their faith. It compels believers to move beyond personal piety to actively seek the establishment of God's kingdom on earth—a kingdom characterized by righteousness, peace, and justice (Matt 6:10). It challenges them to confront societal structures and attitudes that perpetuate inequality and to work towards a more just and equitable world.

by emptying themselves of pride and self-centeredness and allowing God to work in and through them.[7]

The cultivation of these virtues through the process of theosis is not merely a moral imperative but a transformative journey towards becoming more like Christ. It involves cooperation with the grace of God, active participation in the life of the church, and continual striving towards spiritual growth. Ultimately, contemporary Christian ethics emphasizes that the goal of the Christian life is not just moral behavior but the transformation of the whole person, leading to a life of love, compassion, justice, and humility, and reflecting the image of God in which humanity was created.

c. Believers are challenged to apply the principles of theosis to their everyday lives. This includes advocating for the marginalized, standing against injustice, and promoting reconciliation and peace in their communities. Let's unpack each aspect:

   i. *Advocating for the Marginalized*: Theosis entails recognizing the inherent dignity and worth of every human being, as all are created in the image of God. Therefore, believers are called to stand in solidarity with those who are marginalized and oppressed in society. This involves actively working to address systemic injustices such as poverty, discrimination, and inequality. By advocating for the marginalized, believers participate in God's mission of bringing about justice and compassion in the world.

   ii. *Standing Against Injustice*: Just as Christ confronted the powers and principalities of his time, believers are called to challenge injustice wherever it is found. This may involve speaking out against oppressive systems, confronting prejudice and discrimination, and working to dismantle structures that perpetuate inequality. Theosis empowers believers

---

7. In the process of theosis, individuals are called to cultivate humility—a virtue that involves emptying oneself of pride and self-centeredness and allowing God to work in and through oneself. Humility is foundational to Christian spirituality, shaping the believer's character and disposition to align more closely with Christ. By embracing humility, believers participate more fully in God's redemptive work and bear witness to his transforming grace in the world.

to be agents of change in the pursuit of a more just and equitable society.

iii. *Promoting Reconciliation and Peace*: Central to the Christian faith is the message of reconciliation—reconciliation between humanity and God and reconciliation among human beings. Theosis involves embodying this message by actively seeking reconciliation and peace in all relationships and communities. This may require humility, forgiveness, and a commitment to dialogue and understanding across differences. By promoting reconciliation and peace, believers participate in God's work of healing and restoring broken relationships.

In applying the principles of theosis to their everyday lives, believers are called to be transformative agents in the world, bringing about God's kingdom of justice, love, and peace.[8] This requires a holistic approach that integrates spirituality with social action, personal transformation with societal change. By living out the principles of theosis, believers bear witness to the transformative power of God's love and contribute to the ongoing work of redemption and reconciliation in the world.

3. **Interfaith Dialogue and Ecumenical Engagement**

   a. Theosis serves as a point of dialogue and convergence in interfaith and ecumenical discussions, fostering mutual understanding and cooperation among different religious traditions. When exploring theosis in interfaith dialogue, one can uncover parallels with concepts found in other religious traditions. For example, in Hinduism, the concept of moksha or liberation shares similarities with theosis, emphasizing the ultimate goal of union with the divine and the transcendence of individual ego.[9] Similarly, in Sufi Islam, the concept of fanaa, or annihilation of the self in God, reflects a similar journey toward union with the Divine.[10]

---

8. As believers conform to the image of Christ and participate in God's mission, they fulfill their purpose as children of God and ambassadors of his grace (2 Cor 5:20). They reflect God's love and character to the world, proclaiming the transformative power of the gospel through both their words and actions.

9. Sivananda, *Bahgavad Gita*.

10. Chittick, *Sufi Path*; Nasr, *Heart of Islam*.

By recognizing these parallels, interfaith dialogue can transcend theological differences and foster mutual understanding. Rather than focusing solely on doctrinal distinctions, discussions can center on shared spiritual experiences and aspirations. Theosis serves as a bridge, allowing individuals from diverse religious backgrounds to find common ground in their pursuit of spiritual growth and union with the divine.

Furthermore, the concept of theosis encourages humility and openness in interfaith dialogue. Recognizing the limitations of human language and understanding when it comes to describing the divine, individuals are encouraged to approach dialogue with a sense of reverence and awe. This humility enables participants to learn from one another, recognizing the unique insights and perspectives that each tradition brings to the conversation.

In ecumenical discussions within Christianity, theosis offers a unifying vision that transcends denominational differences. While theological nuances may vary between Eastern Orthodox, Catholic, and Protestant traditions, the shared goal of spiritual transformation and union with God remains central. Emphasizing theosis can help Christians focus on their commonalities rather than their divisions, fostering greater unity and cooperation within the body of Christ.

The concept of theosis serves as a powerful catalyst for interfaith and ecumenical dialogue, fostering mutual understanding and cooperation among different religious traditions. By recognizing the shared aspirations for spiritual transformation and union with the divine, individuals can transcend theological differences and work together toward the common good.

b. Believers engage in dialogue with people of other faiths, exploring commonalities and differences in their respective understandings of divine-human union and spiritual transformation. At the heart of this dialogue lies the recognition of the sacred within each tradition. While the specific expressions and conceptualizations of the divine may vary across religions, the underlying quest for transcendence and the longing for spiritual transformation are universal human experiences. By engaging in dialogue, believers can recognize and honor the divine presence in the lives of others, regardless of religious labels.

One key aspect of dialogue is the exploration of different understandings of divine-human union. In Christianity, for example, the concept of union with the divine often centers around the incarnation of God in Jesus Christ and the indwelling of the Holy Spirit in believers. This union is understood as a transformative relationship that shapes the believer's identity and guides their actions in the world.

Spiritual transformation is another central theme that believers can explore in dialogue with people of other faiths. Within Christianity, spiritual transformation is often understood as a process of inner renewal and sanctification, guided by the grace of God and the practice of spiritual disciplines. This transformation leads believers to embody the virtues of love, compassion, and humility, reflecting the image of Christ in their lives.

By engaging in dialogue with people of other faiths, believers have the opportunity to learn from diverse perspectives on spiritual transformation and gain new insights that can deepen their own spiritual practice. Moreover, dialogue can foster a spirit of mutual support and solidarity in the shared struggle for greater spiritual awakening and social justice.

From a theological perspective, engaging in dialogue with people of other faiths can be seen as an expression of the divine call to love our neighbors as ourselves. Jesus Christ himself taught the importance of loving our enemies and welcoming the stranger, of transcending religious boundaries to embrace the universal kinship of all humanity. In this sense, dialogue becomes an act of faithful obedience to the commandment to love, reflecting the divine image implanted within each person, regardless of their religious affiliation.

Believers engage in dialogue with people of other faiths to explore commonalities and differences in their respective understandings of divine-human union and spiritual transformation. Through this dialogue, believers can deepen their own faith, foster mutual respect and understanding, and bear witness to the inclusive love of God that embraces all people, regardless of religious differences.

c. The concept of theosis encourages believers to seek unity and reconciliation within the broader Christian community and to collaborate with people of goodwill in addressing shared concerns and challenges. Theosis emphasizes the dynamic relationship between God and humanity, reflecting the divine desire for communion with his creation. This relational aspect extends not only vertically between individuals and God but also horizontally among members of the Christian community. Just as theosis entails union with God, it also entails unity within the body of Christ. This unity is not merely an abstract concept but a lived reality wherein believers, as they grow in the likeness of God, increasingly embody the values of love, compassion, and reconciliation.

Within the Christian tradition, theosis is intimately linked to the person of Jesus Christ. Through the incarnation, God took on human nature, uniting divinity with humanity in the person of Jesus. The life, death, and resurrection of Christ serve as the ultimate paradigm for theosis, demonstrating the possibility of humanity's union with God and the transformation that ensues. Thus, the Christian journey towards theosis involves conforming to the image of Christ, who reveals the fullness of God's love and the way of reconciliation.[11]

Practically, theosis motivates believers to seek unity and reconciliation within the broader Christian community and beyond. This pursuit is grounded in the recognition of the inherent dignity of every human person as a beloved creation of God. By striving for unity, believers emulate the divine desire for harmony and wholeness. Moreover, theosis fosters collaboration with people of goodwill from diverse backgrounds and traditions in addressing shared concerns and challenges. Such collaboration is guided by the recognition of the divine image in all humanity and the common pursuit of justice, peace, and the common good.

---

11. Through the incarnation, God revealed his desire to unite divinity with humanity in Jesus Christ. The life, death, and resurrection of Christ serve as the ultimate paradigm for theosis—the process by which humanity is called to union with God and transformation into his likeness. By conforming to the image of Christ and participating in God's mission of reconciliation, believers embody God's love and reveal his kingdom on earth, fulfilling their purpose as children of God and ambassadors of his grace.

Theosis, therefore, invites believers to transcend divisions and differences and embrace a vision of unity that reflects the divine unity of Father, Son, and Holy Spirit. This unity is not uniformity but encompasses diversity within a shared commitment to love and reconciliation. As individuals and communities progress in theosis, they become agents of God's transforming grace in the world, working towards the fulfillment of God's kingdom where all are reconciled in Christ.

The concept of theosis offers a profound theological framework for understanding the transformative journey of believers towards union with God and the implications for communal relationships within the Christian community and broader society. Through theosis, believers are called to embody the values of unity, reconciliation, and collaboration, reflecting the divine image and participating in the ongoing work of God's kingdom on earth.

4. **Personal Development and Well-Being**

    a. Theosis promotes personal development and well-being, recognizing the importance of holistic growth in body, mind, and spirit. This pursuit inherently recognizes the importance of holistic growth in body, mind, and spirit.

        i. Particularly in the Eastern Orthodox tradition, theosis is understood as the ultimate goal of human life. It is the process by which humans participate in the divine nature (2 Pet 1:4) and move towards union with God. This understanding implies a journey of transformation, where individuals strive to align their will with the divine will, embodying virtues such as love, compassion, and humility. Theosis thus emphasizes not just the salvation of the soul but the transformation of the entire person, encompassing body, mind, and spirit.

        ii. From a psychological standpoint, theosis aligns with theories of self-actualization and transcendence. Psychologist Abraham Maslow, in his hierarchy of needs, proposes that self-actualization represents the pinnacle of human development, where individuals strive to realize their full potential and achieve a sense of fulfillment.[12] Similarly, theosis can be seen as the highest form of self-actualization, where individuals seek to transcend their ego-driven desires and align themselves with divine purposes.

iii. Theosis promotes holistic well-being by emphasizing the interconnectedness of body, mind, and spirit. Just as physical exercise is essential for bodily health and intellectual stimulation is crucial for mental well-being, spiritual practices such as prayer, meditation, and contemplation are vital for nurturing the spirit. Theosis encourages individuals to cultivate these spiritual disciplines, recognizing that true flourishing comes from the integration of all aspects of the self.

iv. Theosis fosters a sense of community and interconnectedness. In the Christian tradition, the journey towards union with God is not undertaken in isolation but within the context of the church, the body of Christ. This communal aspect of theosis underscores the importance of relationships and mutual support in personal development and spiritual growth. By participating in the life of the church, individuals are nourished by the sacraments, the Scriptures, and the fellowship of believers, all of which contribute to their holistic well-being.

v. Theosis offers a profound framework for personal development and well-being, acknowledging the interconnectedness of body, mind, and spirit. Rooted in theological depth and psychological insight, theosis invites individuals to embark on a transformative journey towards union with the divine, where true flourishing is found in the integration of all aspects of the self and the nurturing of relationships within a supportive community.

b. Believers are encouraged to prioritize self-care, emotional health, and spiritual flourishing, recognizing that their well-being is intimately connected to their relationship with God and their participation in the divine life. At the heart of the statement lies a profound understanding of the interconnectedness between

---

12. Maslow, *Motivation*.

the well-being of individuals and their spiritual journey. Let's delve into each component:

i. *Self-Care*: This involves attending to one's physical, emotional, and mental needs. It recognizes that humans are holistic beings and that neglecting any aspect of oneself can hinder overall well-being. In a theological context, self-care can be seen as stewardship of the body and mind, recognizing them as gifts from God. Just as one would care for a precious gift, believers are called to nurture their bodies and minds to fulfill their potential in serving God and others.

ii. *Emotional Health*: Emotions are integral to human experience, and acknowledging and processing them is essential for emotional health. Christianity affirms the validity of emotions while also providing frameworks for understanding and navigating them. For example, the Psalms are replete with expressions of various emotions, demonstrating that it is acceptable to bring all feelings before God. Prioritizing emotional health involves cultivating emotional intelligence, practicing empathy, and seeking support when needed.

iii. *Spiritual Flourishing*: This concept encompasses growth, maturity, and vitality in one's spiritual life. It's about moving beyond mere adherence to religious practices to experiencing a deep and transformative relationship with the divine. Spiritual flourishing involves practices such as prayer, meditation, study of Scriptures, participation in religious rituals, and engagement with a faith community. It's not merely about accumulating knowledge or performing rituals but experiencing the presence and love of God in one's life.

iv. *Relationship with God*: At the core of Christianity is the belief in a personal relationship with God through Jesus Christ. This relationship is dynamic and transformative, influencing every aspect of a believer's life. Prioritizing self-care and emotional health is not self-centered but rather a recognition that a healthy relationship with oneself is essential for a healthy relationship with God. As Jesus taught, loving one's neighbor as oneself presupposes a healthy self-love.

v. *Participation in the Divine Life*: In Christian theology, believers are called to participate in the divine life through union with Christ. This participation involves sharing in God's love, grace, and mission in the world. It's not merely about individual salvation but also about being agents of God's kingdom on earth. Prioritizing self-care and emotional health enables believers to more fully participate in this divine life, as they are better equipped to love God and others authentically.

The theological reflection on this statement underscores the understanding that God desires wholeness and flourishing for his people. Prioritizing self-care, emotional health, and spiritual flourishing is not antithetical to the Christian life but rather an integral part of it. By nurturing themselves, believers are better able to fulfill their calling to love God and neighbor and thereby participate more fully in the divine life and advance God's kingdom on earth.

c. Practices such as mindfulness, gratitude, and forgiveness can support believers in their journey towards union with God, fostering inner peace, resilience, and joy. When explored within the context of various religious traditions, these practices serve as pathways toward deeper union with the divine, fostering inner peace, resilience, and joy.

i. Mindfulness, rooted in traditions such as Buddhism and various contemplative practices within Christianity, involves paying deliberate attention to the present moment without judgment. From a theological perspective, mindfulness enables believers to cultivate a deeper awareness of the presence of God in their daily lives. By quieting the mind and focusing on the present moment, individuals can become more attuned to the subtle movements of the Spirit and experience a profound sense of connection with the divine. This heightened awareness can lead to a deeper understanding of one's purpose and place within the cosmos, fostering a sense of inner peace and contentment that transcends worldly concerns.[13]

---

13. Mindfulness and spiritual contemplation enable believers to transcend worldly concerns and temporary distractions. By centering their thoughts on God and his

ii. Practicing Gratitude, encouraged in nearly every religious tradition, involves cultivating a thankful disposition towards life and its myriad blessings. From a theological standpoint, gratitude is an acknowledgment of God's abundant grace and provision. By consciously acknowledging and appreciating the gifts that surround them, believers can develop a sense of humility and awe in the face of divine generosity. This attitude of gratitude not only deepens one's relationship with God but also fosters a sense of inner joy and contentment, even in the midst of life's challenges. Moreover, studies have shown that practicing gratitude can have tangible psychological benefits, such as increased happiness and resilience, further reinforcing its importance in the spiritual journey.[14]

iii. Forgiveness is also a central practice in many religious teachings; it involves letting go of resentment and releasing the desire for vengeance. From a theological perspective, forgiveness reflects the divine attribute of mercy and offers believers a pathway towards reconciliation and healing. By extending forgiveness to others and ourselves, individuals participate in the redemptive work of God, breaking the cycle of hurt and resentment and fostering inner peace and freedom. Moreover, forgiveness enables believers to experience the transformative power of grace, allowing them to transcend the limitations of ego and embrace a deeper sense of interconnectedness with all creation.[15]

Practices such as mindfulness, gratitude, and forgiveness are not merely psychological exercises but profound spiritual disciplines that can support believers in their journey towards

---

eternal truths, individuals gain perspective on life's transient nature and prioritize spiritual growth and relational depth over material pursuits (Matt 6:33).

14. Gratitude fosters a sense of inner joy and contentment regardless of external circumstances (Phil 4:4–7). When individuals focus on what they are grateful for, they shift their perspective from scarcity to abundance, from problems to blessings. This mindset cultivates a positive outlook on life and helps maintain emotional resilience amidst life's challenges (Ps 16:11).

15. Forgiveness is integral to spiritual growth and witness. It challenges believers to live out the gospel message of reconciliation and forgiveness (2 Cor 5:18–20). By forgiving others, believers demonstrate the power of God's grace to transform hearts and lives, drawing others closer to him through acts of mercy and compassion.

union with God. By cultivating these virtues, individuals can deepen their awareness of the divine presence, cultivate a thankful disposition towards life, and experience the transformative power of grace. In doing so, they can foster inner peace, resilience, and joy that emanate from a profound sense of union with the divine.

5. **Hope and Meaning in Times of Adversity**

a. Theosis offers hope and meaning in times of adversity, reminding believers that their struggles and sufferings have redemptive significance within the larger narrative of salvation. This union is not one of absorption or annihilation of the individual but is rather a transformative journey towards likeness to God, where human beings are enabled to reflect the divine image more fully.

In times of adversity, theosis offers believers a profound source of hope and meaning. Central to this perspective is the understanding that human suffering and struggles can be infused with redemptive significance. Rather than viewing adversity solely through a lens of pain and despair, believers are encouraged to see it as a pathway towards deeper communion with God.

The idea of redemptive suffering is deeply rooted in Christian theology, particularly in the understanding of Christ's salvific work on the cross. Through his own suffering and death, Christ offers a model for believers to follow, demonstrating that suffering can be imbued with meaning and transformative power. Just as Christ's sacrifice brought about redemption for humanity, believers are invited to participate in this redemptive process through their own experiences of suffering.

Within the framework of theosis, adversity becomes a means through which individuals can grow in virtue, deepen their trust in God, and become more fully aligned with the divine will. Rather than being seen as obstacles to be avoided or overcome, struggles and sufferings are embraced as opportunities for spiritual growth and purification.[16] This perspective

---

16. Adversity challenges individuals to deepen their trust in God's providence and faithfulness. By relying on God's grace and guidance, believers learn to surrender their own plans and desires to his divine will. This trust grows as they experience God's presence and sustaining power amidst life's challenges, fostering a deeper intimacy with him.

challenges believers to reframe their understanding of suffering, recognizing it not as a sign of divine abandonment but as a pathway towards deeper intimacy with God.

The concept of theosis underscores the interconnectedness of individual salvation within the larger narrative of God's plan for humanity. Believers are invited to see their own struggles and sufferings as part of a larger story of redemption, where even the most challenging circumstances can contribute to the fulfillment of God's purposes. In this way, theosis offers believers a sense of purpose and hope amidst adversity, reminding them that their experiences are woven into the fabric of God's redemptive work in the world.

Theosis provides a theological framework through which believers can find hope and meaning in times of adversity. By viewing suffering as a pathway towards deeper communion with God and participation in the divine nature, believers are able to embrace their struggles with a sense of purpose and with trust in God's redemptive plan.

b. Believers can find comfort and strength in the assurance that God is working in and through their circumstances to bring about their ultimate transformation and union with him.

   i. *Divine Providence*: Many theological frameworks adhere to the concept of divine providence, which suggests that God is actively involved in the unfolding of events in the world. This belief is foundational to the idea that even in the midst of trials and challenges, believers can trust that God is at work, orchestrating events for their ultimate good (Rom 8:28).

   ii. *Suffering and Redemption*: Central to many faith traditions is the notion of redemptive suffering, the idea that suffering can have meaning and purpose within the context of a larger divine plan. In Christianity, for example, the suffering of Christ is seen as redemptive, bringing about salvation for humanity. Similarly, believers may see their own suffering as a means of participating in the redemptive work of God.

   iii. *Transformation and Sanctification*: Believers often understand their journey through life as a process of transformation and sanctification, becoming more like God in character and virtue. The apostle Paul frequently speaks of this process in his letters, describing believers as being "transformed into [God's] likeness with ever-increasing glory" (2 Cor 3:18 NKJV). In this view, the trials and challenges faced by believers are seen as opportunities for growth and refinement.

iv. *Union with God*: The ultimate goal of many religious and spiritual traditions is union with the divine. Whether it is described as union with God, enlightenment, or salvation, believers long for a deep and intimate connection with the transcendent. The assurance that God is working in and through their circumstances to bring about this union provides comfort and hope in the midst of life's difficulties.

v. *Faith and Trust*: Believing in God's providence and redemptive power requires a deep sense of faith and trust. It means surrendering control and submitting to God's will, even when it may be difficult to understand or accept. This act of faith is itself transformative, shaping the believer's perspective and character.

The belief that God is working in and through our circumstances for our ultimate transformation and union with him is a source of profound comfort and strength for believers.[17] It provides a framework for understanding suffering, challenges, and trials in the context of a larger divine plan, and it inspires hope for a future characterized by deep communion with the divine.

c. The concept of theosis inspires believers to persevere in faith, trusting that God's grace is sufficient to sustain them through life's challenges and trials. This journey of theosis is not without its challenges. Life is fraught with trials, suffering, and temptations that can derail our spiritual growth. However, the promise of theosis gives believers hope and helps them to persevere in the face of these challenges. They trust that God's grace is sufficient

---

17. Believers find hope in the belief that God's ultimate purpose is our union with him in eternity. The trials and tribulations of this life are seen in the context of preparing us for the glory that awaits us in heaven (2 Cor 4:17–18). This eternal perspective encourages believers to persevere with faith and endurance, knowing that their present sufferings are temporary and that an eternal reward awaits them (Rom 8:18).

to sustain them through every trial, empowering them to overcome sin and grow in holiness.

Theosis reminds believers that their ultimate identity and destiny lie in union with God. As they journey toward greater likeness to Christ, they are drawn ever closer to the divine source of all love, goodness, and perfection. This union with God brings fulfillment and joy that surpasses any earthly pleasure or achievement.

Theological reflection on theosis also has profound implications for our understanding of salvation. It moves beyond a purely legal or forensic framework, in which salvation is seen primarily as the forgiveness of sins and the imputation of Christ's righteousness. Instead, theosis emphasizes the transformative work of the Holy Spirit within the believer, leading to true spiritual renewal and union with God.

The concept of theosis inspires believers to persevere in faith by offering a vision of salvation as union with God and participation in his divine life. It gives them hope and strength to endure life's challenges, trusting in the sufficiency of God's grace to sustain them on their journey toward greater likeness to Christ.[18]

The concept of theosis continues to be relevant in contemporary Christian spirituality and ethics, offering believers a transformative vision of union with God and guiding them in their pursuit of holiness, ethical living, interfaith dialogue, personal development, and resilience in the face of adversity. By embracing theosis as a guiding principle in their lives, believers can experience deeper intimacy with God and participate more fully in his redemptive work in the world.

Relevance in Daily Life

The concept of theosis—the process of becoming one with God or being divinized—is profoundly relevant in contemporary Christian spirituality

---

18. Believers who are grounded in theosis trust in the sufficiency of God's grace to transform their lives. They understand that their efforts in spiritual disciplines and acts of obedience are empowered by God's Spirit working within them (Phil 2:13). This trust fosters humility and dependence on God, acknowledging that true transformation comes from his grace and not from their efforts alone.

and ethics. It offers a transformative vision that can deeply impact how believers live their daily lives and engage with the world. Here's how theosis shapes modern Christian spirituality and moral practices:

1. *Pathway to Holiness and Personal Transformation*: Practicing theosis through daily spiritual disciplines helps believers maintain focus on their higher calling. For instance, setting aside time for prayer and reflection can guide decision making, foster resilience in times of adversity, and promote a deeper sense of connection with God. In practical terms, this might look like a commitment to ethical behavior in one's career, fostering empathy in personal relationships, or maintaining a sense of peace amidst life's challenges.

2. *Development of Virtues*: By embodying virtues such as compassion and justice, Christians can influence their communities positively. This could manifest in acts of kindness, advocacy for social justice, or efforts to support and uplift others. Theosis thus inspires believers to be agents of change, promoting ethical behavior and contributing to the common good.

3. *Ethical Living and Social Responsibility*: Christians guided by theosis might engage in community service, support charitable causes, or practice sustainable living. These actions reflect a commitment to living out divine principles in practical ways, such as advocating for marginalized groups or contributing to environmental conservation efforts.

4. *Enhancing Interfaith Dialogue*: In practice, this might involve participating in interfaith initiatives or dialogues or promoting mutual respect and collaboration on social issues. Embracing theosis can help believers approach interfaith interactions with openness and a commitment to shared values, fostering greater harmony and cooperation across different religious traditions.

5. *Resilience and Hope*: In facing personal or communal difficulties, Christians inspired by theosis can draw strength from their faith, seeing challenges as part of their journey towards greater holiness. This mindset helps them persevere, maintain hope, and find purpose in their trials, leading to a more profound and resilient spiritual life.

The concept of theosis remains a vital and dynamic aspect of contemporary Christian spirituality. It offers a framework for personal transformation, ethical living, and social responsibility, guiding believers in their journey towards holiness and divine union. By integrating the principles of theosis into their daily lives, Christians can experience deeper intimacy with God, contribute positively to their communities, and navigate life's challenges with greater resilience and purpose.

Chapter 10

Theosis in Teilhard de Chardin's Thought

TEILHARD DE CHARDIN WAS a French Jesuit priest, paleontologist, and philosopher who lived from 1881 to 1955. He is best known for his integrated approach to science and spirituality, often referred to as "Theology of Evolution" or "Cosmic Christology."[1] His thought was deeply influenced by his dual interests in science and theology, and he sought to bridge the gap between these seemingly disparate fields.

Teilhard de Chardin's integrative approach to science and spirituality continues to inspire thinkers who seek to reconcile scientific understanding with religious faith. His vision of a universe evolving towards greater complexity, consciousness, and unity remains a powerful and thought-provoking perspective in contemporary discussions of cosmology, evolution, and the relationship between science and religion. I will describe some key aspects of Teilhard de Chardin's thought.

1. **Evolutionary Perspective**

    Teilhard accepted the scientific theory of evolution and saw it not only as a biological process but also as a spiritual one. He believed that evolution is not merely a random process but a directed

---

1. Teilhard de Chardin, *Science and Christ*. Teilhard de Chardin's scientific contributions were significant, particularly in the field of paleontology. He participated in important excavations, most notably in China, where he discovered important fossil remains. His scientific work informed his broader understanding of evolution and the development of life on earth.

movement towards greater complexity and consciousness, ultimately leading towards a point of convergence, or the "Omega Point."[2] His approach can be summarized in several key points:

a. *Acceptance of Evolution*: Teilhard fully embraced the theory of evolution as proposed by Charles Darwin and later refined by modern evolutionary biology. He saw evolution not just as a biological process affecting species over time but as a cosmic principle shaping the entire universe towards greater complexity and consciousness.

b. *Nonrandom Direction:* Unlike some interpretations of evolution as a purely random and undirected process, Teilhard believed that evolution has a purpose and directionality. He saw it as a movement towards increasing complexity, organization, and ultimately towards greater consciousness. This directionality implies a teleological aspect to evolution—a movement towards a specific goal or endpoint.

c. *Spiritual Dimension*: One of the most distinctive aspects of Teilhard's thought is his incorporation of spirituality into the evolutionary process. He viewed evolution as not only a physical unfolding but also a spiritual journey. According to Teilhard, the universe is not just a collection of inert matter evolving by chance; rather, it is imbued with a spiritual energy that drives it towards higher levels of consciousness and unity.

d. *Omega Point*: Central to Teilhard's evolutionary perspective is the concept of the Omega Point. He posited that evolution is converging towards a final point of unity and culmination—a state of maximum complexity and consciousness where all individuals and the cosmos are united with the divine. The Omega Point represents the ultimate goal towards which the evolutionary process is oriented.

---

2. Teilhard de Chardin viewed evolution as a dynamic process guided by a divine principle toward a convergence. He termed the convergence the "Omega Point." Teilhard de Chardin used the term "Christic" to refer to the divine force or energy, which, in his philosophy, is driving creation toward increasing complexity and consciousness, leading to the "Omega Point." Therefore he went beyond the purely biological aspects to propose that evolution is a spiritual journey towards greater complexity and consciousness (1 Cor 15:46). See Teilhard de Chardin, *Divine Milieu* and *Phenomenon of Man*.

e. *Christic Principle*: Teilhard interpreted the Omega Point not only as a cosmic convergence but also as the manifestation of the Christic principle. For him, Christ is both the culmination and fulfillment of cosmic evolution, representing the ultimate unity and coherence that draws all creation toward itself. Teilhard's Christology is unique in that it integrates Christ with the evolutionary process, viewing the Christic principle as the divine force that guides and unites creation, ultimately leading all things toward the Omega Point.[3]

f. *Implications for Humanity*: Teilhard's evolutionary perspective has profound implications for understanding humanity's place in the cosmos. It suggests that humans are not just a random occurrence in evolution but play a significant role in the universe's spiritual journey towards the Omega Point. As conscious beings capable of self-reflection and spiritual growth, humans contribute to the evolution of consciousness and the realization of unity in the cosmos.

This integrative vision of Teilhard de Chardin has indeed become a profound rearticulation of how science harmonizes with spirituality. His work acts as a challenge to transcend the false duality so often positioned between those realms and creates an invitation for us to embrace reality in all its forms. Teilhard challenges a purely mechanical and meaningless universe, advocating for a teleological (purpose-driven) cosmos that is spiritually significant and intrinsically valuable. He proposes a vision of the universe that is evolving toward greater complexity and consciousness, with a definitive goal or end point, which he calls the Omega Point. This reflects his belief in a universe that is meaning oriented and guided by divine purpose rather than being random or mechanistic.[4]

Through this epic evolutionary lens, Teilhard imbues humanity with a new planetary mission. We are not just spectators but players taking part in the cosmic awakening. By adopting such a vantage point, we lend our many forms of agency enormous consequence—every one of us playing one or more parts in helping to shape the noosphere and move toward the Omega Point. Teilhard de Chardin's focus on unity and interconnectedness—which resonates

3. Teilhard de Chardin, *Phenomenon of Man*.
4. Teilhard de Chardin, *Divine Milieu* and *Phenomenon of Man*.

strongly with contemporary ecological and systemic thinking—remains relevant even for those who may not fully accept his ideas universally. This vision is encapsulated in his most famous pronouncement regarding the noosphere, which, while having evolved into the modern global network of communication and collective intelligence, reflects Teilhard's concept of the growing complexity of human consciousness. His insights on complexity scaling and his framework for understanding human cognitive-spiritual evolution continue to offer valuable perspectives in current discussions about the future of humanity and the trajectory of human evolution.

In increasing the emphasis on matter as spiritual and of evolution itself as sacred, Teilhard's thought provides a powerful basis for stewarding our planetary environment. It motivates us to view caring for the earth not simply as a pragmatic matter but also as an ethical one.

Teilhard de Chardin's evolutionary thinking provides a rich framework that could offer insights into different contemporary challenges. His thought offers a mission, which inspires hope, encourages unity, and leads to responsible action in rapidly changing times. This mission encourages understanding of the social process as a human journey through the universe, which moves towards consciousness and unity. Teilhard de Chardin's thought continues to offer valuable insights for our contemporary age, particularly in guiding the understanding of the interconnectedness of humanity and the cosmos. His vision of evolution, emphasizing unity and the spiritual direction of progress, provides a framework for addressing the complexities of global relationships and fostering greater harmony on a global scale.

2. Omega Point

Central to Teilhard's thought is the concept of the Omega Point, which he described as the ultimate goal of evolution. This point represents a state of maximum complexity and consciousness, where all individuals and the entire cosmos are drawn into a transcendent unity with God. It's a convergence of spiritual and material evolution towards unity and completion.[5]

---

5. Central to Teilhard's thought is the concept of the Omega Point, which he described as the ultimate aim of evolution—a point of convergence where all creation, both spiritual and material, reaches its fulfillment in Christ (Col 1:19–20). This idea

a. *Ultimate Goal of Evolution*: According to Teilhard, the Omega Point represents the ultimate aim and culmination of the evolutionary process. It is not merely a theoretical endpoint but a real, teleological goal towards which the universe is progressing. This goal is characterized by maximum complexity and consciousness, reflecting a state of heightened spiritual and material integration.

b. *Maximum Complexity*: Teilhard envisions the Omega Point as a state where complexity reaches its zenith. This complexity encompasses both physical structures (such as biological organisms and ecosystems) and nonphysical structures (such as consciousness and cultural developments). The universe evolves from simpler forms towards increasingly intricate and interconnected systems, culminating in a state of profound unity and coherence.

c. *Convergence of Individuals and Cosmos*: At the Omega Point, Teilhard posits a convergence where all individuals and elements of the cosmos are unified. This unity transcends individuality and diversity, forming a harmonious whole where distinctions between beings dissolve into a profound interconnectedness. It's a vision of cosmic unity where the diversity and multiplicity of creation find their ultimate purpose and fulfillment.[6]

d. *Transcendent Unity with God*: Teilhard's concept of the Omega Point is deeply theological. He sees this state of unity as not only a harmonization of the cosmos but also as a union with God. This is a transcendent unity where the divine presence permeates and integrates all aspects of creation, bringing a profound sense of fulfillment and completeness to the universe.

3. **Christogenesis**

Teilhard proposed the idea of "Christogenesis," meaning the ongoing process of the universe becoming increasingly filled with the presence of Christ. For him, Christ is not only a historical figure but

---

suggests that evolution is progressing towards a state of unity and integration at a cosmic scale, where all elements of creation come together in Christ.

6. Teilhard de Chardin, *Phenomenon of Man*.

also the principle of unity and coherence driving the evolutionary process towards the Omega Point.[7]

a. *Meaning*: Christogenesis, as proposed by Teilhard, refers to the ongoing process through which the universe becomes increasingly imbued with the presence and influence of Christ. It's not merely a static concept but a dynamic principle that informs Teilhard's understanding of evolution and spiritual development.

b. *Christ as Principle of Unity*: For Teilhard, Christ is not only a historical figure but also a cosmic principle of unity and coherence. Christ serves as the driving force behind the evolutionary process, guiding it towards greater complexity, consciousness, and unity. In this sense, Christogenesis depicts Christ as the underlying energy that shapes the universe towards its ultimate fulfillment in the Omega Point.

c. *Integration of Evolution and Christology*: Teilhard's Christogenesis bridges the gap between scientific understanding (evolution) and theological belief (Christology). It proposes that the evolutionary journey of the cosmos is not separate from but intimately connected with the divine plan embodied in Christ. This integration challenges the dichotomy often perceived between scientific explanations of the universe and religious interpretations of divine purpose.

d. *Cosmic and Personal Dimension*: Christogenesis encompasses both the cosmic evolution of the universe and the personal spiritual growth of individuals. It suggests that as the universe evolves towards greater unity with Christ, individuals too are invited to participate in this process through their spiritual awakening and alignment with Christ's principles of love, unity, and compassion.

e. *Teleological Implications*: Similar to Teilhard's concept of the Omega Point, Christogenesis introduces a teleological perspective into the evolutionary narrative. It implies that there is a purposeful direction towards which the universe is evolving—a state where Christ's presence and influence permeate all aspects

---

7. Teilhard de Chardin, *Divine Milieu*. "Christogenesis" suggests that the presence of Christ permeates and animates the entire cosmos. It signifies an ongoing process where the universe becomes increasingly filled with the divine presence and infused with Christ's transformative energy (Eph 1:10).

of creation. This perspective invites a deeper contemplation of the meaning and significance of human existence within the larger cosmic order.

4. **Noosphere**

Teilhard coined the term "noosphere" to describe the sphere of human thought, encompassing all human knowledge, culture, and spirituality. He saw the development of the noosphere as a critical stage in the evolution of the earth, where human consciousness becomes increasingly interconnected and aware of its spiritual dimensions.[8]

   a. *Meaning*: The term "noosphere" derives from the Greek words "nous," or mind, and "sphere," indicating a sphere or layer of human thought. Teilhard coined this term to describe a collective sphere of human consciousness encompassing all human knowledge, culture, and spirituality. Unlike the biosphere (the sphere of biological life) and the geosphere (the sphere of inanimate matter), the noosphere is characterized by the realm of human cognition and cultural development.

   b. *Evolutionary Context*: Teilhard viewed the development of the noosphere as a critical stage in earth's evolution, following the formation and development of the biosphere. He saw it as a natural progression in which human consciousness evolves towards increasing complexity and interconnectedness. The emergence of the noosphere represents a qualitative leap in evolution, where human thought and culture play a transformative role in shaping the planet's future.

   c. *Interconnectedness and Awareness*: Central to Teilhard's concept is the idea that as the noosphere develops, human consciousness becomes more interconnected. This interconnectedness transcends geographical and cultural boundaries, fostering a global awareness of humanity's shared destiny and responsibilities. Teilhard believed that this heightened awareness would lead

---

8. Teilhard de Chardin, *Phenomenon of Man*. Teilhard saw the development of the noosphere as inherently tied to humanity's spiritual evolution. As human consciousness expands and becomes more interconnected globally, Teilhard believed that people would increasingly recognize and explore their spiritual dimensions, seeking deeper meaning and purpose beyond material existence (Eph 1:17–18).

to a deeper understanding of spiritual dimensions and a sense of unity among individuals and societies.[9]

d. *Spiritual Dimensions*: While grounded in scientific observations and evolutionary theory, Teilhard's concept of the noosphere also carries profound spiritual implications. He viewed the noosphere as a realm where spiritual values, ethical principles, and religious insights can converge and enrich human understanding. In this sense, the development of the noosphere is not just a cognitive evolution but also a spiritual awakening, where humanity collectively engages with questions of meaning, purpose, and transcendence.[10]

e. *Technological and Cultural Impact*: Teilhard recognized that the development of the noosphere is influenced by technological advancements and cultural innovations. Technologies such as communication networks, global transportation, and information systems contribute to the interconnectedness of human thought and the acceleration of cultural exchange. Cultural developments, including art, literature, philosophy, and religion, shape the collective consciousness of the noosphere and contribute to its evolution.

5. **Cosmic Vision**

Teilhard had a deeply mystical vision of the cosmos as a dynamic whole, where everything is interconnected and evolving towards greater unity and consciousness. His vision was optimistic, seeing evolution as a process that leads to greater complexity, diversity, and ultimately to union with the divine.[11]

a. *Dynamic Wholeness*: Teilhard perceived the cosmos not as a collection of disparate elements but as a dynamic whole. He saw everything in the universe—from galaxies and stars to planets and living organisms—as interconnected and interdependent. This interconnectedness implies a unity that transcends

---

9. Teilhard de Chardin, *Future of Man*.
10. Teilhard de Chardin, *Divine Milieu*.
11. In Teilhard's theology, Christogenesis implies a vision of cosmic redemption whereby the entire created order, including humanity, participates in the redemptive work of Christ. This cosmic perspective emphasizes the interconnectedness of all created things and underscores the ultimate purpose of creation in glorifying God (Ps 148:1–5). See Teilhard de Chardin, *Divine Milieu*; King, *Spirit of Fire*.

individual entities, suggesting a cosmic symphony of unfolding complexity and harmony.

b. *Evolutionary Process*: Central to Teilhard's cosmic vision is his understanding of evolution as more than a biological process; it's a cosmic principle guiding the universe towards greater complexity and consciousness. Evolution, for Teilhard, is not random but directed towards a purpose—the development of consciousness and the eventual union with the divine. This perspective challenges deterministic views of evolution and emphasizes the creative unfolding of life and consciousness.

c. *Optimism and Purpose*: Teilhard's cosmic vision is infused with optimism. He saw evolution as a progressive journey towards higher states of complexity, diversity, and ultimately towards unity with the divine. This optimism stems from his belief that, despite the challenges and apparent chaos in the world, there is an underlying order and purpose guiding the evolutionary process towards a greater spiritual fulfillment.

d. *Union with the Divine*: At the heart of Teilhard's cosmic vision is the concept of union with the divine. He envisioned evolution as a pathway leading towards a final convergence or Omega Point—a state of complete unity and coherence where the cosmos and all its inhabitants are united with God. This union represents the fulfillment of the universe's evolutionary journey, where individual consciousnesses merge into a collective consciousness in harmony with the divine presence.

6. **Criticism and Controversy**

Teilhard's ideas were controversial within the Catholic Church during his lifetime, partly due to their novelty and the perceived challenge they posed to traditional theology. His works were initially suppressed by the church, but over time, his ideas gained more acceptance and influenced theological and philosophical discourse, especially in the context of science and religion dialogue.[12]

---

12. Haught, *Teilhard de Chardin*.

Spiritual Fulfillment and God's Plan for Creation

Teilhard de Chardin's thought on spiritual fulfillment and God's plan for creation underscores the idea of evolution as a purposeful journey towards unity with God. His concept of the Omega Point represents the culmination of this journey, where the entire cosmos achieves spiritual and cosmic fulfillment in God's loving embrace.

a. *Integration of Evolution and Theology*: Teilhard's Omega Point concept bridges the gap between scientific understanding and theological reflection. He proposes that evolution is not merely a random or purposeless process but a journey guided by divine purpose towards greater complexity, consciousness, and unity. The Omega Point represents the culmination of this evolutionary journey—a state where the entire cosmos, including humanity, reaches its fullest potential in union with God.

b. *Teleological Perspective*: Unlike traditional evolutionary views that often focus solely on physical or biological development, Teilhard introduces a teleological perspective. He sees evolution as progressing towards a definite end—the Omega Point—where all creation is harmonized and unified in God. This perspective underscores a deeper purpose to existence beyond material or temporal considerations, emphasizing the spiritual dimension of evolution.

c. *Journey Towards Spiritual Awareness*: Teilhard envisions evolution as a process that leads humanity towards deeper spiritual awareness and consciousness. This journey involves not only intellectual and moral development but also a transformation of the human spirit towards greater love, compassion, and unity. The Omega Point, therefore, signifies the culmination of humanity's spiritual quest—a state where individuals and the entire cosmos are fully aware of and aligned with God's loving presence.

d. *Fulfillment of Human and Cosmic Destiny*: The Omega Point represents the fulfillment of both human and cosmic destinies in God's loving embrace. It symbolizes the ultimate realization of God's plan for creation, where all aspects of existence—physical, spiritual, and cosmic—are brought into perfect unity and harmony. This fulfillment transcends individual lives and extends to the entire cosmos, affirming Teilhard's vision of a cosmic Christ who draws all creation towards divine communion.

Theosis and Teilhard's Vision: A Theological Reflection

I will outline the connection between Teilhard de Chardin's ideas and the concept of theosis by examining how theosis relates to his notions of the noosphere, Christogenesis, and the integration of theosis with Christogenesis. This will include exploring his cosmic vision and the concept of the Omega Point and their implications for Christology.

1. **Reflection on Theosis and Teilhard's Vision**

    a. *Complementary Perspectives*: Theosis and Teilhard's Omega Point offer complementary perspectives on the journey towards unity with God. While rooted in different theological traditions (Eastern Christian theology, on one hand, and Catholic theology and evolutionary thought, on the other), both concepts emphasize the transformative process of becoming like God and participating in divine life.

    b. *Integration of Evolution and Divine Purpose*: Teilhard's integration of evolutionary theory with theological insights enriches the understanding of theosis by placing it within the context of cosmic evolution. It suggests that the evolutionary journey itself is guided by divine purpose towards a state of cosmic and spiritual fulfillment, where theosis unfolds within the unfolding cosmos.

    c. *Ethical Implications*: Theosis and Teilhard's Omega Point invite ethical reflection on how humans are called to participate in the ongoing transformation towards unity with God. Both emphasize the importance of moral and spiritual growth, cooperation with divine grace, and active engagement in promoting justice, compassion, and harmony in the world.

In Eastern Orthodox theology, theosis involves becoming more like God through divine grace. This requires ongoing moral refinement and spiritual maturity, encouraging believers to adopt virtues such as love, humility, and self-control. The journey towards theosis is not just about personal piety but about growing into a fuller expression of divine goodness in all aspects of life. Teilhard de Chardin's Omega Point envisions the ultimate convergence of all creation in Christ, which implies a continuous process of spiritual evolution. Individuals and societies are called to develop in alignment with this divine trajectory, fostering growth that mirrors the cosmic movement towards unity and harmony.

2. **Reflection on the Noosphere**

    a. *Unity in Diversity*: The concept of the noosphere promotes a vision of unity in diversity, where diverse cultures, beliefs, and ideas contribute to a richer tapestry of human thought and experience. It challenges narrow views of progress and encourages dialogue and collaboration across different perspectives, fostering mutual understanding and respect.

    b. *Responsibility and Stewardship*: Teilhard's concept of the noosphere underscores humanity's responsibility as stewards of the earth and custodians of its evolutionary trajectory. It calls for ethical engagement with technological advancements and cultural developments to ensure that they contribute positively to the flourishing of human consciousness and the sustainability of the planet.

    c. *Hope and Vision*: The idea of the noosphere offers a hopeful vision of human potential and collective evolution. It suggests that through conscious reflection, creativity, and collaboration, humanity can transcend current challenges and contribute to a more harmonious and spiritually aware global community.

    d. *Integration of Science and Spirituality*: By introducing the concept of the noosphere, Teilhard bridges the gap between scientific inquiry and spiritual exploration. He demonstrates that scientific understanding of human cognition and cultural development can coexist with spiritual insights into the nature of consciousness and the interconnectedness of all life.

    Teilhard de Chardin's concept of the noosphere represents a visionary perspective on the evolution of human consciousness and culture. It invites us to consider the profound implications of our interconnectedness and the transformative potential of collective human endeavor in shaping a more unified and spiritually aware future.

3. **Reflection on Christogenesis**

    a. *Cosmic Redemption*: Christogenesis emphasizes the cosmic dimension of redemption, suggesting that Christ's influence extends throughout creation, bringing all aspects of existence into alignment with God's loving purpose.[13] This perspective invites a reevaluation of traditional Christian doctrines in light of cosmic evolution, highlighting the transformative power of Christ's presence in shaping the destiny of the universe.

b. *Integration of Science and Theology*: Teilhard's concept of Christogenesis exemplifies his efforts to integrate scientific discoveries with theological insights. By interpreting evolution as a process infused with Christ's influence, he bridges the gap between empirical observations and spiritual truths, offering a coherent framework for understanding the deeper meaning and purpose of cosmic evolution.

c. *Ethical Implications*: Understanding Christogenesis inspires ethical reflection on humanity's role in contributing to the ongoing process of cosmic transformation towards Christlikeness. It calls for moral responsibility, compassion, and stewardship of the earth, recognizing that our actions have cosmic significance in realizing God's plan for creation.

d. *Hope and Meaning*: Christogenesis provides hope and meaning in a universe that often appears chaotic or indifferent. It suggests that amidst the complexities of evolution, there is an underlying purpose and directionality towards unity in Christ. This vision encourages individuals to participate actively in the unfolding of Christ's influence in the world, fostering a sense of purpose and divine connection in their lives.

Teilhard de Chardin's concept of Christogenesis offers a profound and transformative perspective on the relationship between Christ, evolution, and the cosmos. It invites us to contemplate Christ's ongoing presence and influence in the unfolding story of creation, expanding our understanding of redemption to encompass the entire universe. Christogenesis challenges us to see ourselves as participants in a cosmic journey towards greater unity

---

13. Central to Teilhard's thought is the concept of the "Cosmic Christ," where Christ is understood not only as the historical Jesus but also as the principle of unity and coherence that integrates all of creation. This cosmic dimension of Christology reflects Teilhard's belief in the universal significance of Christ's redemptive work, extending beyond humanity to encompass the entire cosmos. See Teilhard de Chardin, *Phenomenon of Man*.

and consciousness in Christ, inspiring us to live with hope, ethical responsibility, and a deeper sense of spiritual connection with all creation.

4. **Reflection on the Unity of Theosis and Christogenesis**

   a. *Coherence in Divine Plan*: Theosis and Christogenesis together affirm a coherent understanding of God's plan for creation. Theosis focuses on personal and communal transformation towards union with God, while Christogenesis extends this transformation to a cosmic scale, emphasizing Christ's role in guiding all of creation towards its ultimate fulfillment in God.

   b. *Integration of Faith and Life*: Understanding theosis within the context of Christogenesis encourages a holistic integration of faith and life. It invites individuals to discern how their personal spiritual journey contributes to the larger cosmic evolution under Christ's guidance. This integration fosters a sense of purpose, meaning, and responsibility in living out one's faith amidst the complexities of the world.

   c. *Hope Amidst Challenges*: The combined perspective of theosis and Christogenesis offers hope amidst the uncertainties and challenges of life. It reassures believers that God's loving plan is unfolding progressively towards unity and harmony, despite the apparent discord and suffering in the world. This hope inspires perseverance, resilience, and a deeper trust in God's providential care.

Theosis and Christogenesis, when viewed together, provide a profound understanding of God's ongoing work in creation and humanity's role within that divine plan. They offer hope and encouragement by presenting Christ not only as a historical figure but as an active and transformative presence guiding the universe towards unity and fulfillment in God. This combined perspective invites believers to deepen their spiritual journey towards union with God and to participate actively in the cosmic evolution towards greater unity, harmony, and divine communion. It calls for a life of faith, hope, and love rooted in the assurance that God's purpose for creation is being realized under the guidance of Christ's transformative presence.

5. **Reflection on Teilhard's Cosmic Vision**

   a. *Integration of Science and Spirituality*: Teilhard's cosmic vision represents a bold attempt to reconcile scientific understanding with spiritual insight. By viewing evolution as a cosmic journey towards greater unity and consciousness, he demonstrates how scientific observations of the universe's development can harmonize with mystical and theological beliefs about the nature of existence and purpose.

   b. *Challenge to Dualism*: Teilhard challenges dualistic views that separate the physical and spiritual realms. His vision underscores the interconnectedness of all aspects of reality—physical, biological, psychological, and spiritual—suggesting that they are part of a seamless continuum unfolding towards a common destiny.

   c. *Hope and Meaning*: Teilhard's cosmic vision offers hope and meaning in a world often characterized by fragmentation and uncertainty. It invites individuals to see themselves not as isolated beings but as integral parts of a larger cosmic drama—a drama where every action, thought, and relationship contributes to the evolving tapestry of existence towards unity and divine communion.

   d. *Ethical Implications*: Understanding Teilhard's cosmic vision can inspire ethical reflection and action. It emphasizes the responsibility of individuals and societies to contribute positively to the evolution of consciousness and the realization of unity. This includes fostering compassion, justice, and environmental stewardship as integral parts of our participation in the cosmic journey.

   Teilhard de Chardin's cosmic vision presents a profound synthesis of scientific inquiry and spiritual revelation. It invites us to contemplate the universe as a dynamic and interconnected whole evolving towards greater unity, complexity, and consciousness—a vision that holds promise for a deeper understanding of our place in the cosmos and our role in shaping its future.

6. **Reflection on the Omega Point**

   a. *Integration of Science and Spirituality*: Teilhard's concept of the Omega Point bridges the gap between scientific understanding and spiritual insight. It proposes that the evolutionary journey, which science studies through physical and biological processes, is being guided by a deeper spiritual principle towards unity and coherence. This integration challenges the notion of a purely mechanistic universe and invites a holistic understanding where the material and spiritual dimensions are interconnected.

b. *Teleological Perspective*: The idea of the Omega Point introduces a teleological perspective into evolution, suggesting that there is a purposeful direction towards which all of life and existence are moving. This contrasts with some interpretations of evolution that see it as a random or directionless process. Teilhard's teleology implies that there is meaning and significance in the evolutionary journey, culminating in a state of divine fulfillment.

c. *Hope and Meaning*: Teilhard's vision of the Omega Point offers hope and meaning in a world often characterized by complexity, challenges, and uncertainties. It suggests that despite the struggles and conflicts inherent in evolution, there is a transcendent goal towards which humanity and the universe are evolving. This can inspire individuals to see their lives as part of a larger cosmic narrative and to contribute positively towards the realization of unity and harmony.

d. *Implications for Ethics and Human Responsibility*: Understanding the Omega Point challenges humans to consider their ethical responsibilities in the context of a unified and evolving cosmos. It emphasizes the interconnectedness of all life and encourages actions that promote harmony, justice, and the well-being of the planet and its inhabitants. Teilhard's vision invites a sense of stewardship towards creation and a commitment to nurturing the evolution of consciousness towards its fullest potential.

Teilhard de Chardin's concept of the Omega Point offers a visionary and integrative perspective that infuses the evolutionary journey with both spiritual depth and purpose. It encourages us to reflect on the ultimate destiny of the universe as it converges into a unified whole in communion with the divine. This perspective inspires a profound reevaluation of our individual and collective roles within the ongoing cosmic unfolding, urging us to align our actions and values with this grand, divine trajectory.

7. **Reflection on Teilhard's Christology**

    a. *Sacramental Universe*: Teilhard's vision invites us to see the universe as sacramental—a visible sign of God's invisible presence. Christ's permeation of the cosmos suggests that every aspect of creation has the potential to reveal divine glory and participate in God's redemptive plan. This perspective encourages a holistic appreciation of creation's inherent goodness and its role in reflecting God's love and beauty.

    b. *Unity in Diversity*: Teilhard's cosmic Christology emphasizes unity in diversity. It challenges dualistic views that separate the spiritual from the material or the sacred from the secular. Instead, it affirms that Christ's presence unites all dimensions of existence, fostering a deeper sense of interconnectedness and interdependence within creation.

    c. *Ethical Implications*: Understanding Christ's presence in the cosmos inspires ethical reflection and responsibility. It calls us to recognize the sacredness of all life and the interconnectedness of all beings within the cosmic web. This awareness challenges us to care for the earth, promote justice, and cultivate relationships that reflect Christ's love and compassion for all creation.

    d. *Hope and Meaning*: Teilhard's cosmic Christology offers hope and meaning in a world often marked by fragmentation and discord. It assures us that Christ's loving presence permeates even the darkest corners of existence, guiding creation towards unity and fulfillment in God. This vision encourages us to align our lives with God's purposes, trusting that Christ's transformative power can bring healing and reconciliation to a broken world.

Teilhard de Chardin's thought about the existence of Christ permeating all of the cosmos challenges us to see creation as infused with divine presence and purpose. His cosmic Christology invites us to embrace a holistic understanding of reality, where Christ's love and unity encompass the entire universe, guiding evolution towards its ultimate fulfillment in God. This perspective inspires profound reflection on the interconnectedness of all life and calls us to participate actively in God's ongoing work of cosmic and spiritual renewal.

Integrating Christogenesis and Theosis

Integrating Christogenesis with theosis enriches our understanding of how the evolutionary and spiritual dimensions converge in Christian theology. It invites us to see the cosmic and personal dimensions of salvation as interconnected processes leading towards unity in Christ. This integration encourages a holistic view of salvation that encompasses the entire cosmos in its journey towards God.

1. *Unity of Creation and Redemption*: Christogenesis emphasizes the unity of creation and redemption, suggesting that the evolutionary process is not separate from God's salvific plan but an integral part of it. This challenges traditional dichotomies between creation and salvation, proposing instead a seamless narrative where Christ's presence guides and transforms all of creation towards divine fulfillment.[14]

2. *Evolutionary and Cosmic Dimension*: Christogenesis in Teilhard's view extends beyond individual human salvation to encompass the entire cosmos evolving towards union with Christ. This cosmic dimension resonates with the idea of theosis, where all of creation is moving towards participation in the divine life.[15]

3. *Personal Transformation*: Theosis involves the transformation of individuals through grace and spiritual practices, leading to greater conformity to Christ. In Teilhard's framework, this personal transformation aligns with the evolutionary journey towards the Omega Point, where all things are united in Christ.[16]

---

14. Christogenesis posits that the entire cosmos, including the evolutionary development of life, is infused with the presence and purpose of Christ (Col 1:16–17). It emphasizes that creation and redemption are not separate realms but interwoven aspects of God's overarching plan for the universe. In this view, the unfolding of creation through evolutionary processes is understood as participating in the divine drama of redemption.

15. Teilhard's concept of Christogenesis posits that the evolutionary process is not limited to biological development alone but includes the entire cosmos, from the smallest particles to the vast expanses of galaxies (Col 1:16–17). In this view, all of creation is in a state of dynamic movement towards unity and integration in Christ, the Alpha and Omega of creation (Rev 22:13).

16. Teilhard's perspective aligns personal spiritual transformation through theosis with the cosmic evolutionary journey towards the Omega Point. He proposes that as individuals strive for greater conformity to Christ, they participate in and contribute to the overarching process of cosmic evolution towards unity in Christ (Rom 8:21).

4. *Unity in Christ*: Both concepts emphasize unity; Christogenesis sees all creation converging in Christ, while theosis emphasizes unity with God through participation in the divine nature.[17]

5. *Ecological Awareness*: Teilhard's Christogenesis underscores the interconnectedness of all creation, prompting ecological stewardship and care for the earth as part of our journey towards Christ.[18]

6. *Spiritual Growth*: Theosis emphasizes the importance of spiritual disciplines and sacramental life in the Christian journey, fostering personal transformation towards Christlikeness.

    a. *Hope and Transformation*: Christogenesis offers hope and encouragement by presenting Christ not only as a figure of the past but as an active and transformative presence within the ongoing evolution of the universe. It suggests that despite the challenges and complexities of existence, there is a divine purpose unfolding towards unity and harmony under Christ's guidance.

    b. *Ethical and Spiritual Implications*: Understanding Christogenesis can inspire ethical and spiritual reflection among individuals and communities. It invites a deeper commitment to embodying Christ's teachings of love, justice, and reconciliation in personal lives and societal structures. It encourages a holistic approach to spirituality that acknowledges the interconnectedness of all life and the imperative to nurture a world increasingly filled with Christ's presence.

    c. *Dialogue Between Science and Religion*: By integrating Christogenesis with evolutionary theory, Teilhard's thought fosters a fruitful dialogue between science and religion. It demonstrates that scientific understanding of the universe's development can coexist harmoniously with theological interpretations of divine

---

17. The goal of theosis is for believers to become increasingly conformed to the likeness of Christ, reflecting his character and virtues in their lives (Rom 8:29). This transformative process leads to a deepening communion with God and a unity of will and purpose with him, where believers experience union with God's divine nature.

18. Teilhard's Christogenesis bridges the gap between faith and ecological concerns by affirming that our care for the earth is intertwined with our journey towards Christ. This integration challenges Christians to reflect on how their faith informs their relationship with the natural world and motivates them to advocate for environmental justice and sustainability (Isa 24:4–6).

purpose and presence, enriching both perspectives and offering new insights into the nature of reality.

Teilhard de Chardin's concept of Christogenesis presents a compelling vision of the universe evolving towards unity and fulfillment under the guiding influence of Christ. It invites us to explore the dynamic interplay between cosmic evolution and divine presence, encouraging a deeper engagement with the spiritual dimensions of existence and our role within the unfolding cosmic drama.

The main aspects of Christogenesis include:

1. *A Cosmic-Divine Interplay*: It proposes a close link between universal development and God's presence, with divine guidance steering evolution.
2. *Spiritual Dimension*: It emphasizes the spiritual nature of existence alongside the material, viewing spiritual growth as central to cosmic progress.
3. *Humanity's Cosmic Role*: It positions humans as integral to God's universal plan, not mere products of chance.
4. *Science-Spirituality Fusion*: It blends evolutionary science with spiritual concepts, envisioning a universe growing in complexity, unity, and consciousness under divine influence.

While compelling, Christogenesis faces criticism. Some argue it overstates divine involvement in evolution, while others see it as too speculative and lacking empirical support.[19] Despite critiques, Christogenesis remains a provocative theory, challenging us to view our existence and spiritual journey within a broader cosmic framework.

---

19. McDermott, *Teilhard and the Church*.

Chapter 11

Theosis in Social and Environmental Challenges

The concept of theosis, which centers on union with God and participation in the divine life, offers a profound theological framework that can guide and inspire Christian responses to social and environmental challenges. This is especially true when this rich theological and anthropological tradition combines with the newer insights of Teilhard de Chardin, whose thought encompasses heaven, earth, the Christian journey, and how we address challenges to our shared future. Theosis focuses on both union with God and participation in the divine life, leading to an integration of theology and practice. It encourages Christ's followers to reflect the divine and actively engage with current social and environmental issues.

Theosis simply entails that believers should represent the divine in an embodied and participatory way by manifesting to others the goodness, justice, and mercy of God. Such a commitment would mean working for social justice and the rights of those left out, as well as peacemaking activism. And, when believers understand themselves as playing a part in the life of God, they are moved to act for the sake of reflecting that kingdom upon earth. Theosis also promotes a theology that encourages individuals to view themselves as stewards of creation called by God, the Creator of all things and the Provider who sustains life (see Gen 2), calling us to an ecological mission of safeguarding our home planet.

Knowing that they are part of the divine life, believers wish to act in ways that respect and preserve all forms of earthly reality. This means defending sustainable practices, fighting for justice in instances of environmental racism or injustice, and working to manage climate change. The work of communities characterized by theosis is to create a just and compassionate society by loving those around them unconditionally. Knowing themselves to be part of this divine community, their hope is to overcome social and environmental challenges together through God's Spirit within them. This includes volunteering, advocating in support of public policies serving the common good and relationship building across all lines of difference.

The theosis paradigm provides a robust framework for Christian responses to social and ecological predicaments. Because theosis—in stressing union with God and so participation in divine life—impels a reassertion of some communicable properties of God into creaturely transactions. These include serving social justice, promoting ecological stewardship, and enhancing the quality of community life. Christians seeking to live out their faith in the world will find it a great aid in thesis as they attempt to discern what their role might be. This perspective fosters a commitment to addressing social inequalities, protecting the environment, and promoting holistic well-being, all grounded in the vision of living in harmony with God's purposes for creation.[1]

1. **Ethical Imperatives**

   Theosis underscores the ethical imperative for Christians to embody the virtues of love, compassion, justice, and stewardship in their interactions with others and the environment. When considering theosis in relation to the ethical imperative for Christians to embody virtues such as love, compassion, justice, and stewardship, several profound interpretations emerge:

   a. *Love as Divine Union*: At the core of theosis is the idea of union with God through love. Theosis underscores that love is not merely a human emotion but a divine attribute. Therefore, Christians are called to embody love not only in their

---

1. Theosis affirms that the entire cosmos, including the natural world, is created by God and participates in his divine plan (Ps 24:1). This theological perspective challenges Christians to view environmental stewardship not merely as a duty but as a sacred responsibility to care for God's creation, ensuring its sustainability and honoring its intrinsic value (Gen 2:15).

interpersonal relationships but also in their relationship with the entire cosmos, recognizing that all creation is infused with the love of God.

b. *Compassion as Participation in Divine Suffering*: Compassion, understood as suffering with others, takes on a deeper significance in the context of theosis. Just as Christ entered into human suffering to redeem it, Christians are called to participate in the suffering of others, thereby manifesting the compassionate nature of God and contributing to the process of cosmic redemption.

c. *Justice as Divine Harmony*: The pursuit of justice is integral to theosis because it reflects the divine principle of harmony and righteousness. Christians are called to work towards justice not only in human society but also in their relationship with the environment, recognizing that ecological justice is essential for the flourishing of all creation and is reflective of God's desire for shalom, or peace.

d. *Stewardship as Cocreation with God*: Stewardship, understood as responsible caretaking of the earth and its resources, is a central aspect of theosis. Christians are called to recognize their role as cocreators with God and to exercise dominion over the earth in a manner that reflects God's loving and just reign. This entails using resources wisely, promoting sustainability, and advocating for environmental stewardship as an expression of love for God and neighbor.

2. **Reflect the Character of Christ**

Reflecting the character of Christ involves embodying the virtues and principles he exemplified during his earthly ministry. Believers are called to emulate Christ by advocating for the well-being of all people, especially the marginalized and vulnerable, and addressing systemic injustices that perpetuate poverty, oppression, and discrimination.[2]

---

2. Christ's teachings emphasize justice and righteousness, challenging systems of oppression and advocating for fairness and equality (Isa 1:17; Matt 23:23). Christians are called to solidarity in addressing systemic injustices that perpetuate poverty, discrimination, and inequality; they are to strive to transform unjust societal structures (Amos 5:24).

a. *Imitating Christ's Compassion*: Christ's ministry on earth was marked by compassion and solidarity with the marginalized and oppressed. Believers, recognizing their identity as followers of Christ, are compelled to emulate his compassion by advocating for the well-being of those who are marginalized and vulnerable. This imitation of Christ is not only a moral imperative but also a spiritual discipline that deepens one's connection to the divine.

b. *Prophetic Witness Against Injustice*: The call to advocate for the well-being of all people, particularly the marginalized, entails a prophetic witness against systemic injustices. Believers are called to speak truth to power and challenge the structures and systems that perpetuate poverty, oppression, and discrimination. This prophetic witness is grounded in the biblical tradition of justice and righteousness, which calls for the liberation of the oppressed and the establishment of God's kingdom on earth.

c. *Solidarity with the Marginalized*: Believers are called to stand in solidarity with the marginalized and vulnerable, recognizing their inherent dignity and worth as children of God. This solidarity entails actively listening to the voices of the marginalized, amplifying their stories, and advocating for their rights and well-being. It also requires a willingness to confront one's own privilege and complicity in systems of injustice.

d. *Building Kingdom Justice*: Advocating for the well-being of all people, particularly the marginalized, is integral to the mission of building God's kingdom of justice and righteousness on earth. Believers are called to be co-laborers with God in the work of reconciliation and restoration, striving to create a world where all people can flourish and thrive. This work of kingdom justice requires both individual acts of compassion and systemic change that addresses the root causes of poverty, oppression, and discrimination.

3. **Solidarity and Empathy**

Theosis fosters a sense of solidarity and empathy with those who suffer from social and environmental injustices as believers recognize the inherent dignity and worth of every human being and the interconnectedness of all creation. Christians, inspired by their union with God and their participation in his redemptive work, are

THEOSIS IN SOCIAL AND ENVIRONMENTAL CHALLENGES   185

compelled to stand in solidarity with the oppressed, to listen to their voices, and to work alongside them for justice and reconciliation.³

a. *Union with God*: The Christian understanding of salvation emphasizes a transformative union with God, wherein believers become partakers of the divine nature (2 Pet 1:4). This union is not passive but dynamic, involving a participation in God's redemptive work in the world. Through this union, Christians are infused with a deep sense of empathy and solidarity with those who suffer injustice and oppression, mirroring God's own concern for the marginalized.

b. *Listening to the Voices of the Oppressed*: Solidarity with the oppressed requires a willingness to listen attentively to their voices and experiences. In the Christian tradition, God is often portrayed as a compassionate listener who hears the cries of the oppressed and acts on their behalf. Similarly, Christians are called to cultivate a posture of humble listening, acknowledging the dignity and agency of those who have been marginalized and allowing their voices to shape efforts for justice and reconciliation.

c. *Working for Justice and Reconciliation*: Inspired by their participation in God's redemptive work, Christians are compelled to actively engage in the pursuit of justice and reconciliation. This involves not only addressing the symptoms of oppression but also confronting the systemic structures and ideologies that perpetuate injustice. Christians are called to embody the prophetic vision of a world where justice rolls down like waters and righteousness like an ever-flowing stream (Amos 5:24) by working alongside the oppressed to dismantle oppressive systems and build communities of equity and inclusion.

d. *Incarnational Witness*: The Christian ethic of solidarity with the oppressed finds its ultimate expression in the example of Jesus Christ, who identified with the marginalized and confronted the powers of injustice and oppression. Christians are called to embody this incarnational witness, following in the footsteps of

---

3. Christians are called to be a voice for the voiceless—to speak out against oppression and advocate for those who are marginalized and vulnerable (Prov 31:8–9; Isa 58:6–7). This advocacy extends to addressing issues such as human trafficking, racial discrimination, gender inequality, and other forms of social injustice that deny individuals' inherent dignity and rights.

Christ by standing in solidarity with the oppressed, advocating for their rights and dignity, and working towards the realization of God's kingdom of justice and peace.

4. **Environmental Stewardship**

Theosis informs Christian responses to environmental challenges by highlighting humanity's role as stewards of God's creation and the interconnectedness of all living beings. Believers, recognizing their call to care for the earth and its resources, are motivated to adopt sustainable lifestyles, promote environmental conservation, and advocate for policies that protect the planet for future generations.[4]

  a. *Stewardship as Sacred Responsibility*: The biblical narrative portrays humanity as stewards of creation, entrusted with the care and preservation of the earth and its resources (Gen 2:15). This stewardship is not merely a pragmatic obligation but a sacred responsibility grounded in the belief that the earth belongs to God and that humans are accountable for their stewardship of it. Believers are called to view environmental care as an expression of reverence for the Creator and gratitude for his gifts.

  b. *Interconnectedness of Creation*: The Christian understanding of creation emphasizes the interconnectedness and interdependence of all living beings. Just as humanity is created in the image of God, so too is the entire natural world imbued with divine significance and worth. Believers are called to recognize and honor this interconnectedness, understanding that the health and well-being of humanity are intricately linked to the health and well-being of the earth and its ecosystems.

  c. *Justice for the Vulnerable*: Environmental degradation disproportionately impacts marginalized communities and future generations. Believers, motivated by principles of justice and compassion, are called to advocate for environmental policies that prioritize the needs of the most vulnerable and ensure equitable access to clean air, water, and resources. This advocacy is grounded in the biblical imperative to seek justice for the oppressed and care for the least of these (Matt 25:40).

---

4. Theosis encourages a holistic spirituality that integrates personal transformation with engagement in social and environmental issues. By nurturing a deeper relationship with God and embodying Christlike virtues, individuals are empowered to contribute positively to their communities and the natural world (Gal 5:22–23).

d. *Hope for the Future*: Believers are called to embody a vision of hope for the future, rooted in the belief that God is actively working to renew and reconcile all things (Rev 21:5). While the challenges of environmental degradation can be daunting, Christians are motivated by a faith that compels them to work towards a more sustainable and just world. This hope is not passive but catalyzes action, inspiring believers to engage in tangible efforts to mitigate climate change, protect biodiversity, and promote ecological restoration.

5. **Restorative Justice**

Theosis calls Christians to engage in restorative justice efforts that seek to heal broken relationships, restore dignity to the marginalized, and reconcile communities divided by social and environmental injustices. Believers, inspired by their union with God and their commitment to the common good, are called to pursue reconciliation and forgiveness, address the root causes of conflict and inequality, and work towards the restoration of wholeness and harmony in society and the natural world.[5]

a. *Union with God and the Source of Love*: Believers understand that their union with God is not only a personal experience but also a transformative encounter with the source of all love and compassion. Grounded in this divine love, believers are called to extend forgiveness and reconciliation to others, mirroring the boundless mercy and grace of God. This union with God empowers believers to transcend divisions and embrace the inherent worth and dignity of all people, regardless of their backgrounds or beliefs.

b. *Commitment to the Common Good*: Believers are motivated by a deep commitment to the common good, recognizing that their flourishing is intimately connected to the well-being of others and the entire created order. This commitment compels believers to actively seek reconciliation and forgiveness, as well as to address the root causes of conflict and inequality that disrupt the

---

5. Inspired by their union with God, believers are called to discern and address the root causes of systemic injustices such as poverty, discrimination, racism, and economic inequality (Amos 5:24, Mic 6:8). This requires a commitment to challenging unjust social structures and advocating for policies that promote equity, fairness, and dignity for all individuals.

harmony of society and the natural world. Believers understand that true justice and wholeness can only be achieved when all members of society are able to thrive and fulfill their potential.

c. *Addressing Root Causes of Conflict and Inequality*: Believers recognize that reconciliation and forgiveness are not merely individual acts but require addressing the systemic injustices and inequalities that perpetuate conflict and division. This includes confronting structures of oppression and exploitation, advocating for the rights and dignity of marginalized communities, and working towards systemic change that promotes justice and equality for all. Believers are called to be agents of transformation, challenging the status quo and striving to create a more just and equitable society.

d. *Restoration of Wholeness and Harmony*: At the heart of the believer's calling is the vision of restoration—of restoring wholeness and harmony in society and the natural world. This restoration entails healing the wounds of past injustices, reconciling broken relationships, and nurturing a sense of solidarity and interconnectedness among all members of the human family and the wider web of life. Believers understand that true peace and flourishing can only be achieved through reconciliation with God, with one another, and with the earth.

6. **Hope and Resilience**

Theosis offers Christians hope and resilience in the face of social and environmental challenges, reminding them of their ultimate identity as beloved children of God and their participation in his redemptive purposes. Believers, grounded in their union with God and their trust in his providence, are empowered to persevere in the work of justice and reconciliation, even in the midst of adversity and uncertainty.[6]

a. *Union with God as a Source of Strength*: Believers draw strength from their deep union with God, understanding that they are not alone in their endeavors for justice and reconciliation. This

---

6. The biblical concept of shalom encompasses wholeness, peace, and harmony in all dimensions of life—spiritual, social, and environmental (Jer 29:7; Ps 85:10). Inspired by their union with God, believers are called to work towards the restoration of shalom by actively promoting justice, reconciliation, and sustainable practices that contribute to the flourishing of all creation.

union is a source of spiritual nourishment and empowerment, providing believers with the courage, wisdom, and resilience needed to confront injustice and navigate challenges with faith and fortitude. Grounded in this intimate relationship with God, believers find the strength to persevere, trusting in his guidance and sustenance.

b. *Trust in God's Providence*: Believers place their trust in God's providence, believing that he is actively working for the redemption and restoration of the world. This trust enables believers to persevere in the face of adversity and uncertainty, knowing that God's purposes will ultimately prevail. Even when confronted with seemingly insurmountable obstacles, believers maintain confidence in God's faithfulness and sovereignty, finding reassurance in his promises of justice and mercy.

c. *Courage to Confront Injustice*: Grounded in their union with God and trust in his providence, believers are emboldened to confront injustice and work for reconciliation, even when doing so requires courage and sacrifice. Inspired by the example of prophets, saints, and martyrs who have gone before them, believers remain steadfast in their commitment to uphold the principles of righteousness and love, refusing to be deterred by opposition or persecution. Their trust in God's justice gives them the courage to speak truth to power and stand up for the marginalized and oppressed.

d. *Hope in the Midst of Adversity*: Believers find hope in the midst of adversity, anchored in the promise of God's kingdom of justice and peace. Even when confronted with setbacks and disappointments, believers remain hopeful, knowing that God is at work in the world to bring about transformation and renewal. This hope sustains believers and helps them to persevere; it inspires them to continue their efforts for justice and reconciliation with confidence and resilience.

The concept of theosis provides a theological foundation for Christian responses to social and environmental challenges, guiding believers in their efforts to embody love, compassion, justice, and stewardship in their interactions with others and with the environment. By embracing theosis as a guiding principle in their lives, Christians can work towards the flourishing of all creation and the realization of God's kingdom of justice, peace, and shalom. The historical development of theosis in Christian thought reflects the ongoing exploration of the relationship between humanity and the divine, emphasizing the transformative journey toward union with God as the ultimate goal of the Christian life.

7. **Christian Ethics**

Theosis has contemporary relevance for Christian ethics, including implications for social justice, environmental stewardship, interfaith dialogue, and other pressing ethical issues.[7] While it may seem like a lofty and esoteric concept, it holds significant contemporary relevance in Christian ethics for several reasons.

   a. *Human Flourishing and Fulfillment*: Theosis underscores the idea that human beings are meant to grow and develop spiritually, morally, and intellectually. In contemporary ethics, this emphasis on human flourishing provides a framework for understanding ethical decisions and actions. It encourages individuals to strive for moral excellence and to cultivate virtues such as love, compassion, justice, and humility.

   b. *Dignity and Value of Every Person*: Theosis affirms the inherent dignity and value of every human being as a beloved creation of God. In a world where human dignity is often disregarded or violated, the concept of theosis reminds Christians of the sacredness of every individual and calls them to treat others with respect, empathy, and compassion.

   c. *Ethical Transformation*: Theosis involves a process of ethical transformation, wherein individuals are gradually conformed to the image of Christ. This transformation encompasses all aspects of life, including relationships, work, social justice, and environmental stewardship. In contemporary ethics, the idea of ethical transformation challenges individuals to reflect critically on their values, attitudes, and behaviors and to strive for personal and social change in accordance with the teachings of Christ.

---

7. The concept of theosis informs ethical decision making by guiding believers to consider how their actions and choices impact the dignity and well-being of others (Mic 6:8). It encourages a conscientious approach to social issues, prompting Christians to advocate for just policies, support humanitarian efforts, and engage in acts of charity that promote human flourishing.

d. *Community and Communion*: Theosis emphasizes the communal dimension of Christian life, highlighting the interconnectedness of individuals within the body of Christ. In contemporary ethics, this emphasis on community and communion underscores the importance of solidarity, mutual support, and cooperation in addressing social injustices, promoting the common good, and building inclusive and compassionate communities.

e. *Engagement with the World*: Theosis is not a solitary journey but involves active engagement with the world and its challenges. In contemporary ethics, this engagement translates into a commitment to social justice, peacebuilding, reconciliation, and the promotion of human rights and dignity. The concept of theosis inspires Christians to work for the transformation of society and the establishment of God's kingdom of love, justice, and mercy on earth.

The concept of theosis offers a profound vision of human identity, purpose, and destiny, which has enduring relevance for contemporary Christian ethics. It challenges individuals to live lives of moral excellence, compassion, and service, and to work for the realization of God's reign of justice, peace, and reconciliation in the world.

8. **Ecumenical Dialogue**

In ecumenical dialogue between Christian traditions, theosis can prompt an exploration of how a shared understanding of divine-human union can facilitate greater unity and cooperation among different denominations. Theosis holds significant potential for fostering ecumenical dialogue between Christian traditions, as it touches on fundamental aspects of Christian spirituality and theology that are shared across denominational lines. Here's how theosis can play a role in ecumenical dialogue:[8]

a. *Common Ground*: Theosis is a concept that transcends denominational boundaries. While it's most commonly associated with Eastern Orthodox Christianity, elements of theosis can be found in Catholicism, Protestantism, and even in early Christian

---

8. Theosis involves a holistic view of human nature, emphasizing the potential for humans to participate in God's divine life. This perspective can bridge doctrinal differences concerning human nature, grace, and salvation, as it invites dialogue on how Christians understand the relationship between God and humanity.

writings. Recognizing this common ground can provide a starting point for dialogue and mutual understanding among Christians of different traditions.

b. *Focus on Transformation*: Theosis emphasizes the transformative journey of the Christian life, where believers move toward union with God and conformity to the image of Christ. This emphasis on transformation can serve as a unifying theme in ecumenical dialogue, as Christians from various traditions can share their experiences of spiritual growth and the ways in which they seek to become more like Christ.

c. *Shared Spiritual Practices*: Many Christian traditions incorporate spiritual disciplines and practices aimed at fostering theosis, such as prayer, fasting, contemplation, and participation in the sacraments. By exploring these shared spiritual practices together, Christians from different traditions can learn from one another and deepen their own spiritual lives while also recognizing the common goals they share.

d. *Unity in Diversity*: The concept of theosis affirms the unity of all believers in Christ while also acknowledging the diversity of Christian traditions and expressions. Ecumenical dialogue grounded in theosis can therefore embrace both unity and diversity, recognizing the value of different theological emphases and spiritual practices while affirming the essential unity of the body of Christ.

Theosis offers a rich theological framework for ecumenical dialogue among Christians, providing common ground, fostering spiritual growth, and promoting unity in diversity. By exploring the implications of theosis together, Christians from different traditions can deepen their understanding of their faith and enrich their relationships with one another.[9]

9. **Psychological Well-being**

Spiritual practices associated with theosis, such as prayer, meditation, and community engagement, contribute to mental health and

---

9. Theosis invites Christians to contemplate the mystery of God's presence and transformative grace in human life. This contemplative aspect can encourage humility and openness in ecumenical dialogue, as participants acknowledge the limitations of human understanding before the divine mysteries.

resilience.[10] This spiritual journey involves transformation, where individuals strive to embody the virtues of God, such as love, compassion, and holiness, through a life of prayer, worship, and ascetic practices. The relationship between theosis and psychological well-being is multifaceted and can be explored from various angles:

a. *Sense of Purpose and Meaning*: Engaging in spiritual practices associated with theosis can provide individuals with a profound sense of purpose and meaning in life. The pursuit of union with God gives them a transcendent goal to strive for, which can imbue their lives with a sense of direction and fulfillment. Research in psychology consistently shows that having a strong sense of purpose is closely linked to psychological well-being, including lower rates of depression and anxiety.[11]

b. *Connection and Belonging*: Participation in communal spiritual practices, such as liturgical worship and communal prayer, fosters a sense of connection and belonging within a community of believers. This sense of belonging can contribute to feelings of social support and reduce feelings of loneliness and isolation, both of which are important factors in promoting psychological well-being.

c. *Coping Mechanisms*: The spiritual practices associated with theosis often involve forms of prayer, meditation, and contemplation, which can serve as effective coping mechanisms for dealing with stress, adversity, and existential concerns. These practices encourage individuals to cultivate a sense of inner peace, resilience, and acceptance, which can buffer against the negative effects of stress and contribute to overall psychological resilience.

d. *Character Development*: Theosis entails the cultivation of virtues such as love, compassion, humility, and forgiveness, which are not only central to spiritual growth but also closely related to positive psychological functioning. Research in positive psychology has shown that these virtues are associated with

---

10. Theosis emphasizes the integration of spiritual and psychological aspects of human life. Engaging in spiritual practices associated with theosis can promote psychological integration, where individuals experience greater harmony between their beliefs, values, emotions, and actions. This integration is linked to improved psychological well-being and overall life satisfaction.

11. Pargament, *Psychology of Religion*; Emmons, *Psychology of Ultimate Concerns*.

greater life satisfaction, happiness, and overall psychological well-being.[12]

e. *Self-Transcendence*: Theosis involves transcending the ego and the narrow confines of self-interest to align one's will with the divine will. This process of self-transcendence can lead to a shift in perspective from self-centered concerns to a more expansive and inclusive orientation toward others and the world. Such a shift is associated with greater empathy, altruism, and prosocial behavior, all of which contribute to psychological well-being.

The relationship between theosis and psychological well-being is characterized by a synergistic interplay between spiritual growth and psychological flourishing. Engaging in spiritual practices associated with theosis can foster a sense of purpose, belonging, resilience, and character development, ultimately leading to greater psychological well-being and fulfillment.

10. **Literature and Art**

Analyze representations of theosis in contemporary Christian literature, art, and music, examining how artists and writers express themes of divine-human union and spiritual transformation in their creative works.[13] In contemporary Christian literature, art, and music, artists and writers express themes of divine-human union and spiritual transformation through their creative works. Authors such as Metropolitan Kallistos Ware, Fr. Thomas Hopko, and Fr. John Behr have written extensively on theosis, examining its theological significance and practical implications for Christian life.[14] Their writings delve into topics such as the role of grace, prayer, and the sacraments in the process of theosis, as well as the importance of participating in the life of the church community. In art, theosis may be depicted symbolically through images of saints or biblical

---

12. Koenig, "Research on Religion and Aging."

13. In each of these artistic expressions, theosis is portrayed as a dynamic process of spiritual growth and transformation, emphasizing the profound mystery of God's presence in human life. Artists and writers explore the tension between human imperfection and the longing for divine perfection, illustrating how individuals navigate doubts, struggles, and moments of revelation on their journey towards union with God. Through literature, art, and music, representations of theosis invite viewers and listeners to ponder the deeper meaning of life, faith, and the pursuit of spiritual fulfillment.

14. Ware, *Orthodox Way*; Hopko, *Winter Pascha*; Behr, *Mystery of Christ*.

figures portrayed with radiant halos or in heavenly settings, symbolizing their union with God.

Contemporary Christian artists may also explore the theme of theosis through abstract or conceptual artworks that convey the idea of spiritual transformation and union with the divine. Additionally, some artists may draw inspiration from traditional iconography and Eastern Orthodox visual motifs to represent theosis in their work. Music also plays a significant role in expressing the theme of theosis in contemporary Christian worship and composition. Hymns and liturgical chants often contain lyrics that reflect the longing for union with God and the desire for spiritual transformation. Contemporary Christian musicians may incorporate themes of theosis into their lyrics, exploring concepts such as surrendering to God's will, experiencing divine love, and striving for holiness. Some artists may draw from the rich musical traditions of Eastern Orthodox chant or incorporate elements of mysticism and contemplation into their compositions to evoke the sense of transcendence associated with theosis.

While the concept of theosis may not be as widely discussed in contemporary Western Christian circles as it is in Eastern Orthodoxy, it nonetheless remains a profound and compelling theological idea that continues to inspire reflection, creativity, and spiritual growth, as seen in literature, art, and music within the broader Christian tradition.

11. Theosis and Missional Theology

Theosis, the concept of human beings participating in the divine nature and becoming more like God, has profound implications for missional theology. This exploration examines how a deeper understanding of divine-human union shapes Christian mission and evangelism, particularly in cross-cultural contexts.[15] Theosis frames the mission not as merely bringing God to others but as participating in God's ongoing work of drawing all creation into divine union. This perspective shifts the focus from a unidirectional model of mission to a more collaborative approach, which recognizes God's

---

15. Theosis offers a theological framework that deeply informs missional theology, shaping how Christians understand and engage in mission and evangelism, especially in cross-cultural contexts. It challenges missionaries to embody the transformative love of God, respect cultural diversity, pursue holistic redemption, empower discipleship, and engage in dialogue for mutual transformation.

presence and activity in all cultures and encourages missionaries to work alongside local communities rather than imposing external forms of Christianity.

This concept has profound implications for missional theology, especially how it shapes Christian mission and evangelism in cross-cultural contexts.

a. *Incarnational Approach*: Theosis emphasizes the incarnation of Christ, where God took on human flesh to dwell among humanity. This underscores the importance of embodying the message of the gospel in mission work. Just as Christ became human to reach humanity, Christians are called to immerse themselves in the cultural contexts of those they seek to evangelize. This means understanding and respecting the beliefs, values, and practices of different cultures while sharing the transformative message of the gospel.

b. *Relational Engagement*: Theosis emphasizes the intimate union between God and humanity. This relational aspect informs missional theology by highlighting the importance of building authentic relationships with people from different cultural backgrounds. Rather than seeing evangelism as a one-way communication of the gospel message, theosis encourages a mutual exchange where both parties grow together in understanding and faith.

c. *Transformational Ministry*: Theosis teaches that the ultimate goal of human existence is to be transformed into the likeness of Christ. In the context of missional theology, this means that evangelism is not merely about converting individuals to a set of beliefs but about facilitating a journey of spiritual transformation. Missionaries and evangelists, therefore, should focus on holistic ministry that addresses the spiritual, emotional, physical, and social needs of individuals and communities.

d. *Cultural Reconciliation*: Theosis teaches that through union with God, humanity is reconciled to God and to one another. In the context of cross-cultural mission and evangelism, this implies working towards reconciliation and unity among diverse cultural groups. Rather than imposing one's own cultural norms and values, Christians are called to promote reconciliation and understanding across cultural divides, recognizing the inherent dignity and worth of every individual as a reflection of God's image.

e. *Empowerment of Indigenous Leadership*: Theosis emphasizes the indwelling of the Holy Spirit in believers, empowering them to participate in the divine life. In the context of cross-cultural mission, this means recognizing and empowering indigenous leaders within local communities to take ownership of the mission and evangelism efforts. Instead of maintaining a paternalistic approach, missional theology informed by theosis encourages the development of indigenous leadership and contextualized expressions of faith.

The implications of theosis for missional theology are profound, shaping how Christians understand and engage in mission and evangelism, particularly in cross-cultural contexts. By emphasizing the incarnation, relational engagement, transformational ministry, cultural reconciliation, and empowerment of indigenous leadership, theosis encourages a holistic and culturally sensitive approach to sharing the gospel and participating in God's mission in the world.

By emphasizing union with God and participation in the divine life, theosis presents a transformative vision for mission that is rooted in respect, holism, and cultural sensitivity.

1. *Incarnational Mission*: Theosis encourages missionaries to adopt an incarnational approach, to become students of culture and engage deeply with local communities.
2. *Eschatological Focus*: Theosis frames mission within the broader narrative of God's redemptive plan, emphasizing the ultimate goal of union with God.
3. *Sacramental Worldview*: Theosis promotes a sacramental cosmology, recognizing the sacred in all of creation and in diverse cultural expressions.
4. *Community-Focused Mission*: Theosis emphasizes the social nature of human existence and the importance of building vibrant Christian communities.

5. *Spiritual Formation*: Theosis highlights the need for spiritual formation as part of the missional journey, focusing on spiritual disciplines and contemplative practices.

6. *Ecological Concern*: Theosis extends to all of creation, encouraging missionaries to engage in environmental stewardship and promote eco-justice.

7. *Interfaith Dialogue*: Theosis provides a framework for meaningful interfaith dialogue, recognizing the divine presence in diverse traditions.

A missional theology informed by theosis offers a compelling alternative to approaches that have been criticized for their lack of contextual sensitivity or spiritual depth. It presents Christian mission as a holistic and dynamic process that respects the dignity of all peoples and cultures while pointing them towards closer union with the divine. This stance fosters a humble, other-centered learning posture and an honoring of the wide rainbow spectrum of cultural diversity represented in various cross-cultural mission encounters.

— Chapter 12 —

Theosis in the Digital Age

THE DIGITAL AGE EXPRESSION of the human condition is both nuanced and intricate. First, technology has created the potential for communication to be easier and education more accessible with instant global online connectivity, an infinite amount of information at our fingertips, and a tsunami of entertainment and creative outlets. But, this era too has many troubles and worries. For example, digital addiction and privacy breaches are rising concerns; cyberbullying and misinformation represent some of the new challenges society is facing. More and more information shooting out from all spatial corners, so that we feel overwhelmed, which leads to anxiety. On top of that, the general rapid pace at which technology is improving has led to labor market displacement and worry about the future of work.

The digital age has brought about significant advancements, but it has also raised concerns about its impact on mental health, social interactions, and the ability to focus. Theosis, a concept that emphasizes union with God and participation in the divine life, offers a valuable framework for navigating these challenges and promoting well-being in the digital landscape. Theosis can be seen as striving for inner peace, contentment, and spiritual fulfillment. In the context of the digital age, this can be particularly important, as constant exposure to social media can foster feelings of inadequacy, comparison, and anxiety. By focusing on union with God and seeking spiritual growth, individuals can develop a sense of self-worth that is not dependent on external validation.

This can help to counterbalance the negative effects of social media and promote mental health.

Theosis emphasizes the importance of genuine connection and community. While digital technologies can facilitate connections with others, they can also hinder these connections by replacing face-to-face interactions with virtual ones. Theosis can encourage individuals to prioritize meaningful relationships and to seek out opportunities for face-to-face interaction. By cultivating genuine connections with others, individuals can foster a sense of belonging and combat feelings of loneliness and isolation.

Theosis offers a valuable framework for navigating the challenges of the digital age. By focusing on union with God, spiritual growth, and genuine connections with others, individuals can promote mental health, foster meaningful relationships, and live a more fulfilling life. As society continues to adapt to the digital landscape, theosis can provide a guiding principle for navigating these challenges and ensuring the well-being of individuals in the digital age.

However, the realities of the digital age can make engaging in the practices that are foundational for theosis difficult. The relentless stimulation from digital devices can undermine the ability to focus and concentrate, thereby impeding spiritual practices such as meditation, prayer, and contemplation, which are fundamental to theosis. The constant barrage of notifications, emails, and social media can divert individuals away from moments of reflection and introspection, making it difficult to establish a deeper connection with the divine.

While theosis is a spiritual concept centered on achieving union with the divine, it intersects with discussions about how to lessen the harmful effects of digital technologies on mental health, social interactions, and self-esteem in the digital age. Achieving a balance between the advantages of technology and the pursuit of spiritual fulfillment and genuine human connection is crucial for navigating the challenges of the digital era; this is in alignment with the principles of theosis. Exploring theosis in the context of the digital age could be fascinating.

1. **Digital Immortality**

    With advancements in artificial intelligence and virtual reality, there's potential for individuals to create digital personas or avatars that persist beyond their physical existence.[1] This blurs the line

1. Bainbridge, *Interface*.

between the mortal and the divine, as these digital entities may perpetuate a form of existence akin to the eternal.[2] The idea that these digital entitles blur this line has gained traction as advancements in artificial intelligence, virtual reality, and other technologies, enabling the creation of sophisticated digital representations of individuals, have been made.

The concept of digital immortality, the idea of preserving consciousness and identity in a digital form beyond physical death, raises profound philosophical questions about the nature of life, identity, and human existence. This chapter will explore the implications of digital immortality, including its potential to blur the lines between mortality and immortality, its connection to ancient themes of transcendence and eternal life, and the ethical and philosophical questions it raises. Digital immortality challenges traditional notions of mortality and immortality. By digitizing parts of oneself, individuals could potentially transcend the limitations of physical existence, raising questions about what it means to be human. This concept could lead to a blurring of the lines between mortal and immortal beings, as individuals may no longer be bound by the same physical constraints as those who have not been digitized.

The desire to transcend physical limitations and achieve eternal life is a theme that has captivated humanity throughout history. Most spiritual, philosophical, and theological systems have explored the possibility of immortality or visions of all-knowing wisdom as attributes of divinity. Digital immortality offers a new way to explore these ancient themes, as individuals may be able to achieve a form of immortality that was previously reserved for the divine. The concept of digital immortality raises numerous ethical and philosophical questions: What constitutes a person's identity in a digital form? Can a digital consciousness truly be considered alive? What are the implications of digital immortality for concepts such as free will, consciousness, and the soul?

The idea of digital immortality is a fascinating and complex concept that challenges our understanding of life, death, and human

---

2. AI and VR technologies allow for the creation of increasingly sophisticated digital personas or avatars. These entities can simulate human-like intelligence, emotions, and even personalities based on extensive data and algorithms. As these technologies progress, there is potential for these digital entities to persist indefinitely, perhaps even beyond the lifespan of their human creators.

existence. While the technological feasibility of digital immortality remains to be seen, the philosophical and ethical questions it raises are significant. As we continue to explore the possibilities of digital technology, it is essential to consider the implications for our understanding of ourselves and our place in the universe.

On a practical level, digital immortality raises ethical and societal questions: Who would control these digital copies, and how would they be used? What regulations would govern this technology? How might it affect our understanding of loss and the process of grieving? The idea of digital immortality challenges our basic assumptions about life, death, and human nature. It compels us to consider the far-reaching effects of new technologies, not just on individual lives but on our collective understanding of humanity. As technology continues to advance, the quest for digital immortality will likely remain a deeply philosophical and ethically complex pursuit.

2. **Augmented Humanity**

Emerging technologies such as brain-computer interfaces and genetic manipulation have the potential to boost human abilities to seemingly supernatural levels when compared to our ancestors. This technological pursuit of transcendence echoes the search for divinity found in many spiritual practices. It encompasses progress in areas like brain-computer interfaces (BCIs), genetic modification, and biotechnology, which promise to dramatically enhance our physical, mental, and emotional capacities. This notion not only pushes the boundaries of what we believe humans are capable of, but also prompts us to consider the similarities between seeking transcendence through technology and the quest for godhood in various religious beliefs. Many of these technologies seek to realize the concept of Augmented Humanity, which is, itself, a fascinating exploration of human desire for self-enhancement and transcendence.[3] It reflects our ongoing quest to push the boundaries of our existence, both physically and mentally. In the context of religious and philosophical traditions, this often involves a journey towards divinity or enlightenment, a journey aiming to transcend mortal limitations and achieve a state of spiritual completeness.

The digital age has presented a new avenue for pursuing these aspirations. BCIs, for example, offer the possibility of enhancing

---

3. Kurzweil, *Singularity Is Near*; Bostrom, *Superintelligence*.

human cognitive abilities, memory capacity, and sensory perception. This technology blurs the lines between organic and artificial components, raising questions about the nature of human identity and consciousness. As we continue to explore the potential of Augmented Humanity, it is important to consider the ethical implications and societal consequences of these advancements. While the benefits are significant, it is crucial we work to ensure that these technologies are developed and used responsibly, with a focus on enhancing human well-being rather than creating new forms of inequality or discrimination.

Similarly, advances in genetic engineering promise to enhance human traits and capabilities at the fundamental level of our biology. Techniques such as CRISPR[4] allow scientists to edit the human genome with unprecedented precision, opening up the possibility of eliminating genetic diseases, enhancing physical attributes, or even augmenting cognitive functions. The concept of Augmented Humanity has implications that go beyond simply enhancing individual capabilities. It prompts deep ethical, societal, and philosophical debates about what defines human identity, how we ensure equality, and what it truly means to be human. As technology allows people to overcome their biological constraints, unequal access to these enhancements could worsen existing social divides, potentially creating new forms of privilege and discrimination.

The technological pursuit of transcendence challenges us to rethink our concepts of divinity and spirituality in today's world. While religious traditions offer paths to enlightenment or salvation through spiritual practices, technology presents a secular alternative, inviting individuals to seek self-improvement and self-transcendence through scientific and technological means. However, the journey towards Augmented Humanity is not without its risks and challenges. There are significant concerns about potential misuse of technology, loss of human autonomy, and the erosion of our shared humanity. The quest for enhancement through technology also raises

---

4. Doudna and Sternberg, *Crack in Creation*. CRISPR stands for "clustered regularly interspaced short palindromic repeats." It refers to a natural defense mechanism used by bacteria to protect against viruses. Scientists have adapted this system for genetic engineering, allowing precise editing of DNA in various organisms. This has huge implications for medicine, agriculture, and biological research.

ethical quandaries regarding consent, fairness, and the unforeseen consequences of modifying the human genome or brain.

Augmented Humanity represents a significant intersection of technology, spirituality, and human ambition. It prompts us to reassess our understanding of human potential and the nature of divinity in an era characterized by scientific advancements and technological innovation. As we grapple with the ethical and philosophical intricacies of this new frontier, it's crucial to approach the pursuit of enhancement with humility, thoughtfulness, and a dedication to promoting human flourishing for all.

3. **Networked Consciousness**

The interconnectedness facilitated by the internet could be seen as a reflection of a collective consciousness, where individuals contribute to and draw from a shared pool of knowledge and experience. This interconnectedness mirrors the idea of theosis as individuals strive to become part of something greater than themselves. In this interconnected digital landscape, individuals contribute to and draw from a shared pool of knowledge, experiences, and perspectives, blurring the boundaries between individual minds and forming a collective intelligence, sometimes referred to as Networked Consciousness, greater than the sum of its parts.[5] This concept parallels the notion of theosis, where individuals strive to transcend their individual identities and become part of something greater than themselves.

At its core, Networked Consciousness reflects the transformative impact of digital technologies on human society and consciousness. The internet has facilitated unprecedented levels of communication, collaboration, and information exchange, enabling individuals from diverse backgrounds and locations to connect, share ideas, and cocreate knowledge on a global scale. Social media platforms, online communities, and collaborative platforms have further amplified this interconnectedness, fostering virtual spaces where individuals can engage in dialogue, debate, and collective action in real time. From this perspective, the internet can

---

5. Surowiecki, *Wisdom*. Networked Consciousness encapsulates the transformative impact of digital technologies on human society and consciousness. It underscores the power of digital connectivity to foster global communication, collaboration, and knowledge exchange, while also highlighting the need for ethical considerations and responsible use of technology to promote positive societal outcomes.

be seen as a manifestation of a collective human mind, where each individual node contributes to the emergence of a distributed network of knowledge, wisdom, and creativity. Just as neurons in the brain form intricate networks that give rise to consciousness and cognition, individuals interconnected through the internet form a global networked consciousness that transcends geographical, cultural, and linguistic boundaries.

The concept of Networked Consciousness resonates with the idea of theosis in several ways. In the pursuit of theosis, individuals seek to transcend their individual egos and merge with a higher reality or divine presence. Similarly, in the digital realm, individuals contribute to and participate in a collective intelligence that transcends individual perspectives and experiences. Through collaboration, cooperation, and mutual exchange, individuals become part of something greater than themselves, tapping into a shared pool of knowledge and insight that transcends individual limitations.

Furthermore, the notion of Networked Consciousness underscores the transformative potential of digital technologies to foster empathy, understanding, and solidarity across diverse communities. By connecting individuals with different backgrounds, cultures, and worldviews, the internet enables the exchange of diverse perspectives and experiences, fostering a deeper sense of interconnectedness and common humanity.

However, the concept of Networked Consciousness also presents significant questions and challenges. Issues such as digital surveillance, privacy concerns, and the concentration of power among tech giants underscore the necessity for ethical, legal, and regulatory frameworks to protect individual rights and freedoms in the digital era. Additionally, the proliferation of misinformation, echo chambers, and online polarization highlight the need to cultivate critical thinking, media literacy, and digital citizenship skills to effectively navigate the complexities of the digital landscape.

Networked Consciousness offers a compelling framework for understanding the transformative impact of digital technologies on human consciousness and society. By fostering interconnectedness, collaboration, and collective intelligence, the internet enables individuals to transcend their individual limitations and become part of a global network of knowledge, wisdom, and creativity. As we navigate the opportunities and challenges of the digital age, it is essential to harness the power of Networked Consciousness to promote empathy, understanding, and solidarity across diverse communities, fostering a more inclusive, equitable, and sustainable future for all.[6]

4. Ethical Considerations

As we integrate technology more intimately into our lives, questions of morality and responsibility become paramount. Just as theosis implies a transformation of the individual's moral character towards the divine, the digital era raises questions about how our technological advancements shape our ethical framework and understanding of what it means to be human. At the heart of this discussion lies the concept of responsibility—who bears it and to what extent. With great technological power comes an immense responsibility to ensure that its application aligns with ethical principles and serves the common good. The ethical framework within which we operate must adapt and evolve alongside technological advancements to mitigate potential harms and maximize benefits.

Drawing parallels to the concept of theosis, which denotes a transformative journey towards divine likeness in Eastern Christian theology, we can see a similar transformative journey unfolding in the digital era. However, instead of a spiritual transformation, it's a transformation of our moral character and understanding of what it means to be human in light of technological progress. One of the primary ethical considerations revolves around autonomy and consent. As technology permeates our lives more deeply, there's a risk of eroding individual autonomy, whether through pervasive surveillance, algorithmic manipulation, or the usurpation of decision-making processes by artificial intelligence. Safeguarding individual autonomy entails ensuring transparent and informed consent, as well as empowering individuals by giving them control over their data and digital footprint.

The ethical implications of technological innovations extend beyond individual autonomy to societal justice and equity. As technology amplifies existing inequalities and creates new

---

6. The internet has revolutionized communication by enabling instant, global connectivity. People from diverse backgrounds and geographical locations can now interact in real time, share ideas, and collaborate on projects without the constraints of physical proximity. This unprecedented level of connectivity fosters a sense of interconnectedness and collective intelligence, where individuals contribute to and benefit from a shared pool of knowledge and creativity.

ones, there's a moral imperative to address disparities in access, opportunity, and outcomes.[7] Whether it's the digital divide, algorithmic bias, or the impact of automation on employment, these ethical considerations demand a concerted effort to mitigate these disparities and foster a more inclusive technological future. The ethical dimensions of technological development encompass environmental sustainability and responsible stewardship of resources. The rapid pace of innovation often comes at the cost of environmental degradation and resource depletion. Thus, ethical decision making entails prioritizing sustainable practices and minimizing the ecological footprint of technology.

In navigating these ethical considerations, interdisciplinary collaboration and stakeholder engagement are essential. Ethicists, technologists, policymakers, and society at large must engage in ongoing dialogue to anticipate potential ethical dilemmas, develop robust frameworks for ethical decision making, and hold accountable those who wield technological power. Ultimately, the integration of technology into our lives necessitates a profound reflection on our values, priorities, and responsibilities as individuals and as a society. By embracing a human-centered approach to technological innovation and prioritizing ethical considerations, we can harness the transformative potential of technology to advance human flourishing and collective well-being.

5. Digital Religion

The digital era has seen the rise of online communities and virtual spaces where individuals come together around shared beliefs and practices. These digital spaces could be seen as modern-day temples or places of worship, where the quest for spiritual growth and enlightenment takes on new forms. In these digital temples, people may engage in various activities such as sharing inspirational content, participating in virtual rituals or ceremonies, discussing philosophical ideas, and supporting one another through challenges and triumphs. The internet has enabled individuals from diverse backgrounds and geographic locations to come together

---

7. Addressing the ethical implications of technological innovations goes beyond individual autonomy to encompass broader societal considerations of justice and equity. By prioritizing fairness, inclusivity, and ethical responsibility in the development and deployment of technology, we can strive towards a more equitable future where everyone has the opportunity to benefit from and contribute to technological progress.

in ways that were previously impossible, fostering a sense of global community and interconnectedness.

The digitization of religious texts, teachings, and practices has made spiritual knowledge more accessible than ever before. Online platforms offer resources for learning about different faiths, meditation techniques, mindfulness practices, and more, empowering individuals to explore and deepen their spiritual journeys on their own terms. However, like any aspect of the digital world, digital religion also presents its own set of challenges and complexities. Questions regarding authenticity, authority, and the potential for misinformation or manipulation within online spiritual communities are important considerations.[8] Additionally, the digital realm blurs the lines between the sacred and the profane, raising questions about how technology impacts the experience of spirituality and the nature of religious authority.

Digital religion reflects the evolving nature of human spirituality in the digital age, where technology serves as a catalyst for new forms of connection, exploration, and expression of beliefs and practices.

6. Existential Questions

The rapid pace of technological change in the digital era forces us to confront existential questions about our place in the universe and our relationship to the divine. Just as theosis involves a journey towards union with the divine, the digital era prompts us to consider what it means to be human in a world increasingly shaped by technology. The rapid advancements in technology in the digital era have thrust these questions into sharper focus, challenging us to reevaluate our understanding of ourselves and our place in the universe.

One of the central themes in existential thought is the quest for meaning and purpose in life. As technology permeates every aspect of our existence, from how we communicate and work to how we perceive reality itself, we are compelled to confront how these changes affect our sense of purpose. The digital age

---

8. Ethical responsibility in technological innovation necessitates inclusive design practices that consider the diverse needs, perspectives, and capabilities of all users. This includes designing products, services, and platforms that are accessible to individuals with disabilities, accommodating linguistic and cultural diversity, and respect of user privacy and autonomy.

offers unprecedented opportunities for connection, creativity, and knowledge acquisition, but it also brings about profound shifts in how we relate to each other and the world around us. In this context, we must grapple with questions such as, What is the purpose of human existence in a world increasingly mediated by technology?[9] How do we find meaning in a society driven by constant innovation and change?

The digital era challenges traditional notions of human identity and agency. As artificial intelligence, virtual reality, and other technological advancements blur the boundaries between the human and the machine, we are forced to reconsider what it means to be human. Questions of consciousness, autonomy, and freedom will take on new dimensions in a world where algorithms influence our decisions and our online personas may sometimes feel more real than our physical selves. The existential angst that arises from this tension between our biological nature and our technological augmentation prompts us to reflect on the essence of humanity itself.

Furthermore, the digital era prompts us to confront existential questions about our relationship to the divine or transcendent. The digital age challenges us to redefine our understanding of spirituality and transcendence in a technologically mediated world. As we navigate virtual landscapes, engage with digital communities, and explore new forms of religious expression online, we are compelled to reflect on how technology shapes our spiritual experiences and our sense of connection to something greater than ourselves. In essence, the rapid pace of technological change in the digital era forces us to confront existential questions about what it means to be human in a world increasingly shaped by technology. As we grapple with these questions, we are called to cultivate a deeper awareness of ourselves, our values, and our relationship to the world around us, navigating the complexities of the digital age with wisdom, compassion, and integrity.

While theosis is fundamentally a deeply spiritual concept, its implications can extend into various contexts, including technology. We will examine the intersection of theosis and digital spirituality,

9. Digital technologies have revolutionized communication and connectivity, enabling individuals across the globe to connect instantaneously through social media, video conferencing, and online communities. This interconnectedness fosters opportunities for collaboration, cultural exchange, and collective action on global issues.

exploring how digital technologies and online communities influence contemporary understandings and expressions of the divine-human union and spiritual transformation.

1. Just as theosis involves humans becoming more like God, digital technology aims to augment human capabilities. Through tools like artificial intelligence and machine learning, humans can enhance their cognitive abilities, potentially approaching a state of heightened understanding and wisdom akin to divine knowledge. The analogy with theosis, the theological concept of humans becoming more like God, is intriguing. In the context of digital technology, the aspiration is not towards divinity but rather towards a higher state of knowledge and wisdom. Just as theosis entails a transformation of the human spirit towards godliness, augmented intelligence implies a transformation of the human intellect towards a state of heightened understanding and insight.[10]

    The journey towards augmented intelligence involves leveraging the power of artificial-intelligence (AI) and machine-learning (ML) algorithms to process vast amounts of data, recognize patterns, and derive meaningful insights that humans alone might overlook or take much longer to discover. By offloading repetitive tasks and computational heavy lifting to machines, humans are freed to focus on higher-level thinking, creativity, and intuition—qualities that are uniquely human and difficult to replicate in machines.[11]

    a. *Connectivity and Unity*: Theosis often involves a sense of unity with God and fellow humans. Digital technology, particularly the internet and social media, facilitates unprecedented connectivity among people across the globe. This interconnectedness can foster a sense of unity and solidarity, reflecting the divine unity sought in theosis.

---

10. Augmented intelligence refers to the enhancement of human cognitive abilities through artificial intelligence (AI), machine learning (ML), and advanced computing technologies. Unlike traditional AI, which aims to replicate human intelligence, augmented intelligence focuses on amplifying human capabilities by combining human judgment with AI-driven insights and automation.

11. The notion of augmented intelligence raises philosophical questions about the nature of human identity and agency in a world increasingly intertwined with technology. As we integrate AI into our daily lives, where does the boundary between human and machine blur? How do we preserve our autonomy and sense of self in an era of pervasive data collection and algorithmic influence?

Social media, in particular, plays a significant role in fostering connectivity and unity by providing platforms for people to express themselves, engage in dialogue, and form virtual communities around shared interests and values. From grassroots movements advocating for social justice to global campaigns raising awareness about pressing issues, social media has become a powerful tool for mobilizing collective action and fostering a sense of solidarity among individuals united by common causes.

Moreover, the internet has democratized access to information and knowledge, empowering individuals to educate themselves, engage in lifelong learning, and participate in intellectual discourse with others across the globe. This democratization of knowledge fosters a sense of intellectual unity, where people can exchange ideas, challenge each other's perspectives, and collectively advance human understanding and progress.[12]

b. *Creative Expression*: In theosis, individuals strive to reflect divine attributes, including creativity. Digital technology provides vast opportunities for creative expression through platforms like digital art, music production software, and virtual reality experiences. By harnessing these tools, individuals can express themselves in ways that resonate with divine creativity. When individuals engage in creative expression, they tap into a realm of existence that transcends the mundane and connects them with something greater than themselves. It's a process through which they channel their innermost thoughts, emotions, and experiences into tangible forms, whether it be through art, music, literature, or any other medium. In doing so, they participate in a kind of divine dance, becoming cocreators with the universe.

Digital technology has revolutionized the landscape of creative expression, offering vast opportunities for individuals to explore and manifest their inner worlds. Platforms like digital art software, music production tools, and virtual reality

---

12. While the internet has the potential to bring people together, it can also amplify divisions and polarize communities, particularly when misinformation spreads unchecked or when online discourse devolves into echo chambers and ideological bubbles. Moreover, concerns about privacy, data security, and the digital divide raise important questions about who has access to digital connectivity and who gets left behind in an increasingly connected world.

experiences have democratized creativity, making it more accessible to people from diverse backgrounds and skill levels. Through these tools, individuals can break free from the constraints of traditional mediums and experiment with new techniques, styles, and forms of expression.[13]

c. *Ethical Considerations*: Theosis entails moral and ethical transformation towards alignment with divine principles. Similarly, the advent of digital technology raises ethical questions about how we use and develop it. Integrating theosis principles could encourage the development of technology that promotes human flourishing, social justice, and environmental stewardship. By integrating the principles of theosis into our approach to technology, we can strive to create a digital landscape that promotes human flourishing, social justice, and environmental stewardship.

Theosis is about transcending the limitations of the ego and aligning oneself with higher moral and ethical principles. It involves a process of spiritual growth and transformation, wherein individuals strive to embody qualities such as compassion, empathy, and integrity. In the context of digital technology, this means approaching its development and use with a deep sense of responsibility and mindfulness.

One of the key ethical considerations in the digital age is the impact of technology on human well-being. From social media algorithms that prioritize engagement over mental health to surveillance technologies that erode privacy rights, the ethical questions of digital technology are vast and multifaceted. By integrating theosis principles into the design and deployment of technology, we can strive to prioritize the well-being of individuals and communities above all else.[14]

13. In the context of theosis, harnessing digital technology for creative expression can be seen as a way of aligning oneself with divine creativity. Just as the divine is often described as the ultimate Creator, individuals who engage in creative pursuits are, in a sense, emulating this divine act of creation. Whether they're crafting digital paintings, composing electronic music, or building immersive virtual worlds, they're tapping into the same creative energy that permeates the cosmos.

14. By integrating theosis principles into our approach to technology, we can strive to create digital tools and systems that promote equity, inclusivity, and environmental stewardship. This might involve particular initiatives in technological development efforts, such as designing accessible and inclusive user interfaces, minimizing the carbon footprint of digital infrastructure, and prioritizing the needs of marginalized communities.

d. *Spiritual Practices*: Digital technology can also facilitate spiritual practices that aid in theosis. For example, meditation and mindfulness apps help individuals cultivate inner peace and self-awareness, which are essential aspects of spiritual growth. Virtual communities and online resources can also support individuals in their journeys towards union with the divine. From meditation and mindfulness apps to virtual communities and online resources, technology offers a wealth of opportunities for cultivating inner peace, self-awareness, and connection with the divine.

At the heart of many spiritual traditions lies the practice of meditation, which involves quieting the mind, focusing the attention, and cultivating a sense of presence and awareness. In today's fast-paced world, where distractions abound and stress levels are high, digital meditation apps offer a convenient and accessible way for individuals to integrate this ancient practice into their daily lives. These apps provide guided meditations, breathing exercises, and other tools designed to help users relax, center themselves, and cultivate a deeper sense of inner peace.

Similarly, mindfulness apps leverage digital technology to support individuals in developing present-moment awareness and nonjudgmental acceptance of their thoughts, feelings, and sensations. Through features such as mindfulness reminders, gratitude journals, and daily reflection prompts, these apps help users cultivate mindfulness in their everyday activities, fostering greater clarity, resilience, and emotional well-being.[15]

e. *Transcendence of Boundaries*: Theosis involves transcending human limitations to become more godlike. Digital technology enables us to transcend physical and geographical boundaries, allowing for instantaneous communication, access to information, and immersive experiences. This capacity for transcendence mirrors the spiritual aspiration for union with the divine.

---

15. Virtual communities and online resources also play a crucial role in supporting individuals on their spiritual journey. Through forums, social media groups, and online courses, individuals can connect with like-minded seekers, share their experiences, and learn from spiritual teachers and practitioners from around the world. These digital communities provide a sense of belonging and support, allowing individuals to explore their spirituality in a safe and inclusive environment.

Digital technology has revolutionized our ability to transcend physical and geographical limitations in ways that were once unimaginable. Through the internet, social media, and telecommunications, we can instantly connect with people on the other side of the globe, breaking down barriers of distance and enabling communication and collaboration on an unprecedented scale. This instantaneous connectivity not only facilitates the exchange of information and ideas but also fosters a sense of global interconnectedness and solidarity.

Moreover, digital technology offers immersive experiences that transcend the boundaries of space and time, allowing us to explore virtual worlds, interact with simulated environments, and engage with art and culture from diverse traditions and eras. Virtual reality, augmented reality, and mixed reality technologies transport us to realms beyond the confines of the physical world, offering new perspectives and possibilities for exploration and self-discovery.

In many ways, this capacity for transcendence mirrors the spiritual aspiration for union with the divine. Just as theosis involves transcending the limitations of the human condition to become more godlike, digital technology enables us to transcend the limitations of time, space, and physical embodiment, offering glimpses of a reality beyond our immediate sensory experience.[16]

f. *Challenges and Temptations*: Just as theosis involves overcoming obstacles and temptations on the path to union with God, the digital age presents its own set of challenges. These include issues such as digital addiction, information overload, and the erosion of traditional values. Integrating theosis principles may help individuals navigate these challenges with greater resilience and spiritual discernment.

One of the most pressing challenges in the digital age is digital addiction, characterized by compulsive and excessive use of digital devices and platforms. Whether it's constantly checking

---

16. The aspiration for transcendence through digital technology should not be seen as a replacement for spiritual practice or inner growth. While technology can offer valuable tools and resources for personal and collective transformation, true transcendence ultimately involves a deepening of our connection to ourselves, to others, and to the divine.

social media feeds, binge-watching streamed content, or gaming for hours on end, digital addiction can disrupt individuals' lives, relationships, and sense of self-control. Like the temptations encountered on the path to theosis, digital addiction lures individuals away from their higher aspirations and deeper values, trapping them in a cycle of instant gratification and distraction.

Information overload is another challenge that individuals face in the digital age, where an abundance of information is available at our fingertips. While access to information can empower individuals and broaden their horizons, it can also overwhelm them with irrelevant or conflicting information, leading to confusion, anxiety, and cognitive overload. Just as theosis requires discernment and discrimination in navigating the complexities of spiritual teachings and practices, individuals must cultivate discernment and critical thinking skills to sift through the vast sea of information in the digital realm.

Moreover, the digital age has brought about a shift in cultural values and norms, with traditional virtues such as patience, humility, and compassion often taking a backseat to values like instant gratification, self-promotion, and materialism. This erosion of traditional values poses a significant challenge for individuals seeking to cultivate spiritual depth and integrity in a culture that prioritizes superficiality and self-interest. Like the trials and tribulations faced by seekers on the path to theosis, individuals must resist the temptations of ego gratification and societal pressure, staying true to their innermost values and principles.[17]

2. The engagement in spiritual practices through digital platforms—such as virtual worship services, meditation apps, or online retreats—can significantly impact individuals' experiences of divine union and spiritual transformation. These digital tools offer innovative ways to connect with spiritual practices and communities, which may influence the process of achieving theosis. Online

---

17. Integrating the principles of theosis into our approach to navigating these challenges can provide individuals with greater resilience, clarity, and spiritual discernment. Theosis encourages individuals to cultivate virtues such as self-discipline, mindfulness, and humility, which can serve as antidotes to the temptations and distractions of the digital age. By grounding themselves in a deep sense of purpose and a connection to the divine, individuals can transcend the superficialities of digital culture and navigate its complexities with grace and wisdom.

worship allows individuals to participate in communal religious activities from anywhere in the world. This accessibility can enhance spiritual experiences and foster a sense of divine connection, potentially supporting the journey towards theosis. Digital meditation tools provide structured practices that can guide users in their spiritual disciplines. These apps can help deepen personal spiritual experiences and facilitate transformative processes that align with the concept of theosis. Virtual retreats offer immersive spiritual experiences and teachings without geographical constraints. They enable individuals to engage in focused periods of reflection and growth, contributing to their progress in spiritual transformation.

The digital space allows believers from diverse backgrounds to connect and share their spiritual journeys. This global network fosters a broader understanding of communal spiritual experiences and supports the idea of a universal divine union. By facilitating connections between people from different parts of the world, digital platforms reflect the universal nature of theosis. They help cultivate a sense of shared spiritual goals and experiences, highlighting the interconnectedness of all believers in their pursuit of divine unity.

Digital technologies can profoundly affect spiritual practices and communal connections and, so, shape contemporary expressions of theosis and divine transformation. These tools provide new opportunities for engagement and connection, potentially enriching the spiritual journey toward divine union.

Conclusion

THEOSIS, ALSO REFERRED TO as deification or divinization, is a central theological principle in Eastern Orthodox Christianity. While most prominent in Orthodox thought, similar ideas can be found in early Christian texts and within Catholic and Reformed traditions, though often under different names or with varying emphases. This concept draws its foundation from various biblical passages that emphasize the transformative power of the Christian life and the deep connection between believers and God. Throughout the Bible, there are numerous verses that describe the spiritual journey of followers as they grow to reflect more of God's nature through their relationship with Christ and the Holy Spirit's work.

It's crucial to understand that theosis doesn't suggest humans literally become divine beings equivalent to God. Instead, it proposes that believers can participate in and share aspects of God's divine nature in a way that's compatible with their status as created beings. This theological idea highlights the profound intimacy and ultimate purpose of the Christian faith: a transformative journey towards unity with the divine.

The incarnation of Christ played a crucial role in healing the divide between humanity and God, a separation caused by sin, beginning with Adam and Eve. By becoming human, the Son of God bridged this gap, offering humanity a chance to reconnect with the divine. Christianity uniquely posits that salvation and theosis—the process of becoming united with God and transformed into his likeness—are only achievable through Christ. His statement in John 14:6 emphasizes his unique position as the sole path to this divine union.

In Christian theology, Christ acts as both the mediator between God and humanity (as stated in 1 Tim 2:5) and the eternal High Priest who offered himself as a sacrifice for human sins (described in Heb 4:14–16 and 9:11–14). His death and resurrection are fundamental to Christian faith, providing the grace necessary for theosis. The incarnation demonstrates God's dedication to transforming human nature, allowing believers to grow in holiness and become more Christlike. Following Christ's ascension, the Holy Spirit was given to empower believers in their journey of theosis, sanctifying their lives and aligning them with God's will.

The incarnation of Christ is crucial and urgent because it's the definitive way for everyone to receive the grace needed for theosis. Through Christ's death and resurrection, God offers universal salvation, inviting humanity to restore its relationship with him, grow in holiness, and ultimately share in his divine nature. Theosis restores humanity as God's image by transforming believers into Christ's likeness through the Holy Spirit's power and God's grace. This comprehensive renewal—spiritual, moral, and relational—enables believers to reflect God's character and fulfill their original purpose as bearers of his image.

Therefore, theosis isn't just about individual spiritual growth but about restoring humanity's identity and purpose in communion with God. Christ serves as the perfect expression and restoration of God's image, as mentioned in Col 1:15 and Heb 1:3. By believing in Jesus' resurrection, believers are united with Christ in his death and resurrection. This union not only ensures forgiveness of sins but also empowers believers to live a new life in Christ, marked by righteousness and holiness, as described in Rom 6:4–11 and Col 3:1–4. Theosis is the process by which believers, empowered by the Holy Spirit, are transformed into Christ's likeness. This transformation involves growing in holiness, reflecting God's character, and participating in his divine nature, as outlined in 2 Cor 3:18 and 2 Pet 1:4.

The transfiguration and resurrection of Christ affirm God's universal invitation for all people to enter into a relationship with him through Jesus. This invitation extends to individuals from all nations, backgrounds, and life circumstances, as emphasized in John 3:16 and Rev 7:9. God's grace, demonstrated through Jesus' sacrificial death and triumphant resurrection, enables all believers to participate in theosis. It is through Christ's work and the Holy Spirit's indwelling that believers are empowered to grow in faith and become more like Christ, as described in Eph 2:8–10 and Phil 2:12–13. Theosis goes beyond personal transformation.

It involves a deep, intimate communion with God characterized by love, obedience, and spiritual growth. This relationship is highlighted in Scriptures such as John 15:5, Rom 8:29, and Gal 4:6.

In essence, these events and concepts underscore the accessibility of divine transformation to all who believe, emphasizing both the individual journey of becoming Christlike and the profound relational aspect of unity with God.

In Christian thought, theosis is a multifaceted concept that incorporates various principles and viewpoints, influenced by different theological traditions, backgrounds, and doctrinal emphases. This diversity highlights the depth and complexity of Christian understanding regarding the transformative journey towards union with God. Despite these varying perspectives, all major Christian traditions share a fundamental belief in salvation through Christ's work. The sacrificial death of Jesus on the cross and his resurrection are universally recognized as God's means of offering forgiveness and reconciliation to humanity. So, while different traditions may have distinct approaches to applying and interpreting salvation, they all center on a shared faith in Jesus Christ's salvific work as the cornerstone of their beliefs. This unity amidst diversity reflects the richness of Christian theology and practice across different denominations. It demonstrates how various interpretations can coexist within the broader framework of Christian faith, each contributing to a fuller understanding of the transformative journey towards God.

Catholicism places great importance on sacraments as vital conduits of God's grace. These include baptism, confirmation, Eucharist, reconciliation, anointing of the sick, holy orders, and matrimony. Catholics view these sacraments as external signs established by Christ to impart grace and these play a crucial role in a believer's journey to salvation. Catholic doctrine also emphasizes the significance of prayer, both communal (like liturgy) and individual, as a means to deepen one's relationship with God and receive his grace.

On the other hand, the Reformed tradition, rooted in the teachings of reformers like Martin Luther and John Calvin, highlights the concept of *sola fide* or faith alone. This doctrine maintains that salvation is achieved solely through faith in Jesus Christ, independent of any human works or merits. While the Reformed tradition acknowledges the importance of good works as evidence of faith, it asserts that these do not contribute to one's justification before God. Instead, it emphasizes that justification comes by grace alone, through faith alone, in Christ alone. This comparison illustrates the different approaches to salvation within Christian traditions, with Catholicism focusing on sacramental grace and prayer, while the Reformed tradition emphasizes faith as the sole means of justification.

Eastern Orthodox Christianity emphasizes hesychasm as a pathway to experiencing God's salvation. This practice involves contemplative prayer, stillness, and inner quietude, which aim to achieve union with God by purifying the heart and illuminating the mind through the Holy Spirit's work. The Orthodox tradition views salvation as an ongoing process of becoming more Christlike through spiritual disciplines and active participation in church life.

Teilhard de Chardin, a Catholic theologian and scientist, proposed a unique view of Christ's incarnation as a crucial moment in cosmic evolution. He suggested that Christ's presence and redemptive work transform not just humanity but the entire universe. In this view, Christ draws all of creation towards its ultimate fulfillment and perfection in God. Teilhard de Chardin's theology broadens the idea of theosis (divinization) to include not just individual believers but also a universal process initiated by Christ. According to Teilhard, the events of Christ's life—his incarnation, ministry, death, and resurrection—serve as the crucial catalyst for God's redemptive work across the entire cosmos. Through Christ, all of creation is invited to engage in divine life and to move towards a state of greater unity and perfection within God. This perspective presents a grand vision of salvation that extends beyond human spirituality to include the entire created order, emphasizing the cosmic significance of Christ's work.

Teilhard de Chardin's concepts of Christogenesis and the Omega Point offer a comprehensive view of theosis within a cosmic and evolutionary framework. This perspective portrays Christ's salvific work as transformative not just for individuals but for all of creation, as it guides everything towards ultimate unity and perfection in God. This expansive view enriches traditional understandings of theosis by emphasizing the cosmic scope of Christ's redemptive impact and the ongoing evolution of creation towards its divine destiny.

Christian theology, drawing from passages like Col 1:19–20, teaches that God's redemptive plan through Christ extends to all creation, not just humanity. This passage speaks of Christ reconciling all things to himself, both on earth and in heaven, through his sacrificial death. The idea that Christ's salvation permeates all creation and moves it towards theosis has significant implications for Christian engagement with various aspects of life. It encourages a holistic faith approach that combines spiritual growth with actions promoting justice, environmental stewardship, and ethical behavior across all life spheres. This perspective highlights the transformative power of Christ's redemption for both individuals and society as a whole. It guides believers to actively participate in God's ongoing work of renewal and reconciliation in the world, emphasizing the far-reaching effects of Christ's redemptive work, which extends beyond personal salvation to encompass social, environmental, and ethical dimensions of life.

The belief that Christ's salvation extends to all of creation implies a concern for justice and equity in human society. If all humans are seen as participants in God's redemptive plan, it follows that Christians are called to advocate for justice, defend human rights, and promote the dignity of every person. Viewing creation as participating in theosis through Christ's redemptive work encourages a responsible stewardship of the environment. Recognizing the interconnectedness of all created beings and their ultimate destiny in God fosters a sense of reverence and care for the natural world. Christians are called to be caretakers of the earth, mindful of how our actions affect ecosystems, biodiversity, and the well-being of future generations. Theosis implies a transformative process where individuals and communities are called to reflect the divine image in their lives. This includes ethical conduct guided by principles of love, justice, and compassion. Christ's salvific work not only reconciles humanity to God but also empowers believers to live virtuous lives that reflect God's character.

The theological understanding that all of creation is moving towards theosis challenges social structures and systems that perpetuate inequality, exploitation, and injustice. It calls for a transformation of societal norms and practices to align them more closely with God's kingdom values of love, peace, and solidarity. The redemptive work of Christ and its impact in the digital age, particularly concerning AI, presents an intriguing intersection of theology, technology, and ethics. Herein one might explore how Christ's redemption could potentially influence AI and vice versa.

The redemptive work of Christ offers ethical and theological insights that can guide the ethical development and use of AI in the digital age. Conversely, the integration of AI into human experience prompts theological reflection on how technology intersects with spiritual growth and the pursuit of theosis. Striking a balance between technological advancement and ethical considerations rooted in Christ's teachings is crucial for harnessing AI's potential to promote human flourishing and spiritual development in alignment with Christian principles.

> For those God foreknew he also predestined to be conformed to the image of his Son, that he might be the firstborn among many brothers and sisters. And those he predestined, he also called; those he called, he also justified; those he justified, he also glorified. (Rom 8:29–30 NIV)

Glossary

Apostolic succession: A doctrine in some Christian traditions (particularly Catholic, Orthodox, and Anglican) that asserts the uninterrupted transmission of spiritual authority from the apostles to successive bishops through the laying on of hands.

Ascetic practice: Asceticism refers to practices of self-discipline, renunciation, and austerity undertaken voluntarily as a means of spiritual growth and deeper communion with the divine. Ascetic practices can include fasting, solitude, simplicity in lifestyle, physical exertion, and other forms of self-denial. In various religious traditions, including Christianity, Buddhism, and Hinduism, asceticism aims to cultivate inner purity, detachment from worldly distractions, and a focus on spiritual development.

Athanasius of Alexandria: Athanasius (ca. AD 296–373) was a prominent early Christian theologian and bishop of Alexandria. He is best known for his defense of Nicene Christianity against the Arian heresy, which denied the full divinity of Christ. Athanasius played a crucial role in formulating orthodox Christian doctrine, particularly regarding the Trinity and the nature of Christ. His theological works, especially *On the Incarnation*, remain influential in Christian theology.

Augmented Humanity: Refers to the enhancement of human capabilities through technology, such as wearable devices, implants, or genetic modifications. It aims to improve physical, cognitive, or sensory abilities beyond natural human limits.

Augmented Intelligence: Similar to artificial intelligence (AI), augmented intelligence emphasizes the collaboration between humans and machines to enhance cognitive abilities, decision-making processes, and problem-solving capabilities.

Augustine of Hippo: Augustine was a prominent theologian and philosopher in the Christian tradition. His works, such as *Confessions* and *City of God*, profoundly influenced Western Christianity and Western philosophy.

Barlaam of Calabria: He was a Byzantine Greek scholar and theologian from Calabria, Italy. Barlaam was involved in theological controversies, particularly with Gregory Palamas, regarding hesychasm (a mystical tradition of prayer in the Eastern Orthodox Church).

Beatific vision: A term used in Christian theology, particularly in Catholicism, to describe the direct, intuitive knowledge of God enjoyed by souls in heaven. It is the ultimate goal of human existence and represents the highest form of eternal happiness and fulfillment in communion with God.

Biblical analysis: This refers to the study and interpretation of the Bible from a scholarly perspective. It involves examining the texts, contexts, languages, historical backgrounds, literary forms, and theological themes present in the Bible. Biblical analysis aims to uncover the meaning of the biblical texts and their implications for faith and practice.

Byzantine era: Refers to the period of the Byzantine Empire, which was the continuation of the Eastern Roman Empire after the fall of the Western Roman Empire. It lasted from the fourth century AD to AD 1453 (fall of Constantinople).[1]

Cappadocian Fathers: Refers to three prominent Christian theologians and church leaders of the late fourth century AD: Basil the Great, Gregory of Nazianzus (Gregory the Theologian), and Gregory of Nyssa. They played a crucial role in shaping early Christian doctrine and are known for their contributions to the understanding of the Trinity.

Catholic theology: Catholic theology refers to the systematic study and understanding of Christian beliefs, doctrines, and teachings within the Roman Catholic Church. It encompasses the exploration of God, Christ, the Holy Spirit, salvation, sacraments, moral principles, social teachings,

---

1. See Herrin, *Byzantium*.

and the church's role in the world. Catholic theology draws from Scripture, tradition, magisterial teachings (official pronouncements of the church), and the writings of theologians throughout history.

Character development: The process of cultivating virtues, values, and ethical principles that shape an individual's behavior, decisions, and interactions with others. It involves personal reflection, moral education, and experiential learning.

Christian ethics: The principles, values, and moral teachings derived from Christian Scripture (such as the Bible) and tradition. It guides ethical decision making and behavior based on beliefs about God's will, love for others, and justice.

Christian faith: This encompasses the beliefs and practices of Christianity, centered around the life, teachings, death, and resurrection of Jesus Christ. It involves placing trust and reliance on Christ for salvation and living according to biblical principles.

Christogenesis: Christogenesis is the term that Teilhard used to describe the process through which creation unfolds and reaches its fulfillment in Christ. It emphasizes that Christ's presence is not only central to human history but also to the entire cosmos, linking the divine and the material world in an ongoing process of evolution.

Church fathers: This term refers to early Christian theologians, bishops, and writers who lived from the first to the eighth centuries AD and contributed significantly to the development of Christian doctrine, theology, and spirituality. They played a crucial role in shaping the theological frameworks and doctrinal formulations of the Christian church, especially in its formative period.

Conciliar tradition: This phrase refers to the practice of and authority for decision making through councils (ecumenical councils or synods) within a church or religious tradition. These councils discuss and decide matters of doctrine, discipline, and governance.

Connectivity and unity: The idea that global interconnectedness through technology and communication networks can foster greater collaboration, understanding, and unity among individuals and societies worldwide.

Coping mechanisms: Strategies and techniques individuals use to manage stress, adversity, or emotional challenges. These can include both positive behaviors (such as exercise or social support) and negative behaviors (such as substance use) that help regulate emotions and reduce distress.

Cosmic redemption: A theological concept within Christianity that refers to the ultimate reconciliation and restoration of all creation through the redemptive work of Christ. It encompasses the belief in salvation, renewal, and the fulfillment of God's purposes for the universe.

Cosmic vision: This phrase refers to a comprehensive and inclusive view of the cosmos, often associated with philosophical or spiritual perspectives that seek to understand humanity's place in the universe and the interconnectedness of all things.

Councils of Constantinople: These refer to a series of ecumenical councils held in Constantinople (modern-day Istanbul) in the early Christian church. The most significant ones include the First Council of Constantinople (381), which affirmed the Nicene Creed and dealt with theological controversies, the Second Council of Constantinople (553), which addressed controversies over Nestorianism and Origenism, and the Third Council of Constantinople (869–870), which condemned Photius and dealt with the East-West schism.[2]

Creative expression: This refers to the process of using imagination and skill to produce original works of art, literature, music, or other forms of cultural expression. It encompasses personal and cultural identity, emotions, and social commentary.

Cultural reconciliation: This refers to the process of healing and restoring relationships between different cultural groups, often in the context of historical injustices, colonization, or cultural assimilation. It involves acknowledging past harms and promoting mutual understanding and respect.

Deification: This term is often used interchangeably with theosis. It signifies the process by which a person is transformed into a more godly or divine state. It does not imply that humans become gods in the same

---

2. See Socrates, *Ecclesiastical History of Constantinople*.

sense as God but rather that they participate in the divine nature and become increasingly like God in their virtues and spiritual qualities.

Digital immortality: This is the concept of preserving a person's identity, memories, and consciousness in digital form beyond their biological lifespan. It explores possibilities such as uploading minds into virtual environments or creating digital avatars that simulate the person's personality and experiences.

Digital Religion: This refers to religious practices and beliefs expressed and mediated through digital technologies and online platforms. It encompasses virtual communities, online rituals, digital sacred spaces, and religious discourse in digital spaces.

Divinization: Similar to deification, divinization emphasizes the process of becoming divine or godlike. It underscores the idea that humans are called to share in God's nature through grace and participation in the life of God.

Eastern Orthodox theology: This refers to the theological beliefs, doctrines, and practices of the Eastern Orthodox Church. It encompasses a rich tradition of theology that differs in some respects from Western Christian theology, particularly in its emphasis on mystical experience, theosis, and the importance of the early church fathers.

Ecclesial authority: This refers to the influence and teachings of the early church fathers in shaping the doctrines, practices, and governance of the church. Their writings and theological contributions were foundational in defining the church's authority in matters of doctrine, discipline, and ecclesiastical structure. The early church fathers are considered instrumental in preserving and transmitting the faith in the formative centuries of Christianity.

Ecological stewardship: Ecological stewardship refers to the responsible and sustainable management of the earth's natural resources and environment. It emphasizes the ethical responsibility of humans to care for creation, protect biodiversity, conserve ecosystems, and address environmental issues such as pollution, climate change, and habitat destruction. Ecological stewardship is often grounded in religious or ethical principles that recognize the intrinsic value of nature and the interconnectedness of all living beings.

Ecumenical dialogue: Ecumenical dialogue refers to efforts and conversations aimed at promoting understanding, cooperation, and unity among different Christian denominations, traditions, and churches. It seeks to overcome historical divisions, doctrinal differences, and misunderstandings through respectful dialogue, theological exchange, joint prayer, shared projects, and common witness to the Christian faith. Ecumenical dialogue strives towards visible unity among Christians while respecting diverse theological perspectives and ecclesiastical practices.

Engagement with the world: This phrase denotes the active involvement of individuals or communities in addressing social, political, environmental, or ethical issues. It reflects a commitment to making a positive impact and promoting meaningful change in society.

Environmental stewardship: This refers to the responsible management and care of the environment, considering the ethical, ecological, and social aspects of sustainability. It involves actions aimed at preserving and protecting natural resources and ecosystems.

Epithimian pneuma: *Epithimian pneuma* translates from Greek to "the spirit of desire" or "the spirit of longing." In Christian theology, it can refer to the spiritual desire or longing that exists within humans, which can be directed positively towards spiritual growth and communion with God.[3]

Epithimian sarkos: *Epithimian sarkos* translates from Greek to "the desire of the flesh." In theological contexts, it often refers to earthly or sinful desires associated with the physical or material aspects of human nature, which can lead away from spiritual growth or communion with God.[4]

Eschatological hope: Eschatological hope refers to the hope or expectation concerning the ultimate destiny or future fulfillment of humanity and the world, as understood in religious or theological contexts. It often relates to beliefs about the end times, resurrection, judgment, and the establishment of God's kingdom or the final state of existence.

Ethical considerations: Refers to the careful examination of moral principles and values in decision making, particularly in fields such as

---

3. See Climacus, *Ladder of Divine Ascent*.
4. See Ware, *Orthodox Way*.

technology, medicine, and governance. It involves assessing potential impacts on individuals, societies, and the environment.

Ethics: Ethics refers to principles of right conduct and moral behavior that guide individuals or communities in distinguishing between right and wrong actions. Ethical frameworks are shaped by religious teachings, philosophical traditions, cultural norms, and legal principles. In religious contexts, ethics often reflect beliefs about the nature of God, human dignity, justice, compassion, and the responsibilities of individuals towards others and the broader community.

Evolutionary perspective: This can refer to various perspectives, but in a broad sense, it relates to viewing phenomena (such as religious beliefs, moral systems, or cultural practices) through the lens of evolution and adaptation over time. It can also refer to the evolutionary psychology perspective on human behavior and cognition.

Forgiveness: The intentional and voluntary process of letting go of feelings of resentment, anger, or vengeance toward a person or group who has harmed you. It is often viewed as a crucial element of spiritual and emotional healing.

Grace of God: In Christian theology, grace refers to the unmerited favor and divine assistance given to humans by God. It is understood as a gift freely given by God to empower individuals to live according to his will and to attain salvation.

Gratitude: The practice of recognizing and appreciating the positive aspects of life, acknowledging blessings, and expressing thankfulness. It is considered a virtue in many religious and philosophical traditions.

Gregory of Nyssa: Gregory of Nyssa (ca. AD 335–95) was a Christian bishop and theologian, recognized as one of the Cappadocian Fathers, alongside his brother Basil the Great and his friend Gregory Nazianzus. He made significant contributions to Christian theology, particularly in developing the doctrine of the Trinity and the concept of spiritual perfection. Gregory of Nyssa's writings also explore themes of mystical theology and the journey of the soul towards union with God.

Gregory Palamas: Gregory Palamas (AD 1296-1359) was an Eastern Orthodox theologian and monk from Mount Athos. He is best known for his defense of hesychasm, a mystical prayer tradition focusing on inner stillness and contemplative prayer. Palamas articulated the distinction between God's essence and energies, affirming that through participation in God's uncreated energies, humans can experience divine union and transformation. His theological teachings had a significant impact on Eastern Orthodox spirituality.[5]

Hahomer, Yosarenu: *Hahomer* (הַחֹמֶר) is a Hebrew word that translates to "the clay" or "the material." In Isa 64:8, it symbolizes humanity in its basic form, much like clay is the raw material from which pottery or sculptures are made. In this context, *hahome* represents humanity in its initial state—pliable, moldable, and in need of shaping. It emphasizes the relationship between God as the Creator (the potter) and humanity as the created (the clay). The imagery suggests that God has the ability to shape and mold human lives according to his purposes and will.[6]

Hesychasm: A mystical tradition in Eastern Orthodox Christianity that emphasizes quiet, inner prayer and the direct experience of God through stillness (hesychia) and repetitive prayer, particularly the Jesus Prayer ("Lord Jesus Christ, Son of God, have mercy on me, a sinner").

Historical development: This term typically refers to the evolution or progression of ideas, doctrines, practices, or institutions over time. In theological or religious contexts, it often involves tracing how beliefs and teachings have developed from their origins through various stages in history. Understanding historical development helps scholars and theologians grasp how theological concepts have been shaped by cultural, social, and intellectual factors.

Human flourishing: Human flourishing refers to the holistic development and fulfillment of human potential, encompassing physical, emotional, intellectual, social, and spiritual well-being. It involves the realization of individual talents and capacities, meaningful relationships, a sense of purpose and dignity, and participation in flourishing communities. In philosophical and theological contexts, human flourishing is often linked to ethical principles, justice, human rights, and the common good.

---

5. See Meyendorff, *Study of Palamas*.
6. See Brown et al., *Hebrew and English Lexicon*. See also Oswalt, *Book of Isaiah*.

Illumination: Illumination generally refers to the process of enlightenment or spiritual understanding. In religious contexts, it often denotes the reception of divine or spiritual knowledge, insight, or understanding. For example, in Christian mysticism, illumination can refer to a state of spiritual insight or awareness granted by God.

***Imago Dei*:** *Imago Dei* is a Latin term meaning "image of God." It originates from the Christian theological concept that humans are created in the image and likeness of God (Gen 1:26–27). This belief underscores the inherent dignity, worth, and sacredness of every human being.

Imitatio Christi: Latin for "imitation of Christ," this concept refers to the spiritual practice of modeling one's life and actions after Jesus Christ, particularly in terms of virtues, compassion, and moral teachings.

Incarnation: In Christian theology, the incarnation refers to the belief that the Son of God, the Second Person of the Trinity, took on human flesh in the person of Jesus Christ. It is central to Christian faith as it signifies God becoming fully human while remaining fully divine. The incarnation is seen as the pivotal event through which God entered into human history to reconcile humanity to himself.

Indigenous leadership: Leadership within indigenous communities that draws on traditional values, knowledge, and practices. It often emphasizes community consensus, stewardship of natural resources, and cultural preservation.

***Kidmutenu*:** *Kidmutenu* (כִּדְמוּתֵנוּ) is a Hebrew word that can be translated as "likeness" or "similarity" (Gen 1:26). In the context of the theology, particularly in Christian theology and Jewish thought, it denotes not only a physical resemblance but also a moral and spiritual likeness to God.

Liturgical worship: Liturgical worship refers to formal religious worship conducted according to prescribed rituals, prayers, and ceremonies. It often follows a set order or liturgy, which may vary depending on the Christian tradition (e.g., Eastern Orthodox, Roman Catholic, Anglican). Liturgical worship emphasizes participation in communal prayer, sacraments (such as Eucharist or Communion), Scripture readings, hymns, and symbolic actions that express faith and devotion. It serves to unite believers in worship and strengthen their spiritual life through shared rituals and sacred practices.

Maximus the Confessor: A Christian monk, theologian, and scholar who lived in the seventh century AD. He is known for his profound mystical theology and defense of Orthodox Christian doctrine, particularly against Monothelitism.[7]

Mindfulness: A Buddhist concept that has been secularized and adopted widely, mindfulness refers to the practice of being present and aware in the current moment, without judgment. It involves paying attention to thoughts, feelings, sensations, and the environment.

Missional theology: A theological perspective that emphasizes the church's mission or purpose in the world; it focuses on outreach, evangelism, and social justice. It seeks to understand and engage with contemporary culture and contexts in spreading the message of faith.

Mystical body of Christ: A theological concept within Christianity that describes the unity of believers as a spiritual body or organism with Christ as its head. It emphasizes the interconnectedness and shared identity of all Christians, who together form the church.

Mystical experience: Mystical experience refers to direct encounters or communion with the divine or ultimate reality that transcends ordinary sensory perception and rational understanding. Mystical experiences often involve a sense of union with God, spiritual illumination, profound insight into the nature of existence, or a heightened awareness of spiritual truths. Mysticism is found in various religious traditions and is characterized by practices such as contemplative prayer, meditation, and asceticism.

Nature of God: The nature of God refers to the fundamental characteristics or attributes that define the divine essence in various religious traditions. In monotheistic religions such as Christianity, Islam, and Judaism, the nature of God often includes qualities such as omnipotence (all-powerful), omniscience (all-knowing), omnipresence (present everywhere), eternal existence, goodness, justice, and love. Understanding the nature of God is central to theological inquiry and shapes beliefs about God's relationship with humanity and the universe.

---

7. See Maximus the Confessor, *Cosmic Mystery of Christ*.

Networked Consciousness: The idea that interconnected technologies and devices could lead to a collective or shared consciousness, where information and experiences are seamlessly shared among individuals and machines.

Noosphere: Coined by Pierre Teilhard de Chardin, the noosphere refers to the sphere of human thought, encompassing all human knowledge, culture, and communication. It represents the next stage of evolution beyond the biosphere.[8]

Omega Point: A concept proposed by Pierre Teilhard de Chardin, Omega Point suggests a maximum level of complexity and consciousness, towards which he believed the universe was evolving. It's a speculative idea in the philosophy of science and metaphysics.

Orthodox Theology: Refers to the theological beliefs and teachings of Eastern Orthodox Christianity. It includes doctrines, practices, and interpretations of scripture that are traditionally held by Orthodox Christian communities.

Partakers of the divine nature: The phrase "partakers of the divine nature" is found in 2 Pet 1:4 of the New Testament. In Greek, it is *Theias koinonoi physeōs* (θείας κοινωνοὶ φύσεως). This verse highlights that through God's promises, believers are enabled to partake in the divine nature, escaping the corruption of the world caused by sinful desires. The promises referred to in the passage are God's gifts and assurances—specifically, the promise of salvation through Jesus Christ, which includes the gift of the Holy Spirit and the transformative power of faith. Through these promises, Christians are spiritually transformed, enabling them to reflect God's character and attributes, growing in holiness and virtue.

Prayer: Prayer is a form of communication with the divine or spiritual entities, expressing reverence, supplication, thanksgiving, or worship. In religious contexts, prayer serves as a means of seeking guidance, solace, forgiveness, and communion with God or gods. It can take various forms, including spoken words, meditation, contemplation, and ritualized gestures. Prayer plays a central role in the spiritual life of believers across different religions and denominations.

---

8. See Teilhard de Chardin, *Phenomenon of Man*.

Priesthood of all believers: A Protestant Christian doctrine that asserts the equal spiritual priesthood of all believers, emphasizing direct access to God and the responsibility of all Christians to serve as priests to one another.

Prophetic fulfillment: In religious contexts, particularly in Judaism and Christianity, this refers to the belief that certain prophecies (predictions made by prophets) have been fulfilled by subsequent events or the actions of specific individuals.

Prophetic fulfillment: Refers to the belief in the fulfillment of prophecies or predictions made by prophets in religious traditions. It often signifies the realization of divine promises or the accomplishment of God's purposes through historical events or spiritual revelations.

Protestant theology: Protestant theology encompasses the diverse theological perspectives and beliefs within Protestant Christianity, which emerged from the Protestant Reformation in the sixteenth century. It includes various denominations and theological traditions such as Lutheranism, Calvinism, Anglicanism, Methodism, Baptist, and others. Protestant theology emphasizes principles such as *sola scriptura* (Scripture alone as the basis for faith and practice), justification by faith alone, the priesthood of all believers, and the authority of conscience in interpreting Scripture.

Psychological well-being: Refers to an individual's emotional, social, and psychological state of being. It encompasses factors such as life satisfaction, positive emotions, resilience, and self-fulfillment.

Purification: In religious and spiritual contexts, purification typically refers to the process of removing impurities or sins, often through rituals, practices, or inner spiritual transformation. For example, in Christianity, purification can refer to the cleansing of sins through confession or baptism.

Restorative justice: A system of criminal justice that focuses on the rehabilitation of offenders through reconciliation with victims and the community. It seeks to repair the harm caused by crime rather than just punishing offenders.

Sacraments: Sacraments are sacred rituals or ceremonies recognized as outward signs of inward spiritual grace, instituted by Christ or established by tradition within Christian churches. Common sacraments include baptism, Eucharist (Communion), confirmation, penance (confession), anointing of the sick (and last rites), matrimony, and holy orders (ordination). Through sacraments, participants believe they receive spiritual blessings and are united more closely with God and the Christian community.

Salvation: Salvation is the theological concept concerning deliverance from sin and its consequences, resulting in reconciliation with God and eternal life. It is a central theme in Christianity, which emphasizes God's grace and the redemptive work of Jesus Christ through his life, death, and resurrection. Salvation encompasses forgiveness, justification, regeneration, adoption into God's family, and the hope of eternal life.

Sanctification: Sanctification refers to the process by which believers are progressively transformed into the image of Christ. It involves the work of the Holy Spirit in the life of a Christian, enabling them to grow in holiness, righteousness, and conformity to God's will. Sanctification is understood as a lifelong journey of spiritual growth and moral purification.

Self-transcendence: The concept of moving beyond one's individual concerns and limitations to connect with broader or higher realities, such as spiritual or communal values. It involves personal growth, spiritual development, and a sense of purpose beyond oneself.

Social justice: Social justice refers to the fair and equitable distribution of resources, opportunities, and rights within society, ensuring that all individuals have access to basic needs, dignity, and equal treatment. It involves addressing systemic inequalities, advocating for the rights of marginalized groups, and promoting policies that foster inclusivity, human rights, and economic fairness. Social justice is rooted in ethical principles and is a core concern in many religious traditions, prompting believers to engage in activism and advocacy for societal change.

***Sola fide*:** Latin for "faith alone," *sola fide* is a Protestant theological doctrine that asserts that faith in Jesus Christ is the only means by which a person can receive God's grace and salvation, as opposed to reliance on good works.

***Sola gratia*:** Latin for "grace alone," this doctrine emphasizes that salvation comes by God's grace alone, apart from any human effort or merit.

***Sola scriptura*:** Latin for "Scripture alone," it is the Protestant doctrine that the Bible contains all knowledge necessary for salvation and holiness and is the sole authority in matters of faith and practice.

Spiritual life: Spiritual life refers to the lived experience of faith and relationship with God within a religious or spiritual context. It encompasses practices, beliefs, experiences, and disciplines that deepen one's connection to the divine and foster personal transformation. Spiritual life often involves prayer, meditation, worship, ethical living, and engagement with sacred texts, traditions, and community.

Spiritual transformation: This refers to the process by which a person undergoes significant change in their inner being, beliefs, and behaviors through the work of the Holy Spirit. It involves becoming more Christlike in character and aligning one's life with the teachings and principles of Christianity.

***Tamunateka*:** This word is derived from the root תמונה (*temunah*), which means "likeness" or "image." *Tamunateka* can be translated as "your likeness" or "your form." It is found in Ps 17:15. In this verse, the psalmist expresses a deep longing and assurance of being satisfied by seeing God's face in righteousness. The phrase "when I awake" (בְּעִירֹתִי, *beiruti*) suggests a state of awakening or enlightenment. This awakening implies not merely physical awakening from sleep, but a spiritual awakening or awareness. It denotes a moment of heightened consciousness where one perceives and experiences God's presence and righteousness fully.[9]

Early church fathers: These are influential Christian theologians, writers, and leaders from the first few centuries of Christianity, whose writings and teachings helped shape early Christian doctrine and practices. Examples include Augustine, Jerome, Gregory the Great, and Athanasius.

Theological significance: This refers to the importance or relevance of a theological concept, doctrine, or belief within the framework of a particular religious tradition or system. It involves considering how a theological idea contributes to the understanding of God, human existence,

---

9. See Barker, *NIV Study Bible*.

salvation, ethics, and other aspects of faith. Theological significance often explores the implications and applications of beliefs for personal spirituality and communal life.

Theophany: This term signifies a visible manifestation of a deity to a human being. In religious contexts, it often refers to the appearance of God or a god to a person, conveying a divine message or presence.

***Theosis*:** Also known as divinization or deification, *theosis* is the process of a Christian becoming more like God and ultimately sharing in his divine nature. It's a central theme in Eastern Orthodox theology and involves the idea of humans being transformed and united with God in a profound way.

Transcendence of boundaries: The concept of overcoming physical, cultural, or philosophical limitations through technological advancements, social change, or spiritual growth. It explores the idea of expanding perspectives and possibilities beyond conventional limits.

Transfiguration of Christ: The transfiguration of Christ refers to an event described in the New Testament where Jesus undergoes a profound spiritual and physical change in appearance while on a mountain with three of his disciples (Matt 17:1-9; Mark 9:2-8; Luke 9:28-36). During this event, Jesus' face and clothes are said to have shone brightly, and he is seen conversing with Moses and Elijah. This event is significant in affirming Jesus' divine nature and mission.

Union with Christ: Union with Christ refers to the mystical or spiritual bond between believers and Jesus Christ, understood as central to Christian salvation and spiritual life. It encompasses the idea that through faith and baptism, Christians are united with Christ in his death and resurrection, and, so, share in his divine life and become partakers of his grace, righteousness, and eternal life. Union with Christ is a foundational concept in Christian spirituality and theological reflection.

Bibliography

Alexander, T. Desmond, and Brian S. Rosner, eds. *The New Dictionary of Biblical Theology: Exploring the Unity and Diversity of Scripture*. InterVarsity, 2000.

Anastos, Thomas L. "Gregory Palamas' Radicalization of the Essence, Energies, and Hypostasis Model of God." *Greek Orthodox Theological Review* 38.1–4 (1993) 335–49.

Anatolios, Khaled. *Athanasius and the Early Development of Trinitarian Theology*. Oxford: Oxford University Press, 2007.

Aquinas, Thomas. *Summa Theologiae*. 2nd ed. Translated by Fathers of the English Dominican Province. Revised by Kevin Knight. https://www.newadvent.org/summa/.

Athanasius. *The Incarnation of the Word*. In vol. 4 of *The Nicene and Post-Nicene Fathers*, Series 2. Edited by Philip Schaff and Henry Wace. 1886–89. 14 vols. Reprint, Peabody, MA: Hendrickson, 1995. https://ccel.org/ccel/schaff/npnf204/npnf204.vii.i.html.

Augustine. "Homily 7 on the First Epistle of John." Translated by H. Browne. From vol. 7 of *The Nicene and Post-Nicene Fathers*, Series 1. Buffalo, NY: Christian Literature Publishing, 1888. Revised by Kevin Knight. https://www.newadvent.org/fathers/170207.htm.

———. "Tractate 17." Translated by John Gibb. From vol. 7 of *The Nicene and Post-Nicene Fathers*, Series 1. Buffalo, NY: Christian Literature Publishing, 1888. Revised by Kevin Knight. https://www.newadvent.org/fathers/1701017.htm.

Ayres, Lewis. "Deification and the Dynamics of Nicene Theology: The Contribution of Gregory of Nyssa." *St. Vladimir's Theological Quarterly* 49.4 (2005) 375–94.

Bainbridge, W. S. *The Interface Between Science and Religion*. Cambridge: Cambridge University Press, 2007.

Barker, Kenneth L., ed. *NIV Study Bible*. Grand Rapids: Zondervan, 2002.

Barnes, Albert. *Notes on the New Testament, Explanatory and Practical: James, Peter, John, and Jude*. Edited by Robert Frew. Grand Rapids: Baker, 1959.

Barnett, Paul. *The Second Epistle to the Corinthians*. New International Commentary on the New Testament. Grand Rapids: Eerdmans, 1997.

Barth, Karl. *Church Dogmatics*. Vol. IV/1. *The Doctrine of Reconciliation*. Edited by Thomas F. Torrance and Geoffrey W. Bromiley. Translated by Geoffrey W. Bromiley. Edinburgh: T&T Clark, 1956.

Bauckham, Richard J. *2 Peter, Jude*. Word Biblical Commentary 50. Waco, TX: Word, 1983.

Blue Letter Bible. "μεταμορφόω." https://www.blueletterbible.org/lexicon/g3339/kjv/tr/0-1/.

Böhme, Jacob. *Mysterium Magnum*. Vol. 1. Translated by John Sparrow. London: Theosophical, 1962.

Bostrom, Nick. *Superintelligence: Paths, Dangers, Strategies*. Oxford: Oxford University Press, 2014.

Bradshaw, David. "The Concept of Divine Energies." *Philosophy and Theology* 18.1 (2006) 93–120.

Brown, F., et al. *The Brown-Driver-Briggs Hebrew and English Lexicon*. Peabody, MA: Hendrickson Academic, 1994.

Bruggeman, Walter. *Genesis*. Interpretation. Louisville: John Knox, 1982.

———. *The Message of the Psalms: A Theological Commentary*. Minneapolis: Augsburg Fortress, 1984.

———. *Peace: The Biblical Message of Shalom*. Nashville: Abingdon, 2001.

Calvin, John. *Institutes of the Christian Religion*. 2 vols. Edited by John T. McNeill. Translated by Ford Lewis Battles. Louisville: Westminster John Knox, 1960.

Carson, D. A. *The Difficult Doctrine of the Love of God*. Wheaton, IL: Crossway, 2000.

Catechism of the Catholic Church. 2nd ed. Vatican City: Vatican Press, 1997.

Chistyakova, Olga. "Eastern Church Fathers on Being Human—Dichotomy in Essence and Wholeness in Deification." *Religions* 12.8.575 (2021) 1–11. https://doi.org/10.3390/rel12080575.

Chittick, William C. *The Sufi Path of Love: The Spiritual Teachings of Rumi*. New York: State University of New York Press, 1983.

Clendenin, Daniel B. *Eastern Orthodox Christianity: A Western Perspective*. 2nd ed. Grand Rapids: Baker Academic, 2003.

———. "Partakers of Divinity: The Orthodox Doctrine of Theosis." *Journal of the Evangelical Theological Society* 37.3 (Sept. 1994) 365–79.

Climacus, John. *The Ladder of Divine Ascent*. Translated by Lazarus Moore. Edited by Holy Transfiguration Monastery. Boston: Holy Transfiguration Monastery, 1959.

Collins, Kenneth J. *The Theology of John Wesley: Holy Love and the Shape of Grace*. Nashville: Abingdon, 2007.

Congar, Yves. *The Meaning of Traditon*. Translated by Herbert Beichner. 2nd ed. New York: Seabury, 1964.

Corbin-Reuschling, Wyndy. "The Means and End in 2 Peter 1:3–11: The Theological and Moral Significance of 'Theōsis.'" *Journal of Theological Interpretation* 8.2 (Sept. 2014) 275–86.

Cross, F. L., and E. A. Livingstone, eds. *The Oxford Dictionary of the Christian Church*. 3rd ed. Oxford: Oxford University Press, 2005.

Daley, Brian. *Gregory of Nazianzus*. London: Routledge, 2006.

Davids, Peter H. *The Letters of 2 Peter and Jude*. Pillar New Testament Commentary. Grand Rapids: Eerdmans, 2006.

Doudna, Jennifer A., and Samuel H. Sternberg. *A Crack in Creation: Gene Editing and the Unthinkable Power to Control Evolution*. Boston: Mariner, 2017.

Emmons, R. A. *The Psychology of Ultimate Concerns: Motivation and Spirituality in Personality*. New York: Guilford, 2000.

Evans, Gillian, ed. *The First Christian Theologians*. Oxford: Blackwell, 2007.

George, Archimandrite. *Theosis: The True Purpose of Human Life*. 4th ed. Mount Athos: Holy Monastery of St. Gregorios, 2006.

Gorman, Michael J. *Inhabiting the Cruciform God: Kenosis, Justification, and Theosis in Paul's Narrative Soteriology*. Grand Rapids: Eerdmans, 2009. Kindle.

Gregory of Nazianzus. *On God and Christ: The Five Theological Orations and Two Letters to Cledonius*. Popular Patristics. Crestwood, NY: SVSP, 2002.

Gregory of Nyssa. *On the Making of Man*. In vol. 5 of *The Nicene and Post-Nicene Fathers*, Series 2. Edited by Philip Schaff. 1886–89. 14 vols. Reprint, Peabody, MA: Hendrickson, 1995.

———. *On the Soul and the Resurrection*. Translated by Catherine P. Roth. Crestwood, NY: SVSP, 1993.

Hamilton, Victor P. *The Book of Genesis: Chapters 1–17*. Grand Rapids: Eerdmans, 1990.

Haught, John F. *Teilhard de Chardin: Theology, Humanity, and the Cosmos*. Berkeley: University of California Press, 1981.

Hausherr, Irénée. *The Name of Jesus: The Names of Jesus Used by Early Christians and the Development of the "Jesus Prayer."* Translated by Charles Cummings. Collegeville, MN: Cistercian, 1978.

Haynes, Daniel. "The Metaphysics of Christian Ethics: Radical Orthodoxy and Theosis." *Heythrop* 52.4 (2011) 659–71.

Hays, Richard. *2 Corinthians: A Commentary*. Louisville: Westminster John Knox Press, 2012.

Henry, Matthew. *Commentary on the Whole Bible*. Peabody, MA: Hendrickson, 2008.

Herrin, Judith. *Byzantium: The Surprising Life of a Medieval Empire*. Princeton: Princeton University Press, 2007.

Hopko, Thomas. *The Winter Pascha: Readings for the Lenten Triodion*. SVSP, 2008.

Horton, Michael. *A Better Way: Rediscovering the Drama of Scripture*. Wheaton, IL: Crossway, 2012.

Irenaeus. *Against Heresies*. In vol. 1 of *The Ante-Nicene Fathers*. Edited by Alexander Roberts and James Donaldson. 1885–87. 10 vols. Reprint, Peabody, MA: Hendrickson, 1994.

Kharlamov, Vladimir. "*Theosis* in Patristic Thought." *Theology Today* 65.2 (2008) 158–68. https://doi.org/10.1177/004057360806500203.

King, Ursula. *Spirit of Fire: The Life and Vision of Pierre Teilhard de Chardin*. Maryknoll, NY: Orbis, 2015.

Koenig, H. G. "Research on Religion and Aging: Emerging Theoretical Perspectives and Findings." *Journal of Aging and Health* 21.1 (2009) 181–211.

Krivocheine, Basil. *In the Light of Christ: Saint Symeon the New Theologian*. Crestwood, NY: SVSP, 1986.

Kurzweil, Ray. *The Singularity Is Near*. New York: Penguin, 2005.

Leliovskyi, Mykola. "Eastern Orthodox Doctrine of Theosis." Paper presented in partial fulfillment of requirements for BTS 571, Contemporary Issues in Theology, Master's College, 2011. https://www.academia.edu/10941891/THE_EASTERN_ORTHODOX_DOCTRINE_OF_THEOSIS.

Litwa, M. David. *We Are Being Transformed: Deification in Paul's Soteriology*. Berlin: De Gruyter, 2012.

Lollini, Massimo. "The Blind Spot of the Future." *Humanist Studies & the Digital Age* 7.1 (2022) 1–6. https://journals.oregondigital.org/hsda/index.

Lossky, Vladimir. *The Mystical Theology of the Eastern Church*. London: James Clarke, 1968.

———. *Orthodox Theology: An Introduction*. Translated by Ian and Ihita Kesarcodi-Watson. Crestwood, NY: SVSP, 1978.

Louth, Andrew. *The Origins of the Christian Mystical Tradition: From Plato to Denys*. Oxford: Clarendon Press, 1981.

Luther, Martin. *Commentary on Galatians*. Translated by A. T. W. Steinhaeuser. Grand Rapids: Baker, 1953.

MacDonald, William. *Believer's Bible Commentary*. Nashville: Thomas Nelson, 1995.

MacLaren, Alexander. "Partakers of the Divine Nature (2 Peter 1:4)" Blue Letter Bible. https://www.blueletterbible.org/comm/maclaren_alexander/expositions-of-holy-scripture/2-peter/partakers-of-the-divine-nature.cfm.

Marion, Jim. *Putting on the Mind of Christ: The Inner Work of Christian Spirituality*. Charlottesville, VA: Hampton Roads, 2011.

Marshall, Howard I. *The Letters of John*. New International Commentary on the New Testament. Grand Rapids: Eerdmans, 1978.

Maslow, Abraham H. *Motivation and Personality*. 3rd ed. New York: Harper & Row, 1987.

Maximus the Confessor. *On the Cosmic Mystery of Christ*. Translated by Paul M. Blowers. Crestwood, NY: SVSP, 2003.

———. *The Writings of Saint Maximus the Confessor*. Vol. 1. Translated by George C. Berthold. Chicago: University of Chicago Press, 2015.

McDermott, John L. *Teilhard de Chardin and the Church*. New York: Fordham University Press, 1975.

McGrath, Alister E. *Christian Theology: An Introduction*. 6th ed. Hoboken, NJ: Wiley-Blackwell, 2017.

McGuckin, John A. "Christian Spirituality in Byzantium and the East (600–1700)." In *The Blackwell Companion to Christian Spirituality*, edited by Arthur Holder. London: Blackwell, 2005.

Medved, Goran. "Theosis (Deification) as a New Testament and Evangelical Doctrine." KAIROS 13.2 (2019) 159–82. https://doi.org/10.32862/k.13.2.1.

Meyendorff, John. *Byzantine Hesychasm: Historical, Theological, and Social Problems*. London: Variorum, 1974.

———. *Byzantine Theology: Historical Trends and Doctrinal Themes*. New York: Fordham University Press, 1974.

———. *Introduction a l'étude de Grégoire Palamas*. Paris: Éditions du Seuil, 1959.

———. *St. Gregory Palamas and Orthodox Spirituality*. Crestwood, NY: SVSP, 1974.

———. *A Study of Gregory Palamas*. Translated by George Lawrence. London: Faith, 1974.

Milligan, Ian. *The Transformation of Historical Research in the Digital Age*. Cambridge University Press, 2022.

Moo, Douglas J. *The Letter to the Romans*. New International Commentary on the New Testament. Grand Rapids: Eerdmans, 1996.

Nasr, Seyyed Hossein. *The Heart of Islam: Enduring Values for Humanity*. New York: HarperOne, 2002.

Nodes, Daniel J. "A Witness to Theosis Effected: Maximus Confessor on the Lord's Prayer." *St. Vladimir's Theological Quarterly* 54.1 (2010) 69–83.

Olson, Roger E. "Deification." In *Encyclopedia of Christian Theology*, edited by Jean-Yves Lacoste, 1:342–44. London: Routledge, 2005.

Oswalt, John N. *Book of Isaiah: Chapters 40–66*. New International Commentary on the Old Testament. Grand Rapids: Eerdmans, 1998.
Packer, J. I. "What Did the Cross Achieve? The Logic of Penal Substitution." *Tyndale Bulletin* 25 (1974) 3–45.
Palamas, Gregory. *The Triads*. Translated by John Meyendorff. Mahwah, NJ: Paulist, 1983.
Palmer, G. E. H., et al., eds. *Philokalia*. 5 vols. Translated by G. E. H. Palmer. London: Faber & Faber, 1981.
Pargament, K. I. *The Psychology of Religion and Coping: Theory, Research, Practice*. New York: Guilford, 1997.
Plummer, Alfred. "The Second Epistle of St. Peter." Bible.org., *Ellicott's Commentary for English Readers*. https://biblehub.com/commentaries/ellicott/2_peter/1.htm.>.
Powell, Mark A. *The New Testament: A Historical and Theological Introduction*. Grand Rapids: Baker Academic, 2018.
Rakestraw, Robert V. "Becoming Like God: An Evangelical Doctrine of Theosis." *Journal of the Evangelical Theological Society* 40.2 (June 1997) 257–69.
Rossi, Andrew Del. "Teilhard's Catholicity: An Evolution of Consciousness." *Religions* 12.9.728 (2021) 1–8. https://doi.org/10.3390/rel12090728.
Russell, Norman. *The Doctrine of Deification in the Greek Patristic Tradition*. Oxford: Oxford University Press, 2006. Kindle.
Schreiner, Thomas R. *1, 2 Peter, Jude*. Nashville: Holman Reference, 2003.
Sider, Ronald J. *The Scandal of the Evangelical Conscience: Why Are Christians Living Just Like the World?* Grand Rapids: Baker, 2005.
Sivananda, Swami, ed and trans. *The Bhagavad Gita*. Rishikesh: DLS, 2010.
Socrates. *The Ecclesiastical History of Socrates Scholasticus*. Translated by A. C. Zenos. In vol. 2 of *The Nicene and Post-Nicene Fathers*, Series 2. Edited by Philip Schaff and Henry Wace. 1886–89. 14 vols. Reprint, Peabody, MA: Hendrickson, 1995.
Stavropoulos, Christoforos. *Partakers of Divine Nature*. Minneapolis: Light & Life, 1976.
Stott, John R. W. *The Cross of Christ*. Downers Grove, IL: InterVarsity, 1987.
Surowiecki, James. *The Wisdom of Crowds*. New York: Doubleday, 2004.
Teilhard de Chardin, Pierre. *Christianity and Evolution*. Translated by René Hague. New York: Harcourt, 1969.
———. *The Divine Milieu*. New York: HarperCollins, 1960.
———. *The Future of Man*. New York: HarperCollins, 1964.
———. *The Phenomenon of Man*. Translated by Bernard Wall. New York: Harper & Row, 1959.
———. *Science and Christ*. Translated by René Hague. New York: Harper & Row, 1968.
Thomas, Stephen. *Deification in the Eastern Orthodox Tradition: A Biblical Perspective*. Gorgias Eastern Christian Studies 2. Piscataway, NJ: Gorgias, 2007.
Thunberg, Lars. *Microcosm and Mediator: The Theological Anthropology of Maximus the Confessor*. Lund: C. W. K. Gleerup, 1965.
Toulis, Petros N. "Orthodox Understanding of Religions: The Role of Contextual Theology." Paper presented at the Eupropean Intensive Programme, Constanța, Sept. 9–22, 2012. https://www.academia.edu/2642828/Orthodox_understanding_of_other_religions_The_role_of_contextual_theology_.
van Rossum, Joost. "Deification in Palamas and Aquinas." *St. Vladimir's Theological Quarterly* 47.3 (2003) 365–82.

Vishnevskaya, Elena. *Divinization as Perichoretic Embrace in Maximus the Confessor*. In Partakers of the Divine Nature: The History and Development of Deification in the Christian Traditions, edited by Michael J. Christensen and Jeffery A. Wittung, 132–45. Grand Rapids: Baker Academic, 2008.

Ware, Kallistos. *The Orthodox Church: An Introduction to Eastern Christianity*. New York: Penguin, 1963.

———. *The Orthodox Way*. Crestwood, NY: SVSP, 1995.

———. *The Power of the Name: The Jesus Prayer in Orthodox Spirituality*. 2nd ed. Oxford: SLG, 1986.

The Way of a Pilgrim. Translated by R. M. French. London: Faber & Faber, 1954.

Zhang, Jie, and Zhisheng Chen. "Exploring Human Rersource Management Digital Transformation in the Digital Age." *Journal of the Knowledge Economy* 15 (2024) 1482–98. https://doi.org/10.1007/s13132-023-01214-y.

Zizioulas, John D. *Being as Communion: Studies in Personhood and the Church*. Crestwood, NY: SVSP, 1985.

Subject Index

Adoption, 5, 5n5
Augmented Humanity, 200, 202
Augmented intelligence, 210n11
Auten, 64

Baptism, 36, 128
Byzantine era, 42, 49

Chrismation, 36
Christian ethics, 190
Christic principle, 163
Christogenesis, 165, 166n7, 168n11, 172, 178n14
Compassion, 144
Conciliarity, 133n22
Conciliar tradition, 133
Confession, 37
Cosmic Vision, 168, 175

Digital age, 199–200
Digital immortality, 200
Digital religion, 207
Dilige et quod vis fac, 44n6
Divine energies, 125, 125n10
Divine essence, 125, 125n10
Divine Nature, 6n7, 65
Divinization, 16, 89, 102n7, 102, 104
Doxes eis doxan, 64, 65

Ecumenical dialog, 112, 191
Eikonos, 63, 64
Elijah, 81

Elohim Attem, 59–60
Environmental stewardship, 186
Ephanerothe, 67
Epiphany, 89
Epithimia pneuma, 22
Epithimia sarkikos, 22
Eschatological fulfillment, 37–38, 38n6
Eschatological hope, 13–14, 107, 109
Esometha, 67
Ethical imperatives, 182
Ethical living, 142
Eucharist, 37, 128, 129
ex opere operato, 130

Hahomer, 61
Hesychasm, 49–51
Holiness, 71, 71n27, 99
Homoioi, 67, 68n23
Hoti, 67
Huiou, 63
Human dignity, 71
Humility, 144

Illumination, 7
Imago Dei, 7, 8, 10n9
Imitatio Christi, 139
Incarnation, 26, 122, 122n8, 149n10

Justice, 144
Justification by faith, 42, 42n2, 45, 73, 96, 126

Kidmutenu, 59
Koinonoi, 31
Ktisis, 21

Love, 143

Maiestas dei, 4
Marriage and holy order, 37
Maximum complexity, 165
Metamorphoumetha, 64
Misconstruing theosis, 19
Missional Theology, 195
Moses, 81
Mysterium magnum, 97

Networked Consciousness, 204–5
Noosphere, 167, 172

Omega point, 162, 164, 175–76
Opsometha, 67

Partakers, 65
Philokalia, 6n8, 19n3–4
Physeos, 32
Priesthood of all believers, 135n24
Proorizen, 63
Prophetic Fulfillment, 82
Protestant Reformation, 44
Psychological well-being, 192
Purification, 7

Resurrection, 80
Rada, 58n3
Restorative justice, 187

Sacramental universe, 177
Sanctification, 106–7
Self-Transcendence, 194
Social justice, 143
Solafide, 44, 45, 105, 105n10, 131
Soligratia, 131
Sola scriptura, 131
Symmorphous, 63

Tamunateka, 61
Theias, 31
Theosis, 1–4, 68–70
Theophany, 78, 82–83
Transcendent unity with God, 165
Transfiguration, 78–79, 80n1–4, 81n5, 82–85, 87–92
Transformation, 8, 66
Tselem, 58

Ultimate Goal, 118
Unbridgeable chasm, 18
Unio Mystica, 7, 96, 116, 116n1

Virtue, 138

Yosarenu, 61

Author Index

Anastos, Thomas, 16, 16n1
Aquinas, Thomas, 43, 43n14
Athanasius of Alexandria, 25n14, 48
Augustine of Hippo, 43, 43n4, 44, 44n5–6

Barlaam of Calabria, 52
Barnes, Albert, 31
Barth, Karl, 97
Basil the Great, 47
Bruner, Emil, 136n25

Calvin, Johannes, 105n9
Cappadocian Fathers, 47, 47n10
Clendenin, Daniel B., 1, 3n3
Congar, Yves, 131n18

Gregory of Nazianzus, 47, 47n12
Gregory of Nyssa, 22, 47n11

Henry, Matthew, 29

Irenaeus, 19n5

kainē ktisis, 21

Leliovskyi, Mykola, xiin1
Lossky, Vladimir, 20n6, 26n14
Luther, Martin, 105n9

Maclaren, Alexander, 30
Maximus the Confessor, 49n16–17, 88, 49n17

Palamas, Gregory, 42, 49, 51, 51n23, 52n23, 52n24, 53–54, 130, 130n15
Plummer, Alfred, 30

Russel, Norman, 75n28

Surowiecki, James, 20n5
Stavropoulos, Christoforos, 2, 5, 5n6, 6n7, 23n11
Stott, John, 17n2

Teilhard de Chardin, 161

Wesley, John, 44n7

Zizioulas, John, 125n11

Scripture Index

Genesis
1:26–27   13, 57, 58
2:15   182n1

Exodus
24   83

Psalms
17:15   60, 61
24:1   182n1
82:6   59, 60n7
148:1–5   168n11

Isaiah
24:4–6   179n18
64:8   61, 62

Daniel
7:13–14   82

Amos
5:24   183n2

Micah
6:8   190n7

Matthew
3:17   80, 83
5:17–48   82
5:48   25
17:2   79
17:5   80, 86
22:34–40   82

Luke
9:31   84

John
1:12   57
14:10   57
15:1–5   110

Acts
10:34–35   94n10

SCRIPTURE INDEX

Romans

4:25	92
5:12–21	93
6:3–4	109
6:6	109
8:1	110
8:11	110
8:18–25	38
8:29	62, 63, 63n14, 111, 222
10:12–13	94n10

1 Corinthians

15:20–23	108
15:46	162n2

2 Corinthians

3:18	9, 63, 123, 157
4:17–18	157n17
5:17	21, 93, 128
5:18–20	111, 154n15
5:20	146n8

Galatians

2:20	109, 111
5:16	22
5:22–23	66, 186n4

Ephesians

1:10	166n7
1:17–18	167n8
2:8–9	105

Philippians

2:5–8	142
2:13	158n18
4:4–7	154n14

Colossians

1:15–20	57
1:16–17	178n14–15
1:19–20	220

Hebrews

8:6–13	82

2 Peter

1:4	3, 6, 9, 23, 24n12, 29, 31, 32, 41, 65, 66, 75, 84, 85, 99, 119, 120, 150

1 John

1:12	5
3:1	41
3:2	67, 100
3:8	67, 68

Revelation

7:9–10	95n11
21:3–4	13
21:5	94
22:13	178n15

www.ingramcontent.com/pod-product-compliance
Lightning Source LLC
Chambersburg PA
CBHW050845230426
43667CB00012B/2158